IRAN'S UNRESOLVED REVOLUTION

Dedicated to all those who dare to dream in the darkness of night.

Iran's Unresolved Revolution

MARK DOWNES

LONDON AND NEW YORK

First published 2002 by Ashgate Publishing

Reissued 2018 by Routledge
2 Park Square, Milton Park, Abingdon, Oxon OX14 4RN
711 Third Avenue, New York, NY 10017, USA

Routledge is an imprint of the Taylor & Francis Group, an informa business

Copyright © Mark Downes 2002

The author has asserted his moral right under the Copyright, Designs and Patents Act, 1988, to be identified as the author of this work.

All rights reserved. No part of this book may be reprinted or reproduced or utilised in any form or by any electronic, mechanical, or other means, now known or hereafter invented, including photocopying and recording, or in any information storage or retrieval system, without permission in writing from the publishers.

Notice:
Product or corporate names may be trademarks or registered trademarks, and are used only for identification and explanation without intent to infringe.

Publisher's Note
The publisher has gone to great lengths to ensure the quality of this reprint but points out that some imperfections in the original copies may be apparent.

Disclaimer
The publisher has made every effort to trace copyright holders and welcomes correspondence from those they have been unable to contact.

A Library of Congress record exists under LC control number: 2002074707

ISBN 13: 978-1-138-72029-9 (hbk)
ISBN 13: 978-1-138-72019-0 (pbk)
ISBN 13: 978-1-315-19514-8 (ebk)

Contents

Preface *vii*

Introduction ix

1 Muhammad and the Islamic Movement 1

2 The Islamic Movement – in Resurgence or in Decline? 23

3 Revolution in Review 43

4 Revolution, Power and Binary Opposition 65

5 Ideologies of the Iranian Revolution; the Rise of Khomeinism 82

6 A Great Revolution of the 20th Century – the Installation of an Islamic Theocracy 105

7 The Election of Khatami – Iran from Revolution to Realpolitik 132

Conclusion – Iran Today, Edging towards Unrest 157

Glossary I – People, Places and Organisations in Pre- and Post-1979 Iran *174*
Glossary II – Terms, Dates and Expressions *180*
Bibliography *183*
Index *192*

Map of Iran and the Middle East

Preface

Since September 11th 2001 the goals of the Islamic movement and Islamic government has been called into question. Their compatibility with the ideals of western society and concepts such as democracy and human rights have been openly queried. No country has epitomised the ideals of Islamic governance and the spirit of the Islamic movement more that the Islamic Republic of Iran. It has been accused by the Bush administration of being a sponsor of terrorism, yet in the aftermath of the event of September 2001 it was viewed, for the first time in over two decades, as a reflection of the moderate face of the Islamic movement. It is very possible that Iran could reflect both of these ideas, for its is a fractured society. It has a government that is factionalised to the extent that its left hand does not know, although it may suspect, what the right hand is doing. Invariably in Iran, it is the right hand that pulls the internal strings of government that reflect negatively in Iran abroad.

Broadly speaking this work began as an attempt to understand the development of Iran revolutionary movement and ended up being much more. It is a both a study of Iran's various movement, both Islamic and revolutionary and a snap shot of Iranian society as we enter into the third decade since the overthrow of the Shah and his authoritarian government. It is a reflection on Iran's structure of governance and the prospects of President Khatami's attempts at reforming the system from within. The theory of revolution takes up a substantial part of this work. The events in Iran have led to a significant development in revolutionary theory and this work is an attempt to take these changes into account. A new approach to measuring socio-political unrest in society has been developed utilising Derrida's concept of binary opposition and marrying it to an analysis of political structures.

This book divides into eight chapters. The first two chapters are largely historical, dealing with the development of Shi'ism as part of the Iranian character and a critique of the top-down approach to Islamising Iranian society that was taken by the post-1979 ruling administration. In chapters three and four a review of revolutionary theory is provided, which forms the basis of a theoretical model that I use to measure the level and continuation of socio-political unrest and Iran's revolutionary movement in the post-1979 period. Chapters five to eight concentrate upon contemporary Iran, the socio-political changes that have occurred since the revolution and the current societal friction that is the product of the dichotomy between the reformist desires of the people and the political structure's apparent incapacity to change. Chapter seven maps the development of Iran from the politics of revolution to that of realpolitik. The hopes and aspirations associated with Khatami's second term as President and the potential for social unrest that is ever present in Iranian society will also be dealt with here.

This book is based broadly upon my PhD. Much of the content has also been presented at international conferences in Tehran, Timisoara, Belgrade, the ECPR in Canterbury and in Limerick. This work was made possible by the unyielding support and friendship of both Dr. Rory Keane (Belgrade Open School, Yugoslavia) and Jack Anderson (University of Limerick) with whom I shared some interesting times in Iran and who suffered through numerous discussions of revolutionary theory and Iranian politics. I must also single out Ali, whose friendship is one of the major by-products of this work. Furthermore, I wish to thank my colleagues Dr. Barrie Wharton and John A. Loonam (University of Limerick). In addition, Professor Moxon-Browne and the Center for European Studies at the University of Limerick have always been immensely supportive. I also wish to thank my current employers, the Department of Accounting and Finance at the University of Limerick and the International Agency for Civic Diplomacy and Democratisation (IACDD) for affording me the time to complete this work. A special acknowledgement must go to Leanne Smith for her tireless support and timely interjections during the latter stages of this work, both of which have significantly enhanced the final product. And finally, I wish to thank Susanne for being so special.

Mark A. Downes
Belgrade, October 2002

Introduction

With the world's attention drawn once again towards the Persian Gulf and with Islam's motives regarding western society again being called into question, it is both timely and necessary to bring our understanding of the Islamic movement and Islamic governance up to date. The Islamic Republic of Iran provides us with an interesting case for study Borne out of a revolution that saw the overthrow of a secular western leaning autocrat, the political and social environment in Iran is unique in its attempts to simultaneously embrace the concept of representative government with Islamic institutions. It is easy to simply categorise Iran's Islamic government as being a fundamentalist attempt to drag Iranian society back to the time and the practices of the Prophet Muhammad. It is more difficult to understand the underlying tension that is present in Iranian society, as it attempts to define itself in response to the modern era, in a way that does not forsake its vibrant cultural and religious heritage.

The importance of Iran's strategic position on the Eastern Shore of the Persian Gulf has never been in doubt. Its ability to curtail traffic passing through the Straits of Hormuz, means that Iran and its government are of vital importance to successive western administrations dependant on oil exports from the region. Iran, whose history is marked by a series of invasions, has played an important role in the balance of power and security in the region. If one places Iran in its geo-political context, surrounded as it is to the East by Iraq and the erratic regime of Saddam Hussein, to the South-East by Afghanistan and the still unstable post-Taleban administration, to the North by the increasingly unstable Republics of the former Soviet Unions, it becomes evident how important the government and politics of Iran is for the peace and security of the region.

More importantly, however, is the role that Iran has played as ideological leader to a relatively small but vocal segment of the Islamic world. Ayatollah Khomeini in the aftermath of the establishment of the Islamic Republic offered Iran as an example not only to the Islamic community but also to all oppressed people of the world. Initially alienated, Iran aligned itself to fringe groups; some might say radical or fundamental groups, intent on overthrowing the current international system. That said, with time Iran has established itself as a mature international actor, as was seen in their neutrality with regard to the US bombardment of Afghanistan post-September 11th and their former role as chairperson of the OIC

(Organisation of the Islamic Conference). At the same time Iran has persistently refused to partake in an international system to which it is ideologically opposed. It is Iran's refusal to adhere to the current international system, which makes any study of the Iranian system not only interesting but also vital. The alternative or 'third way' proposed by Ayatollah Khomeini and enshrined in the political life of Iran warrants further scrutiny.

While Iranian society has seen significant changes over recent years, Iran remains a closed society. Therefore, it remains difficult to comprehend the exact nature of Iran's internal politics and how this affects its dealings with the outside world. This analysis of Iran's policies and politics some two decades after the overthrow of the Shah's regime, based on first hand experience, will provide us with a deeper understanding of the evolution of the Iranian revolution. Such an understanding will enable us to comprehend the reasons for the continued socio-political unrest throughout Iranian society and the divisions within Iranian society that threaten to edge Iran towards civil unrest. The following chapters will trace the roots of the present unrest in Iranian society to the inability of the current social and political structures to fulfil the aspirations of the revolutionary movement. The imprisoned reformist Abdullah Nouri caught the essence of this idea when he stated that 'the (Iranian) revolution has come full circle'. By this he meant that the same revolutionaries who manned the barricades in 1979 are now being imprisoned for their opposition to the current political structure and interestingly most of them come from within the ranks of the ruling clergy. It is for that reason and the fact that Iranian society has the potential for increased civil unrest that the time has come to re-evaluate our understanding of the outcome and the impact of the Iranian revolution. Through fusing both theory and practice this work attempts to understand Iran's current political situation in terms of its revolutionary history, its Islamic movement, its unique political system, together with the current political realities of the Iranian political environment.

Many authors have attempted to categorise Iran in terms of its religion or its history. Through utilising revolutionary theory, Islamic ideology, the writings of political and religious ideologues of Iranian society together with an analysis of Iran's political environment and structure of governance, this book provides a holistic, realistic and original understanding of contemporary Iran. Understanding the changes in contemporary Iranian society inevitably forces us to rethinking our understanding of the concept of revolution and the changes that it effects on society. Revolution is a topic that has fascinated scholars and political scientists alike. Perhaps it is the volcanic eruption of violence, or the social upheaval that results, that has attracted adherents to this area of study. Even though there has been a multitude of work published on the subject, a universally acceptable definition of revolution has never been formulated. This is because of the multifaceted nature of a revolution and disagreement as to how and why a revolution occurs. The Islamic revolution in Iran has not only changed the geo-political map of Middle Eastern politics, but coming as it did on a wave of Islamic revivalism, it has struck fear into the hearts of western governments. It led directly to the Soviet invasion of Afghanistan; the destructive 8 year war with Iraq; and some would say also led to the Iraqi invasion of Kuwait and the events that ensued, all of which continue to destabilise the entire region.

The Iranian Revolution has all the criteria necessary for it to be dubbed one of the 'Great Revolutions'.[1] In tandem with the fall of the Soviet Union, it is one of the defining moments in the latter half of the twentieth century. The fact that it was a revolution that was caught on film has meant that it has had a last impression on the western psyche. The scenes of the masses rising up against their tyrannical ruler, openly challenging one of the world's superpowers, and succeeding on both counts, sent shock waves both East and West. The Iranian revolution also brought, for the first time, the ideology of Ayatollah Khomeini and his views on Islam and politics, into the limelight. His perception of the world, the region and his template for Islamic governance, were most unsettling for his Arab neighbours, whom like the Shah had a narrow political base. Khomeini's unyielding, anti-western demeanour together with scenes of religious 'fanatics' threatening to declare *jihad* or holy war on the world made the secular governments of the west and the atheist government of the Soviet bloc uneasy. Religion played a devastating role in the political world of the Middle Ages, however its use as a means of mobilising the masses has since been in a steady decline. The 1979 revolution in Iran brought forward onto the world stage the changes that had been sweeping the Islamic world since the early 1970s. Islam had regained political legitimacy and the cry of 'Allah Akbar' (God is Great), became a cry for political change from Indonesia, to the Philippines and from Sudan to Algeria.[2] In the aftermath of the success of the Islamic revolution, Iran became something of an ideological leader to the Islamic revival. The age of Islamic 'fundamentalism' had arrived and Islamic communities throughout the world had an ideologue in Khomeini and an example in the Islamic Republic of Iran.

Over twenty years have passed since the revolution and the spectre of Islamic 'fundamentalism' remains with us. There are those who argue that Islam as a political ideology has been in decline since the late 1990s,[3] however the current political turmoil in Iran and throughout the Middle East[4] would appear to dispute such a viewpoint. While Islamic fundamentalism has spawned a plethora of debates, discussions, theories and movies, we are still quite a distance from comprehensively understanding the significance of the Iranian Revolution and the impact that it will have on world politics. There are a number of reasons for this, not least the fact that many observers approach the subject from a western perspective, thereby failing to understand the true context of Iranian politics and society. The truth, in fact, is that the roots of the current political situation in Iran can be traced to a mixture of ideas encompassing revolutionary theory and the Islamic movement as well as a number of additional factors. Describing the revolution of 1979 as solely Islamic in nature is to ignore the vast differences that make up this vibrant faith. An understanding of the Shia Islam, its background and the vast differences of opinion that exist concerning the functioning of the state and the role of the clergy, has to be attained. In addition, Iran is an overwhelmingly Shia country, a sect of Islam which is not well understood by most European commentators. Furthermore, Farsi is a language not well known outside of Iran and some parts of Central Asia, so little use has been made by western writers of Iranian sources of information. Finally, the revolution in Iran and its aftermath remains misunderstood because Iran is still a relatively closed society. While international travel is on the increase, few commentators have truly penetrated Iranian society, a society that, like its political life, is highly complex and factionalised. Views from a western perspective often confuse political rhetoric with the reality that is present-day Iran. Iran's internal politics is in a state of constant flux, conservatives and reformers are battling inch by inch for the hearts and minds of the Iranian people. Iran's unique political structure,[5] together with the precarious balance of power between the Supreme Leader and the President also results in much misanalysis, especially regarding the influence that domestic politics can play on the country's foreign policy. This lack of a comprehensive understanding of the Iranian system and its society has meant that western policy towards the region has been misguided. The current US policy towards Iran that varies between containment and open verbal hostility and its persistence in maintaining economic sanctions could convincingly be argued to be counter-productive to the cause of encouraging the development of a democratic society.

    This disagreement regarding Iranian intentions towards the West and whether US sanctions should be revoked, takes on greater significance when we view the current conflict developing within Iran's borders. The election of President Khatami in 1997 (and his successful re-election in

2001) marked a new stage in the development of the Islamic State. It also defined the divisions within the ruling clergy and marked the change from Khomeini's ideology of isolation to Khatami's ideology of engagement. For the West, its response to these developments are based on the question of whether Iran should continue to be treated as a 'rogue' state, or whether it should be welcomed back into the international community as an equal partner. Incorporated into these two perspectives are a number of issues that define Iran's current society and its political stance.

This work will analyse the contemporary political environment of Iran by examining three of these different influences that have shaped Iranian policy and society since 1979. This work will show that contemporary Iran is the product of a revolutionary process that remains incomplete, an Islamic movement that has lost its direction and a political structure that does not reflect the values of the society it serves. Given that the current political structure in the Islamic Republic was born out of a revolution, the study of revolutionary theory and an understanding of the progress or evolution of a revolutionary situation are central to understanding Iranian politics, policy and social development in the post-1979 era. Likewise an understanding of post-1979 Iran will provide a unique insight into the evolutionary nature of a revolutionary situation. While much of the present literature of revolutionary theory looks at revolution in terms of its causes, this is inadequate when attempting to understand the outcome of a revolutionary process. While accepting the general definition put forward by Pettee, that a revolution is 'a reconstitution of the state',[6] this work will develop a new understanding of revolution as a process rather than an event in time, based on the goals of revolutionary activity rather then its causes. For this purpose revolution will be viewed as a means of re-distributing power within a political structure.

While Pettee and his contemporaries define the reconstitution of the state in terms of institutional and elite change, this work shall be terming it in relation to the level of interaction and influence between the populace and the state. Using the literary idea of binary opposition,[7] revolution shall be defined as the reconstitution of the state in terms of institutional and elite change but more significantly in terms of the change in the role played by the population in the governance of the state. By doing this, the term revolution will discount those events which do not result in political evolution and power redistribution, or where the original ideals of the revolutionary movement are misappropriated by an organised elite intent on reorganising political power in the hands of a few. In such situations, of which Iran is one, the very reasoning behind the revolutionary movement has not been fulfilled and if that is so, how could one argue that the revolution has been complete. While the use of binary opposition is not new to political science,[8] its application in the study of the theory of revolution is. Understanding revolution in terms of the relationship between the state and the populace leads to the development of revolutionary theory and to a better understanding of revolutionary societies such as Iran.

Interwoven into the analysis of the Iranian revolution are the various ideologies, Islamic and otherwise,[9] that have directed Iranian society before and after 1979, from Shariati to Khomeini and Soroush.[10] Each of these ideologies have a different perspective on the role of Islam in society and it is to these that we must turn to assist our understanding of the fault lines in Iranian society today. While Khomeini can be said to have been the architect of the early period of Iran's revolution, today there are much more diverse opinions guiding Iranian society. Not least amongst these is President Khatami's theory of 'dialogue amongst civilisations'. Having been elected in 1997 with a landslide victory, gaining over seventy percent of the votes cast, President Khatami has set about redefining the values that shape Iranian society. It will be argued that these 'new values' are in fact a mirror image of the ones espoused by the revolutionaries' over twenty years ago. Notions such as political pluralism, civil society and democratic values are terms used currently by the reformist movement in Iran to define their objectives. It will be shown that these objectives are mere echoes of the goals of the pre-1979 movement to oust the Shah.

A further section of this study is concentrated on analysing Iran as an Islamic movement. The origins of the 1970s Islamic movement will be traced, together with Khomeini's leadership in the latter part of that decade. In addition, the influences that the Islamic movement has had on the current political structure will be reviewed. While it is acknowledged that Islam is a political religion, it will be argued that it is political in a micro sense rather than a macro one. In many ways this is what differentiates the Shia and Sunni Islamic movements. The Sunni movement of the Arab world, for example, attempts to Islamise society from below, by encouraging individual members of society to be better Muslims. The Shia movement, on the other hand, tries to create an Islamic society from above, by developing Islamic structures for society. It will be argued that this attempt is failing. Placing the clergy in a direct political role has politicised Islam rather than Islamising politics.

The third section of this thesis will deal with the analysis of the current political structure and environment in Iran and will be used to evaluate the future of the Islamic regime in Iran. While Khatami's 1997 election has been hailed a victory for greater democracy,[11] his ability to change Iranian society from what some might call a 'theocratic autocracy' to a pluralist society is hampered by the very institutional framework in which he must work. For this reason, the study of Ayatollah Khomeini's philosophy on government, together with the governmental legacy he has left behind must be studied in order to fully comprehend the predicament facing the reformist movement. The ideological battle, which is being waged in the corridors of power, has recently spilled onto the streets of Tehran and other major cities. The student movement's unwillingness to accept the slow pace of reform by the Khatami government has lead to major protests against the conservative positions. They in turn led a crackdown on the press[12] and the reformist movement.[13] While the constitution clearly lays out the roles and powers of each institution of government, the reality is that over time, these positions have shifted significantly. Having held power for the initial period of the revolution and having taken advantage of the chaos that surrounded the ensuing war with Iraq, conservative factions have been able to significantly re-write the balance of power within Iranian society. Khatami's attempts to centralise decision making and to implement a policy of reform that is supported by a majority of the people[14] have been hampered in many cases by conservative factions outside the official decision making process.[15] It is these unofficial influences on both sides of the political divide that hold the key to the future of Iranian society. In many respects the reform movement is hampered by its leader President Khatami. While he is sympathetic to the calls for reform, his political philosophy does not include any serious reform of the Islamic structures that define the Islamic Republic. While there has been much opposition within Iran to the comparison of Khatami's position to that of Gorbachov's in the latter days of the Soviet Union, there is much substance to this perspective. Whether his attempts to reform society, while maintaining the system of government, will be successful have yet to be seen. Khatami's major success since his election has been the reduction of Iran's international isolation.[16] In turn this has had serious consequences for the perception of Islam abroad and the prospect of the survival of the political system at home. In fact, following the Iranian administration's proposal, the United Nations pronounced 2001 as the year of 'Dialogue Amongst Civilisations'.[17] Khatami's ideas, as developed by the concept of 'Dialogue Amongst Civilisations', have the possibility, not only, of revitalising the Islamic movement but also of increasing its international credibility.

Our understanding of the causes and effects of this last 'great revolution of the twentieth century',[18] can further our understanding of the phenomena of revolution. Indeed, by analysing the developments that have occurred in the twenty-something years since 1979, we can in some way enhance our understanding of the evolutionary nature of a revolutionary movement. Furthermore, the ideologies that have surrounded these changes in Iranian society have effects far beyond its borders. The revolution in Iran was arguably the turning point in the Islamic revival that was sweeping the Muslim world. To many, Khomeini and his ideas became an example to be followed. Iran throughout the early period of the revolution took an active part in the development of the Islamic movement; those in the West received Khomeini's policy of 'exporting the revolution' with varying degrees of distrust. Khomeini's policy incorporated not only Islamic revolutions but his message was for all the 'oppressed of the world',[19] he was an anti-imperialist who believed that Islam called on everybody to assist the overthrow of tyranny. In many ways it defined the early period of the revolution and resulted in Iran being given the ominous title of a 'rogue' state, for its alleged support of terrorist groups abroad. In many ways Ayatollah Khomeini's political and ideological legacy is central to our understanding of Iranian politics today. While much has been written on Khomeini, arguably the most radical Muslim leader of his age, in many ways it has been tainted by the subjectiveness of approaching him from a western perspective. To fully understand Khomeini and his impact on Iran and the Islamic world it is first necessary to understanding the cultural and political environment in which his views developed. Khomeini is a complex figure. He was not, as is often cited in western texts, an Islamic traditionalist, but forged his theory of government and society upon a *mélange* of socialism, mysticism, utopianism and a radical interpretation of Shia Islamic beliefs. He was militant whilst being pragmatic; he was at times contradictory being populist whilst at others stringently sticking to his beliefs. Indeed he was as complex as the political system he left behind, a system which attempts to simultaneously espouse the seemly dichotomous philosophies of Islam and democracy.

In many ways the rise of Khomeini and his Islamic ideology tinged with nationalism should have been predicted. By putting Iran into its historical context, with a series of erratic and at times autocratic leaders and having been a victim throughout modern history of the imperialist pursuits of western powers, it was inevitable that Iran would eventually turn away from the West that was solely interested in an abusive relationship, in both economic and political terms. Surrounded by apparent adversaries, in the aftermath of the revolution Iran attempted simultaneously to create a self-sufficient state free from outside interference, at the same time challenging what they considered to be the colonialist attitudes of western powers. The contentious Persian Gulf borders Iran to the south, from whence the Arab invasion in the 14th century led to the Islamisation of the country, to the

East by Iraq an historical and ever present enemy. To the north was the now-defunct Soviet Union, who had a long and varied history in Iran including their occupation of Iran with the aid of Britain during the Second World War and their role in the forced abdication of Reza Shah in 1941 in favour of his son. To the west is the predominantly Sunni dominated government of Afghanistan until the late 1980s a dominion of the Soviet Union and Pakistan, a country thereafter controlled by the radical Taleban movement and currently hosts an unstable western supported government.[20] This valid threat perception and the belief that western powers were only interesting in having a colonial/exploitative view of 'third world' countries including Iran, led the Islamic Republic to formulate policies that western observers interpreted as a direct assault on the West and its values.

Notes

[1] Theorists such as Pettee, Neumann and Marx would define *'Great Revolutions'* as those which lead to a 'reconstitution of the state'. See further Marx, K. (1983), *Karl Marx and Fredrick Engels, Selected Works, Vol. 1* (Moscow: Progress Publishers), Neumann, S. (1948-49), 'The International Civil War', *World Politic, 1* and for the exact use of the term 'reconstitution of the State' see Pettee, G. (1971), *The Process of Revolution* (New York: Harper), p.3.

[2] For a overview of the Islamic movement in the above countries, see further Gowing, P. (1988), *Understanding Islam and Muslims in the Philippines* (Quezon City: New Day Publishers); Boland, B.J. (1982), *The struggle of Islam in modern Indonesia* (The Hague: Nijhoff); Younessi, B. (1995: Summer) *L'islamisme algerien: nebuleuse ou movement social?* Politique-Etrangere 60, pp.365-76, and Simone, T. (1994). *In whose image: Political Islam and urban practices in Sudan* (London: University of Chicago Press).

[3] For a compelling account of such an argument see further Kepel, G. (2000), *Jihad, expansion et déclin de l'Islamisme* (Paris: Gallimard).

[4] Examples of the continued presence of Islam in world politics include the Palestinian crisis with Israel over control of Jerusalem, the continuing civil wars in Sudan and Algeria. Furthermore the use of Islam in the ethnic conflicts of Indonesia and the Philippines is a sign that the political Islam is still very much a part of global politics.

[5] For an overview of Iran's political system see further Appendix 2, suffice to say at this stage that it is 'unique' in the sense that it is the only modern theocratic state, where the clergy are the predominant political elite and where the highest office in the land must be held by a clerical figure. Furthermore, the Iranian political system is not only an attempt to fuse religion and politics, but also tries to adapt democracy to the tenets of the Islamic faith and as such creates a hybrid political structure never seen before in the modern world.

[6] Pettee, G. (1971), *The Process of Revolution* (New York: Harper), p.3.

[7] Binary opposition is a literary device developed by Jacques Derrida to explain interrelated ideas within the same essence. For an expanded explanation, see further Derrida, J. (1995), *Writing and Difference* (London: Routledge).

[8] See further Beardsworth, R. (1996), *Derrida and the Political* (London: Routledge), and Keane, R. (2000), *Reconstituting Sovereignty* (Ashgate: 2002).

[9] In an Islamic sense the major pre-revolutionary ideologues were Khomeini and Shariati. Other influences on pre-revolutionary Iran include Marxist-Leninist groups, groups espousing parliamentary democracy and economic nationalism, while other ideologies represented a mixture of some or all of the above. All of these influences are covered in detail in chapter 6.

[10] See further the glossary in Appendix V for an explanation of the major personalities involved in Iran's political environment over the last four decades.

[11] See for example, Ramazani, R. (1998: Spring), 'The shifting premise of Iran's foreign policy: towards a democratic peace?' *Middle East Journal;* 52, pp.177-87. Masci, D. (1998), 'Reform in Iran: are moderates changing the Islamic Republic?' *CQ-Researcher;* 8, pp. 1099-1119.

[12] See further Hicks, H. (1998: Nov 8), 'As fragile as a crystal glass: press freedom in Iran', *Human-Rights Watch.*

[13] See further (1998: August 6), 'Power Struggle: Khatami liberalism under conservative attack', *Middle East Reporter Weekly;* 88, pp.12-13 and (1998: October 19), 'Khatami fights back the radicals', *Middle East Reporter Weekly;* 88, pp.12-14.

[14] As evidenced by the overwhelming victory of his supporters in the Local Elections held in March 1999 and the Parliamentary Elections in February 2000. See further Joffe, G. (1999, April), 'At a turning point', *World Today;* 55, pp.11-13.

[15] Such as the revolutionary guards and the 'Islamic Foundations' whose control over the Iranian economy gives them the ability to have much political influence. This topic is covered in more detail in chapter 8.

[16] See further (1999: June 24), 'Khatami scores a foreign policy triumph', *Middle-East Reporter Weekly;* 90, pp.12-13; Amuzegar, J. (1998), 'Khatami's Iran, one year later', *Middle East Policy;* 6, pp.76-94; Naufal, M. (1997), 'Iran: Khatami joue a quitte ou double', *Arabies;* pp.20-5.

[17] See further (2000: September 5), 'United Nations year of Dialogue amongst civilisatios, 2001 launched with headquarters roundtable discussion', *UN Press Release GA/9747.*

[18] Robin Wright used this term in the title of her book, see further Wright, R. (2000), *The Last Great Revolution: turmoil and transformation in Iran* (New York, Random House).

[19] See further Iranian Constitution, Item C Article 2.

[20] For an analysis of geopolitics of the Persian Gulf from an Iranian perspective see further Jones, P. (1998: Autumn), 'Iran's threat perceptions and arms control policies, Non-proliferation-Review'; 6, pp.39-55; Arnett, E. (1998), 'Reassurance versus deterrence: expanding Iranian participation in confidence-building measures', *Middle-East-Policy;* 6, pp.137-56; Cordesman, A. (1998), 'The changing military balance in the Gulf', *Middle-East-Policy;* 6, pp.25-44.

Chapter 1
Muhammad and the Islamic Movement

The political folklore of the West has a long and embittered fear of the concept of Islam. The medieval military might of Islam survived and eventually routed the papal, and not so papal, crusades of the 11th and 12th centuries.[1] Indeed, during the Middle Ages, Muslims occupied large parts of Spain and at one point knocked at the very ramparts of Vienna, which was then, as now, the gateway to Western Europe. Even today in large parts of the West, when the word Islam is used it is implicitly, albeit incorrectly, associated with fear, fundamentalism and terror.[2]

From its humble beginnings in the arid planes of Arabia in the beginning of the 6th century, it is now estimated that about one-fifth of the world's population is of the Islamic faith. Muslims can now be found throughout the world; in the Asia in places such as Indonesia; in the Middle East territories such as Iraq, Iran and Afghanistan and in Africa, particularly in the northern half of that continent. Indeed Islam is fast becoming one of the major religions in Western Europe.[3]

Though it seems to some of the more alarmist political commentators that Islam and Muslims are on the march, the aim of this chapter is to provide an introduction to the vibrant faith that is Islam. In addition, it is important for this body of work that the ideological roots of the contemporary Islamic movement be reviewed.

Muhammad and the Birth of Islam

It was from the forbidding and barren land of Arabia that the founder of Islam hailed.[4] Whilst it is known that he was born in Mecca[5] in modern day Saudi Arabia to Abdallah ibn Abd al-Muttalib and his wife Aminah, the exact date of his birth is still an issue of contention amongst historians. There is a saying ascribed to Muhammad that gives us a clue of the date, 'I was born during the reign of the just king', the king in question was the Sasanian monarch Chosroes I, who reigned from AD 531 to 579.[6] It is generally accept that the man who would dramatically alter the course of modern religion was born around circa 570 AD.

Orphaned at the age of six, he was entrusted into the care first of his grandfather and later his uncle, Abu Talib. During his youth he undoubtedly came into contact with monotheist faiths, as the conflict between the Christian Byzantine and Zoroastrian Sasanian Empires was in full swing to the north of the Arabian peninsula. Mecca, a thriving commercial crossroad between the worlds of East and West was the focal point for the idol worshipping Arabs. Muhammad was born into the Quraysh tribe which had control over Mecca at the time. In fact during the early years of his life he lived with the Abd Manaf family who were the custodians of the Ka'bah,[7] the Meccan shrine. While it appears that most of the Arabian Peninsula could have been termed backward or primitive in comparison to their regional contemporaries, most notably the Byzantine or Sasanian Empires, Mecca by contrast had a well-organised system of administration and a thriving economy.

Our knowledge of Muhammad's early childhood is scant. We know that he joined his Uncle Abu Talib in his trading business. At the age of twenty-five, he married a widow of considerable wealth named Khadijah Bint Khuwaylid. She had many trading concerns and Muhammad eventually managed her flourishing business interests. It is said that eight children were born to Muhammad and his wife, four sons and four daughters. The sons did not outlive their infancy and three of the daughters all died childless before the age thirty. His remaining daughter, Fatimah, was married to Ali the son of Muhammad's uncle and guardian Abu Talib. Little is know of this period of Muhammad's life when he was a trader. However, while travelling north to Syria and south to Yemen, it is fair to assume that he came in contact with and was influenced by the culture and practices of the monotheist religions of the region. While it is claimed that Muhammad was illiterate, the early period of his life would have given him an understanding of the requirements of functioning state, knowledge he would require in later years.

Tradition has it that with time, Muhammad became more reflective and suffered from bouts of internal doubts and questioning.[8] During this period of contemplation Muhammad received a revelation from the Angel Gabriel containing his mission for the world. While Muhammad's initial mission would appear to have been to warn his people[9] and to act as a prophet or holy man whose revelations were to enhance the existing doctrine of the monotheist faiths what was to eventually occur was more in line with a religious revolution. The resultant faith, Islam, went far beyond the previous parameters of monotheist faiths and formulated principles and practices that would encompass not only issues of faith and religion but also the economic, political and social lives of its adherents. Islam, from the very beginning, did not allow its followers to have a life outside of Islam and Muhammad was not only a religious leader but became the political, military and social leader of his followers. The legacy left by the all encompassing leadership of Muhammad, has been incorporated into the Islamic faith and has given weight to the argument that Islam is a political doctrine with a political and social ideology.

In the early years following Muhammad's revelations his followers only numbered around fifty and came mostly from his immediate family.[10] Others within the family circle however were less supportive and at times attempted to undermine Muhammad. Sometime in the fourth year of this mission, he made a public declaration to the people of Mecca that he was sent as a messenger from the 'One God'. This intensified the persecution of his followers but also brought with it the conversion of many of his fellow Meccans. During the years that followed, Muhammad's religious and socio-political doctrine developed into a comprehensive framework of ideas on which the future society of Islam could be based. This appealed to a larger cross section of society and provided the fledgling faith of Islam with adherents from all classes of Meccan society. In tandem with the development of the tenants of Islam, a change occurred with the persona of Muhammad, from preacher to leader, from hermit to warrior.[11]

The Birth of the First Islamic Society

The turning point in Islam history occurred around 620 AD when Muhammad made contact with a group of pilgrims from Yathrib, who accepted him as the Prophet of God. In time their numbers grew. This coincided with an increasingly hostile and indifferent reception by the people of Mecca. As a result the prophet decided to leave his hometown of Mecca and move with his supporters to the northern city of Yathrib. This *hijrah*[12] (or withdrawal) to Yathrib occurred in the year 622 AD and is an integral part of the Islamic consciousness, even today.

On the Prophet's arrival the people of Yathrib changed the name of the city to al-Madínah an-Nabí (or Medina in English), which means the 'City of the Prophet'.[13] The arrival of the Muslims of Mecca to join their compatriots in Medina, marks not only the beginning of the Muslim calendar but also marks the beginning of the victory of Islam and the fulfilment of the prophesies of Muhammad. The difficulties and triumph over adversity experienced during the *hijrah* has remained a cornerstone of the Islamic faith and psyche throughout the ages. The eight years spent in Medina further developed the Islamic way of life, together with the religious, political, economic and social practices that were necessary to maintain it. The development of a community beyond tribal or kinship bonds produced a religion that transcends class or family bonds,[14] giving it mass appeal.

Even though Muhammad was brought up in the punishing Arabian Peninsula where tribal laws and wars reigned supreme, he was not a man accustomed to combat. Now, however, as the leader of the people of Medina, he had an obligation to guarantee their safety and protection. As a result of this obligation, Muhammad and a number of his followers had taken up arms against the idolaters in defence of the Muslim way of life.[15] What started as a series of skirmishes, turned into a fully-fledged battle between the Muslim community of Medina and their opponents in Mecca. Alliances were made and battles were fought to protect and further the Muslim community's way of life. The Battles of Badr and Uhud and the failed siege of Medina in 627 AD were all decisive in the development of Islam from merely a religious ideology to that of a strong political and military force.[16] While receiving full devotion from his followers, Muhammad can also be seen as a pragmatic political leader. In total Muhammad had twelve wives, his first was the widow Khadijah, to whom he remained faithful until her death after 24 years of marriage. Muhammad's later marriages, however, facilitated the establishment of system of alliances, with tribal or nomadic groups who were perceived to be a possible threat to the Muslim community.[17]

That Islam had become a political force is further strengthened by the fact that Muhammad sent emissaries to neighbouring leaders from the Monarch Negus of Ethiopia, to Chosroes II the Sasssanian Monarch, Heraclius the Byzantine Emperor, the rulers of Egypt, Syria and, tradition has it, to Pope Honorius I of Campania,[18] to summon them all to Islam. His responses were met with varying degrees of success. While it is claimed that a favourable response was received from the Ethiopian Emperor and the ruler of Yemen, other territories had to be won over by both force of arms and military conquest.

Initially while Muhammad was building his Islamic society in Medina, he sought a truce with the people of Mecca to allow his followers to visit this holy site.[19] However, such tranquil relations with their neighbours were short-lived and following the breaking of the truce of al-Hudaybíyya[20] it became inevitable that a final victory over the idolaters was necessary. Amassing an army of ten thousand men, Muhammad marched towards Mecca and returned to the city of his birth in triumph, as leader of his Muslim force, some eight years after the *hijrah*. Thereafter, he established the new Muslim community in the cities of Mecca and Medina. While Muhammad died two years later in 632 AD the trend of Muslim expansion had begun.

The March towards an Islamic Empire

Following on the heels of their victory in Mecca, the forces of Islam swept through Arabian Peninsula and not long afterwards, with a small force, they overran the mighty Sasanian Empire, bringing Islam to Persia in 637 AD. This decisive victory was followed by the Arab conquest over the Byzantine provinces of Syria and Egypt in 656 AD, the conquest of North Africa occurred in 711 AD and the Muslim forces knocked on the gates of Vienna in 1699.[21] As the conquering Muslim armies swept out of the Arabian Peninsula they brought with them the Arabic language and their new faith, a faith that was readily accepted by their new subjects. Islam with its emphasis on equality and justice for all won mass appeal in societies ridden with class differences and social injustice. There are many theories as to why Islam experienced such a meteoritic rise engulfing not only the Arabian Peninsula but overcame the Byzantine and Sasanian Empires, the most plausible is that Mecca and Medina were highly developed cities on the verge of statehood and merely needed an ideology to galvanise its population. Once the Arab tribes were united in Islam, their tribal warfare, which had previously managed to weaken their peoples, ceased. The united tribes of the Arabian Peninsula still possessed the skills of warfare but now they utilised it for the benefit of Islam. Islam's march through Arabia gave it a warlike doctrine, which has best described by the term '*jihad*' or Holy war. This term has been misused in modern times, it does not mean conversion to Islam through conquest but in this context rather a desire to expand the faith and territories where Islam is found.[22]

While in the new Islamic territories polytheists were not allowed to practice their faith, other monotheists or 'people of the book' such as Christian and Jews were allowed to fulfil their religious obligations in return for a special tax. This policy allowed the Arab armies to give religious freedom to large Christian groups in both Egypt and Syria, groups who were perceived as heretics by the Byzantine Empire and persecuted as such. This practice led to the near peaceful surrender of these territories to the advancing Arab armies and, together with the decline of the great empires explains the rapid expansion of the Arab Empire. While the Muslim community shared some of the theology of Judaism and Christianity, they were convinced of the totality of Muhammad's message and in his role as the final seal of all-previous prophets and revelations. This revolutionary conviction in the completeness of Muhammad's message formed the cornerstone of the Muslim belief system and is still of paramount importance today.[23]

The march towards the new Arab/Islamic Empire that began with the taking of Mecca signified the dawn of what is known as the 'Golden Age' of Islam.[24] This era remains a powerful utopian image that Islamic leaders utilised throughout contemporary Islamic history. Even though today Islam has split into numerous sects with differing opinions on the interpretation of Muhammad's message, each perceives the creation of the first Islamic community as a utopian ideal to be upheld and when possible replicated. Ayatollah Khomeini saw this period in Islamic history, when society's political and spiritual leadership were united in the personage of Muhammad, as being a template on which any modern Islamic state could be designed.

The Divisions Within Islam: The Shia-Sunni Divide

It is generally accepted that Islam, like most modern monotheist religions, has divided with time into a multitude of varying interpretations. In the early days of Islam, directly after the Prophet received his calling, it was the cohesiveness of his followers that enabled Islam to survive and prosper. With the death of the Prophet this cohesiveness was substituted by divisions that are still prevalent today. The roots of these divisions can be found in the rites of succession to the leadership of the Islamic people following the death of the Prophet Muhammad and in time this resulted in disputes regarding the interpretation of his words and actions.

Nowhere is this division depicted more clearly than in the dispute which has engulfed the two main groups within the Islam faith. The divide between Sunni and Shia[25] stems from the belief of who had the right of succession following the death of the Prophet Muhammad. There is much literature available from both sides purporting to speak the truth in the defence of their positions.[26] Therefore it can be difficult to provide an objective account of what happened prior and immediately after the Prophet's passing. What is not in contention is that Muhammad performed his final pilgrimage to Mecca in the spring of 632 AD, eleven years after the *hijrah*. The designation of Ali, as understood from Shia literature, as the successor to the Prophet Mohammed is believed to have taken place during return of the Prophet from his pilgrimage on the 18th day of the month of Dhu'l-hijjah in 632 AD.[27] The proclamation itself has been reported and interpreted in many ways, with the most popular being 'He for whom I was the master, should hence have Ali as his master.'[28] This statement has formed the basis of the Shia conviction that Ali was the designated heir of the Prophet. On his return to Medina and after preparing for a strike into

Byzantine territory to the North, Muhammad fell ill. Unable to lead his faithful in prayer, both the Shia and the Sunni's contend that Ali[29] and Abu Bakr[30] respectively were appointed by the Prophet to lead the congregation in his absence. This point as to who should lead the faithful in prayer during Muhammad's illness is of vital importance. For this would have shown the Prophet's trust in the wisdom and leadership of either of the above parties, skills which were essential for the person who would lead the Muslim community after his passing.

Consensus on the exact date of the Prophets death has never been achieved, however it is generally accepted that it occurred somewhere in May/June of 632 AD.[31] For a time the succession to the prophet remained uncontested, however, once word of Muhammad's death spread, confusion reigned throughout the Muslim community. After a number of contenders for the right to succeed the Prophet came forward, Abu Bakr who was only too aware that tribal and clan differences had the potential to divide the Muslim community and threaten the unity of Islam intervened. In the midst of the ensuing melee the right of Ali as the closest living male relative to the Prophet was forgotten. As the debate began to get out of hand Abu Bakr took the hands of Umar and Abu-'Ubaydah, two potential candidates for the position of Muslim leader, and said 'here are two honourable men; choose either of them that he may rule over you and I shall be the first to pledge my loyalty to him'.[32] Both refused Abu Bakr's nomination and instead pledged their loyalty to him, they were followed by the rest of the congregation. Ali who saw the need to preserve the unity of Islam over his own rights also followed suit. And so, the community based the choice of the first successor to the Prophet or *khalifah* (Caliph) on the principle of general consensus through a vote by the faithful. Abu Bakr was to survive only two years in his position and on his deathbed named Umar as his successor, thereby deviating from the original principle, which established him in the position of Caliph. Umar in turn appointed a six-member council, on his deathbed, which chose Uthman as his successor. It has been alleged that an assassin claiming to be a Shia attacked and killed Umar. It is further alleged that this assassin made his way to Iran, where it is believed he lived out the rest of this days amongst his fellow adherents to Ali, a revered grave in Kashan is supposed to mark his resting place.[33]

The reign of Uthman was a turning point in the history of Islam. The hitherto united community broke apart during the corrupt and divisive reign of Uthman. Abu Bakar and Umar were both said to be just and impartial rulers, with the unity of the Muslim community and the words of the Prophets being their guidance throughout their time of leadership. It is even said that Umar did not spare his own son, when a transgression of the law occurred. By comparison the Caliphate of Uthman was far more politically motivated, power and the maintenance of that power were the main focus of his years of leadership. Being inclined to favouritism and nepotism meant that many of his appointments were based on tribal identity, which for the first time resulted in the return of tribal affiliations to the Muslim consciousness, causing division and discord. This led to uprisings in a number of Muslim territories and eventually led to dissenters coming to Medina and attacking the house of Uthman, killing him.

The death of Uthman left the Muslim community in chaos and without a leader. Uthman had neither named his successor nor established a council who could choose one. During the discussions that took place within the Muslim community concerning who should lead the Muslim community Ali's name was the one that found the greatest consensus amongst the people of Medina. Initially he was not inclined to accept the position of leader, however, eventually he reluctantly agreed. The ascension of Ali to the position of Caliph, for the first time, the right of hereditary rule was united with that of electoral consensus. Such a situation could have united the various factions within Islam; however, this was not to be the case. From the beginning of his reign Ali was beset by opposition from within the Islamic community. The reign of Ali was not the unifying force it should have been but instead it resulted in internal political conflict within the once united Muslim community.

It was Ali's attempts to bring cohesion back to the Islamic community, through righting the wrongs committed during the reign of Uthman, which radicalised the opposition against him. He dismissed the corrupt governors appointed by Uthman, but met tough opposition to such action, especially in Syria where members of Uthman's tribe (the Umayyad) and supporters of the former Caliph had fled following his death. Demands by the 'House of Umayyad' to avenge the death of Uthman were soon heard from Basrah to within the very walls of Medina. Ali was a compassionate leader who preferred to deal with the opposition to his rule through mediation rather than battle. He did everything possible to avoid a clash of arms between the divided Muslim community. The fate, which had befallen Christendom, was to be avoided at all cost. The House of Umayyad however refused to listen to Ali's pleas against the disintegration of Muslim unity. The scene was therefore set for the inevitable clash, which was to pit Muslim against Muslim. The resultant echoes of this conflict are still heard throughout the Muslim community today.

It was during this time that we see the emergence of a third sect within Islam known as the Khawarji.[34] They believed strictly in the word of the Quran and are of importance here because of their unwillingness to follow either of the above groups. In 661 AD, just 40 years after Muhammad took his followers to Medina, followers of the Khawarji decided to kill both the Caliph Ali and the contender to his position from the House of Umayyad, Mu'áwíyah.[35] While Mu'áwíyah escaped the assassin's sword, on the 19th Day of Ramadan in the year 40 AH[36] (661 AD) Ali, the first Imam of the Shia's and the fourth Caliph, the cousin and son in law of the Prophet Muhammad, was killed. The assassins' blow was one from which Ali and Islam would not recover. While Hasan the elder son of Ali, did try to ensure the succession to the position of Caliph was held within the House of Ali, in the face of superior forces from the House of Umayyad, he was compelled to concede and abdicate his claim to the position of Caliph. The House of Umayyad has been depicted as tyrants and usurpers[37] and being more political than religious. They widened the gap between the divisions of Islam rather than trying to heal the wounds that cause such a divide. When Hasan, the elder son of Ali abdicated, he did so on the agreement that the Caliphate would pass to Husayn,[38] Ali's younger son, in the event of Mu'áwíyah's death. However, wanting his lineage to remain in the position of Caliph, Mu'áwíyah broke this agreement with Hasan and named his son Yazíd as his heir. Mu'áwíyah died in 680 AD and although his father assured Yazíd's succession, many Muslims were unwilling to submit to his rule. Husayn freed from the bonds that his brother's agreement had placed on him made his claim as the rightful heir of the Prophet. People from the city of Kúfah, who had earlier supported his brother, sent a deputation to pledge their allegiance to the cause of Husayn. Husayn sent a delegation to Kúfah, who were put to death by the governor of the city, who had been appointed by Yazíd. Hearing this news and in the face of grave danger Husayn made his way to Kúfah with a small number of followers, the male contingent of which is estimated to be around seventy. On the morning of the tenth day of the month of Muharram in 680 AD, Husayn and his small band of followers were met at Karbála by an overwhelming force loyal to the Caliph Yazíd. Heavily outnumbered, Husayn and his followers perished but this date became a watershed in Islamic history. This event has cast the differences between the Sunni and Shia sects of Islam in stone and unleashed passions that have not dissipated in the centuries that have followed. *Áshúrá*, as the 10th day of Muharram has come to be called, symbolises in the Shia faith the need to fight against injustice even in the face of overwhelming odds. Husayn the third Imam of Shi'ism has become a strong and symbolic force in Shia political and religious doctrine. The massacre at Karbála has also been used as an example of the constant battle of Shia's against adversity from within their own society and from without.

And so within sixty years of the death of the Prophet Muhammad, internal division and conflict beset the Islamic faith. The Prophet created a coherent and well functioning nation of Islam, from the multitude of tribes, clans and polytheists that roamed the Arabian Peninsula. He created a nation based upon a series of laws, which brought with it order and peace to this restless and barren land. The factions that emerged upon his death were not unlike those that ripped apart the world of Christendom following the death of Jesus. In brief, the Sunni's believe that the Prophet Muhammad died without designating an heir, leaving his followers to select his successor. While the Shia community contends that Mohammed indicated that Ali, his closest living relative, should be his successor. It is further contended by Shia's that given God's sense of justice and benevolence towards the human race how could he have left the issue of leadership undecided in the wake of Muhammad's death.[39] Shia's also claim that the Prophet would not leave such an important decision as his successor to the deliberations of the whole community, as in the Sunni principle of consensus rule, as there is always the possibility that they might choose incorrectly. This is a theme that re-occurs throughout Shia political ideology, that only God is aware of the qualities of individuals and only he therefore can choose a successor to Muhammad.[40] That is how the Shia argument maintains that only those directly related to the Prophet possess the qualities to lead the faithful. Twelver Shi'ism, which forms the ideological basis of the government in Iran today, and the major focus of this body of work, believes that leadership came directly from the Prophet to Ali and through him to his eleven male descendants. The last of which, Imam Mahdi, has gone into occultation and will return at the end of time to create a just society.

As we have seen there is a third major branch of Islam, which has played an important role in the early years of Islam, the Khawarji.[41] This group was formed about a quarter of a century after the death of the prophet and stemmed from its rejection of the stances of both the Shia and Sunni sects and their total belief in following the literal word of the Quran. Allied to their strict adherence to the word of the Quran was the belief that any Muslim, irrespective of their race or origin could be elected as the head of the faith. This put them at odds with the Sunni's who confined the Calipate to the House of the Prophet and the Shia's who restricted it to the male descendants of the Prophet through his son-in-law Ali. The Khawariji's propensity for radicalism and violence has resulted in many fundamentalist groups today being associated with this sect.[42] Most of the contemporary followers of this sect can be found in Algeria, Tunisia, Oman and East Africa.

While most of the geographic and military gains of Islam occurred during the reign of the Umayyads, their focus on the political rather than the religious aspects of Islam caused discord and conflict within the ranks of the faithful. The divisions within Islam, which materialised such a short time after the death of the Prophet, have intensified over time and to some extent have weakened the potential impact of Islam. The period of Islamic history presided over by the Prophet himself, is looked upon by Muslims as a period of near perfection. Islam's role as the political, social and moral guide of the people was unquestioned. Muhammad's position as political and spiritual leader ensured a society united in its beliefs and unwavering in its purpose.

Shi'ism as a Political Movement

Over the past quarter of a century we have witness a broad based Islamic revival from Egypt to Indonesia and from Turkey to Chechnya. This revival has been misinterpreted in many ways, it does not mean that more people are showing a greater degree of religious commitment, instead it is due to the fact that Islam has begun to re-enter the political spectrum.[43] Islam has been used by opposition groups to highlight the injustice in their society and by those in power to maintain a base of popular support. In most cases the re-emergence of Islam in a political sense has not occurred at the behest of the religious leaders, in fact it is the politicians, the army or the opposition groups who has begun to use Islam as a political weapon to galvanise the population to their cause. In Turkey, for example the Islamic opposition *Refah* or Virtue Party has espoused Islamic ideals and by doing so have attempted to highlight that the causes for the moral and social decline in their society lie in the State's increased secularism. The 'Islamic Brotherhood' in Egypt has used Islam and its inherent quest against injustice to gain popular support for their cause. While in Saudi Arabia, the ruling monarchy has always espoused Islamic ideals through which it could unite a fractured society and lend legitimacy to their rule.

Iran is quite unique in that the ulema[44] or religious classes spearheaded the Islamic revival. This difference between the Islamic movement in Iran and elsewhere stems from the fact that Iranians are followers of the Shia sect of Islam, while the vast majority of the rest of the world are Sunni's. What initially started as differing perspectives on the rights of succession following the Prophet Muhammad, have over time resulted in both groups developing their own theories concerning Islam, the State and society. This is true to the extent that much of Shia theory has been developed in recent centuries and does not necessarily find its roots in the time of the Prophet. This is especially true when we consider Ayatollah Khomeini's often unique and radical ideas on the role of Islam and the State. That said however, much of the theory surrounding the establishment of the Islamic Republic of Iran is based or takes its influence for the earliest period of Islamic history. It is for this reason that it is important for us to trace the development of Shia's thought from that time.

Islam has often been described as a political religion. By doing so, it is as if we are describing Islam and politics as different entities, as if Islam is being politicised by an outside force. In fact for followers of Islam, there is no difference between the practice of their faith and their politics, they are one and the same. Unlike his predecessors, many of Muhammad's revelations are political or legal in nature. This was especially true of the revelations, which occurred after Muhammad and his followers migrated to Medina. Muhammad's position as leader of his people was as much, if not more, a political position than a religious one. The initial division between Shia's and Sunni's over the rights of succession was more of a political disagreement, which took on religious overtones only years later.[45] It was under the Caliphate of the Umayyad and after the massacre of Karbála that much of the religio-political sectarian character of Shi'ism developed.[46] In opposition to the often tyrannical rule of the Umayyads a variety of groups espousing allegiance to a number of Ali's descendants revolted.

Husayn's only surviving son Alí, who was at Karbála but spared because he was extremely ill at the time and not expected to live, became the fourth Imam of the Shia's. Viewing the position of Imam as being descended directly from the Prophet Muhammad and therefore chosen directly by God, Shia's began increasingly to view their leaders as being infallible. In addition, one of the core beliefs of the Shia faith the concept of the *mahdi* or 'rightly guided one', who will return at the end of time to bring justice to the world, was a serious transgression from the original writings of the Quran. Shi'ism, however, was not in any way an organised cohesive group and therefore during the reign of the Abbasids (746 to 1256 AD), it splintered into a number of diverse groupings. While all believe in the succession of Ali, the main bone of contention is the number of Imams that followed Ali as spiritual leader of the faithful. The smallest group known as the 'Fivers' or *Zaidis* is the more moderate of the splinters. They are also closest in thought to the Sunni's having a similar legal system and do not claim that the Imams are infallible. They get their name from the reverence they hold for the fifth Imam and are mainly found today in northern Yemen. The two remaining groups are known as the 'Seveners' or *Isma'ilis* and the 'Twelvers' or *Imamis*. It was the issue of succession after the death of the sixth Imam, Ja'far as-Sadeq, which led to this latest split in

Shi'ism. The Isma'ilists believed that Isma'il was the legitimate successor to his father. There is a continuous line of succession within the Isma'ilis sect up to the present day with the original rights of the Imams being placed in the personage of the Agha Khan. The largest group, the 'Twelvers' followed the succession of Músá, a more moderate son of the Sixth Imam. The Twelvers believe that the son of the eleventh Imam went into occultation and will re-appear as the *Mahdi*, as discussed earlier, at the end of time to bring justice to the oppressed.

The doctrine of occultation was first put forward during the Abbasid Caliphate, by a wealthy Shia leader of the court.[47] This doctrine resulted in a form of compromise between the contenders for Shia and Sunni political control. By suggesting that there was no living leader with full infallibility to interpret the Imams' writings or to rule in their absence, it implied that there was no direct basis to counter the rule of the Caliph. However, in more recent times there was a movement away from this quietist approach as the doctrine of occultation was used to suggest that no temporal leaders have the right to rule in the absence of the Imam. By definition only the religious leaders had the knowledge to interpret the will of the Imams and therefore had more right to rule than any temporal leader. That said, during the Abbasid Caliphate the Twelver Shia movement did not directly attack the Caliph's legitimacy to govern, in fact on some occasions they were allied to the Abbasid's against the Isma'ilists. Examples of this quietist approach to temporal rulers can be seen even in the contemporary writings Ayatollah Khomeini. While he argued for more control for the *ulema* in relation to religious affairs, it was not until 1963 that he call for the direct overthrow of the Shah's regime. It was only after persistent and direct attacks on the very basis of Shia support and authority that revolution against the temporal rulers became the preferred and, in his eyes, the only option. This development of Khomeini's thought from quietism to revolution will be dealt with in more detail in later chapters.

Shi'ism and Iran

Iran[48] or Persia, as it was termed by the Greeks, had a wide and varied history before the Arab invasion and conquest which begun in 637 AD The Achemenian (circa 559-339 BC) and Sasanian (AD 224-651 AD) dynasties provided much of the cultural history from which Iran has benefited.[49] The main religious influence from the pre-Islamic period came from Zoroastrianism.[50] This complex religion is based on the duality of good and evil and the inherent battle between the two. This belief is augmented by a system of punishments and rewards that will be accorded in the afterlife based upon ones deeds and actions in the present. Another religious influence during the pre-Islamic time in Iran was the Mazdak.[51] This was an offshoot of the larger Manichaeism, which was found in the eastern sector of the Persian Empire (i.e. in modern day Iraq) and was also based upon the duality of good and evil.[52] It preached a form of communism of material goods and revolted against the class system, against poverty and general economic decline, which characterised the latter part of the Sasanian period. These themes found in the pre-Islamic religions of Persia found great similarity with the teachings of Muhammad and it was of no great surprise that the people of Iran became avid supporters and subsequently defenders of the Islamic faith.

The Islamic belief in the battle against injustice and tyranny can be seen to have found echoes in Iran's pre-Islamic society. The economic and social decline of the Sasasian period made the Muslim conquest of Iran relatively easy. The religious doctrines of Islam espousing greater equality found fertile ground amongst the people of Persia and they became committed followers of their newfound religion. Looking at the Islamic revival that gripped Iran during the latter years of the Pahlavi monarchy (1925-1979), we can see that many of the ideas are new and based upon Ayatollah Khomeini's interpretation of Shia doctrine, others however can be viewed in a more traditional context. This context is the eternal battle between good and evil, which transcends time and circumstances. Socio-economic and cultural decline, are grievances that have been felt through the centuries. Religion or in this context Islam, promised to muster the forces of good and by doing so bring justice to the oppressed and freedom to the downtrodden.

Today Iran has become synonymous with Shi'ism; however originally this was not the case. The early adherents to Shi'ism were from the area north of Yemen. And while the story goes that the assassin of Caliph Umar fled to Persia, where he lived amongst people of his kind, the vast majority of modern day Iran remained Sunni until the declaration of a Shia state by the Safavids in 1501 AD The Safavids (1501-1742) were a nomadic group originally espousing a form of Islam that incorporated both Sunni and Shia elements. However, by the mid-fifteenth century after travelling amongst the Anatolian nomadic tribes, the Safavids became extremists brandishing a form of Islam reminiscent of the early days of the Shia faith. Once in power the Safavids brand of Shi'ism became less extreme following its contact with the more orthodox views of the followers of Twelver Shi'ism. The declaration of the Shia state under the Safavids also marked another turning point in Islamic history, that being the renewal of the confrontation between Shi'ism and Sunnism that has remained in place until this day. Under the Abbasid caliphate (749-1248 AD) while there were revolutionary Shia groups, the vast majority of the Shia faithful adhered to the political leadership of the Sunni Caliph. This was especially true following the occultation of the Twelfth Imam. The leadership vacuum that was left by his disappearance led to the vast majority of Shia's taking a quietist approach to temporal leadership. This quietist approach of Shi'ism changed with the Safavids belief in ideological conformity and in conversion through conquest. This led the first Safavid ruler of Iran to demand that the Shia ulema publicly criticise and curse the first three Sunni Caliphs. In part, this stemmed from religious vigour and in part, was due to the desire to create a distinction from the ideology and territory of the Sunni Ottoman controlled world. This antagonism between the Safavid (Shia) and Ottoman (Sunni) Empires brought the ideological differences between these two sects of Islam onto a political level.[53] By the end of the Safavid period in 1722, the vast majority of Iranians identified strongly with Twelver Shi'ism.

Twelver Shi'ism follows a line of twelve Imams, the twelfth of which is believed to have gone into seclusion in around 874 AD, his followers await his return as a *Mahdi*, or messianic guide, who will bring an end to tyranny and corruption and restore just rule. While awaiting the re-appearance of the 'Hidden Imam' both the religious leaders (the ulema) and the political leaders of Iran contended with each other for the right to guide society on behalf of the hidden Imam, until his return. Whilst the ulema never accepted the right of a succession of Shahs (Emperors) to rule in the name of God, their imperial rule was all but accepted. This can be seen during the reign of Shah Ismail Safavi[54] the founder of the Safavid dynasty (1501-1742). He established Shia Islam as the official religion of an Islamic Empire and claimed to be the Imam's representative on earth, the Shia ulema subsequently approving his royal title of the 'Shadow of God on Earth'.[55] At the same time the ulema carved out their own niche as religious leaders of the Shia community. The ulema affirmed their role as guardians and interpreters (*mujtahids*) of religious texts and as living sources of emulation (*marja-i-taqlid*) whose example and teaching should be followed until the coming of the *Mahdi*.[56]

The relationship between the temporal rulers and the ulema vacillated between passive acceptance of the regime and outright rebellion. Under the strong hand of the Safavids, the ulema were relatively quiet. While during the reign of the weaker Qajars,[57] the ulema reasserted itself as the rightful heirs and guardians of the Islamic faith. This increased influence of the ulema in religious, as well as political matters can evidently be seen in their involvement in the *bazaari* protest of 1891-92 against the selling of a tobacco concession to a foreign national. The involvement of the ulema in the protest gave religious legitimacy to the cause and forced the cancellation of the concession, the penalty incurred resulted in the creation of Iran's first foreign debt. The ulema's increasing influence on Iranian society can be further seen in their involvement in the Constitutional Revolution of 1905-11. The ulema led a diverse group of opposition activists including intellectuals and secular nationalists in demanding constitutional reforms that would curb and limit the power of the Qajar rulers. The Constitutional Revolution was a significant learning experience for the Iranian ulema. While being paramount to the success of the protest, the ulema were not willing to capitalise on the leadership vacuum that resulted. Instead they returned to their mosques and religious school leaving the political leadership of Iran to secular politicians. The Shia ulema being in a minority throughout Islamic history perceived themselves as being in a position of perpetual opposition. Regarding themselves as representatives of the oppressed and the downtrodden, they preferred to remain detached from political leadership, which they viewed as being corrupt. While the Shia ulema of the early nineteenth century were willing to entrust temporal leadership onto others, the clergy following the 1979 revolution took a more active role in creating a just society based on the philosophy of Ayatollah Khomeini.

Today the Shia community accounts for just 15% of the world's Muslim population, it has always remained a minority sect, believing itself to be disenfranchised and oppressed by the majority Sunni's.[58] This feeling of being constantly oppressed at the hands of others has prevailed throughout the history of the Shia faith and has resulted, in part, in the formation of its reactionary character. For the vast majority of Islamic history it has been the Sunni Caliphate that has prevailed as the leader of the Muslim world. From the time of Husayn's defeat at Karbála and under the divisive rule of the house of Umayyad, Shia revolutionary groups directly opposed and resisted Sunni rule. These groups continued their opposition after the fall of the Umayyads (749 AD), under the subsequent rule of the Abbasid Caliphate.

Many writers have successfully outlined the differences in the ideology and the practice of the Shia and Sunni sects. Some such as Henri Corbin have contrasted these differences as an encounter between the two cultures from which they stem, those being the Arab and Iranian cultures.[59] While the original Shia communities were of Arab origin, Shi'ism did not take on political significance until the declaration by the Safavids of the first Shia state (1501 AD). Much of Shia ideology has developed since this period and as such Corbin's basis of comparison between Sunnism and Shi'ism can be seen to have some validity. Others have taken the view that the social origins of the Shia faith have been tantamount in the formation of their political practices. Especially as Shia's have come mostly from the tribes of southern Arabia whose tradition of a 'semi-divine king' has developed into a cornerstone of Shia political thought.[60] Enayat puts forward the idea that Shia ideology was partially formed as a reaction to Sunni dominance. He contends that each school of thought has been affected in some way by the development of the other and as such the doctrinal difference between the two is the not the abyss that is sometimes portrayed.[61]

The evolution of the fundamentals of the Shia faith and by consequence of Shia political thought has resulted from their individual interpretation of the Quran and the experience of living as a minority under Sunni rule. One of the most important tenets of the Shia faith is the refusal to concur with, or believe that, the opinion of the majority is necessarily right, or conversely as Enayat explains this, as a belief in 'a rationalised defence of the moral excellence of an embattled minority'.[62] It has been argued by Shia's that the Quran too took a negative view of majority rule and rarely accepts it as a factor of legitimacy'.[63] Enayat goes further to suggest that with Shia ideology there is a belief in the inherent virtue of 'belonging to a militant minority'.[64] This idea of defiance against a majority and being the oppressed transcends Shia thought even to the present day. In reference to the Islamic revolution, the lone opposition stance of Ayatollah Khomeini against the seemingly secure but unjust rule of the Pahlavi regime can be likened to the Shia admiration of the defiance and martyrdom of Imam Husayn.

In contrast Sunnism is based on the tenets of consensus rule. This belief in community rule is based upon the claim that the prophet Muhammad is quoted as being of the opinion that 'my community will never agree in error'. Sunnisn thereby confers upon the community of rulers the same infallibility that the Shia places upon the line of twelve Imams or their representatives.[65] While any minority that has been constantly ostracised and persecuted will gradually pull away from the majority view and formulate their own attitudes and opinion, we can trace the origins of the Shia view on majority rule to the theory of succession to the prophet being confined to members of the Prophet Muhammad's House. This had lead some to argue that this reflects the elitist nature within the doctrine of Shi'ism.

Shia's and Sunni's also differ in their opinion of Islamic government. While both sides agree that the Islamic history since the beginning of the reign of the Umayyads was far removed from the 'Golden Age' of Islam, they disagree about the direction taken since this time. For the Sunnis the 'Golden Age' of Islam is viewed in utopian terms, Islamic history since this time has been a movement away from this ideal state. For Shia's, as they await the return of the hidden Imam who will bring justice and equality, for them Islamic history is rather a movement towards the creation of the ideal state. This sense of idealism or utopianism is prevalent through Shia ideology. The belief that at the end of time God will create the perfect state filled with virtue and equality almost puts such a state outside the bounds of human creation. Believing that the creation of a true Islamic society can only be possible with the return of the hidden Imam, for centuries the Shia ulema were content to continue under the political leadership of the Sunni Caliphate. While the above statement is true, taken in the context of being a minority this could also be termed a pragmatic approach towards their survival. In any case the Shia ulema did not openly support the Sunni leadership, nor did they actively opposed it. As Enayat points out 'the dividing line between idealism and apathy can be a very thin one',[66] which meant that following the absence of a living Imam, Shia's were apt to remain out of politics and Shi'ism remained within the realms of a theological endeavour. At least that is until the politicisation of Shi'ism by the Safavids in Iran in the sixteenth century.

Much of the Islamic world has been ruled throughout the ages by governments that are not based structurally on the teachings of Islam but who espouse Islam as a means of legitimising their rule.[67] In Shi'ism there is the belief that all temporal rulers are illegitimate, this together with the conviction in the fallibility of man and natural dark side of man's personality, heightens the view that only God can directly rule and create the idealistic state to which Shia's aspire to. Therefore, in the absence of a living Imam to guide the Shia community, who should have the right to rule? While the Safavids in Iran were able to legitimise their rule through claiming that they were directly descended from the family of the Prophet Muhammad, subsequent rulers were not as fortunate. The Qajar dynasty had no direct linkage to the house of the Prophet and therefore lacked any form of legitimacy in the eyes of the Shia ulema. It was during the time of the Qajar dynasty that the ulema began to reassert their influence over the Islamic community and undermined the authority of the political rulers of Iran. While the Pahlavi dynasty was decidedly anti-ulema and use autocratic means to legitimise their rule, it was under Mohammad Reza Shah that the ulema began to reassert itself in a political sense. Ayatollah Khomeini appealed to the masses and the junior clergy to save Iran and Islam from the tyrannical rule of the Pahlavi's. This was a call that united much of the opposition against the incumbent regime and set in motion a series of events that would see the establishment of the first modern theocratic state. Iran's modern Islamic movement was unique in that it was led by the clergy and was the only movement of the 1970s to gain political control. The reasons for this are developed further in the next chapter when the Shia and Sunni perspectives on government are reviewed and their differing views analysed, so that an assessment of the role of the Islamic movement in modern society can be made.

Notes

[1] See further Riley, S., Jonathan, S. (1987), *The Crusades: a short history* (New Haven: Yale University Press), and Kernaghan, P. (1993), *The Crusades: cultures in conflict* (New York: Cambridge University Press).
[2] An interesting book in this regard is by Said, E. (1997), *Covering Islam: How the media and the experts determine how we see the rest of the world* (London: Vintage).
[3] See further Reeves, M. (2000), *Muhammad in Europe* (Reading: Garnet); Nielsen, J. (1994), *Islam and Europe* (Birmingham: Center for the Study of Islam and Christian-Muslim Relations); Anders, J. and Jorgen, B. (Eds) (1997), *Islam in a changing world: Europe and the Middle East* (Richmond: Curzon); Bistolfi, R. (1995), *Islam: a new element in the culture of Europe* (Birmingham: Centre for the Study of Islam and Christian-Muslim Relations).
[4] For a truly academic and enlightening text on this subject see Balyuzi, H. (1976), *Muhammad and the Course of Islam* (Oxford: George Ronald). Another good account of the Prophet Muhammad's life is by Andrae, T. (1960), *Mohammad, the Man and his Faith*, (New York: Harper and Row). Also available is Hakeem, F. (1988), *La vie de Mohammad* (London: Islam International), or Sliman, I.B. (1990), *The life of Mohammad: Prophet of Allah* (London: Studio Editions).
[5] Mecca is the form used in English from the Arabic version al-Makkah.
[6] This information was obtained through primary research interviews, quoted from the book *Kanzol Amal* by Montafeg Hendi.
[7] The Ka'bah, is Arabia's and Islam's most holy shrine, it contains the Black Stone, reputedly brought to Abraham by the Angel Gabriel.
[8] Wharton, B. (1998), *The Islamic resurgence in Egypt and its relationship with the EU* (Limerick: University of Limerick), p.40.
[9] Muhammad is often referred to in the Quran as *Nadhir*, which means 'He who warns'. This is substantiated by the 19th verse number of the fifth chapter which called Maidah (translated means Food).
[10] For an account of the early period of Muhammad's life see further; al-Tabari, Abu (1988), *Muhammad at Mecca* (Albany: State University of New York Press), or Peters, F.E. (1994), *Muhammad and the origins of Islam* (Albany: State University of New York Press).
[11] The different aspects of Muhammad's character, together with his role as socio-political leader of the Islamic society can be seen in the following; Watt, W.M. (1974), *Muhammad: prophet and statesman* (London: Galaxy Books), Muir, W. (1912), *The life of Mohammad: from original sources* (Edinburgh: Grant).

[12] The *hijrah* (or its English variants hegira, *hijra* or *hejira*) from Mecca by Muhammad and his followers is often mistranslated as a 'flight', when in fact it was a well-organised and planned withdrawal or emigration from the city.

[13] For an account of the Prophet's time in Medina, see further Watt, W.M. (1981), *Muhammad at Medina* (Oxford: Oxford University Press).

[14] This can especially be seen when after the siege of Medina in 627 AD when Sa'd ibn-Mu'adh head of the Aws clan, sentenced the male members of the Banú-Qurayzah to death for their treachery during the siege. This decision was against the advice of most of his clan members but showed that allegiance to the Islamic community was to be set above all other alliances, even those owed to their clan.

[15] For one perspective on Muhammad the warrior, his military campaign and defence of Islam, see further Rahman, A. (1980), *Muhammad as a military leader* (London: Muslim Schools Trust).

[16] Balyuzi, H.M. (1976), p.53.

[17] For example, Muhammad's marriage in 627 AD to the daughter of the chief of the al-Hárith tribe, led to the tribe, who were previously hostile, converting to Islam and allying themselves to the Muslim community in Medina.

[18] While there is a debate as to whether Muhammad's emissaries when as far as Pope Honorius I of Compania, it is fair to say that Muhammad's emissaries travelled from Persian to Northern Africa and into parts of Eastern Europe. See further Balyuzi, H.M. (1976), Chapter 2.

[19] Watt, W.M. (1981), p.122.

[20] This was a treaty signed by Muhammad with the Quraysh leaders of Mecca, allowing Muhammad and his followers to go on pilgrimage to Mecca. It also forbade hostilities between Muslims and the people of Mecca. Many of Muhammad's followers saw this as a defeat but as time would show, it allowed Muslims to mix with the population of Mecca, proselytising and winning many converts. See further Balyuzi, H.M. (1976), p.127.

[21] See further Gabrieli, F. (1968), *Muhammad and the conquests of Islam* (London: Weidenfeld & Nicolson), or Bishai, W. (1968), *Islamic history of the Middle East: backgrounds, development, and fall of the Arab Empire* (Boston: Allyn and Bacon).

[22] On an individual level 'jihad' has more to do with personal sacrifice and effort.

[23] Wharton, B. (1998), p.43.

[24] For a more in-depth view of this period see, Lombard, M. (1975), *The Golden Age of Islam* (Oxford: North-Holland Publishing Co).

[25] Shia (also spelt Shi'a or Shi'ite) literally means a follower of Ali.

[26] For the Shia perspective on Islam, see Jafri, S. (1979), *Origins and early development of Shi'a Islam* (London: Longman); Tabataba'i, M. (1975), *Shi'ite Islam* (London: Allen & Unwin); and Halm, H. (1997), *Shi'a Islam: from religion to revolution* (Princeton: Markus Wiener). For a comparative analysis see Salamah, A. (1991), *Shia & Sunni Perspective on Islam* (Riyadh: Abul-Qasim) or Qutm, M., *Islam the Misunderstood Religion* (Kuwait City: Ministry of Awqaf & Islamic affairs).

[27] Balyuzi, H.M. (1976), p. 220.

[28] This information was obtained during primary research interviews, it was quoted from the book *Al Gadier* by Allameh Amini.

[29] Ali was Muhammad's cousin and son-in law. He was married to Fatimah the Prophet's daughter (the Prophet had sons and so Ali was the closest living relative). His children Hasan and Hussein were the only two male surviving grandsons of the Prophet Muhammad. Ali practically grew up in the Prophet's household and was the closest relation to the Prophet and for this reason those of the Shia faith believe that he would be the natural successor to the Muhammad.

[30] Abu Bakr was Muhammad's uncle and one of the first converts to Islam. He accompanied Muhammad on his exodus from Mecca and remained a close confidante of the Prophet throughout his life. The Sunni's contend that as the most senior member of the prophet's family, it was he who had the right to succeed the Prophet on his death.
[31] Balyuzi, H.M. (1976), p. 227.
[32] Watt, W.M. (1981), p.141.
[33] Interview with an Iranian cleric March 1999.
[34] Khawarji literally means outsiders but they have also been known as 'Pietists' or 'Reciters of the Quran', they could be viewed as Islamic puritans.
[35] Mu'áwíyah was the chief counsel for the Caliph Uthman and has been seen as the instigator of much of the Caliph's unjust decisions. Following Uthman's death he escaped to Syria, where he roused the people against Ali and demanded vengeance for Uthman's murder. Power hungry, he refused to swear allegiance of Ali and commenced a rebellion against him, claiming the position of Caliph for himself and the House of Umayyad.
[36] A.H. refers to 'After the Hirjah'.
[37] This point, together with the disastrous consequences for Islam that the rule of the House of Umayyad's had, was depicted by Ameer, A. (1949), *A Short History of the Saracens* (London: Macmillan and Co), and Balyuzi, H.M. (1976), *Muhammad and the Course of Islam* (London: George Ronald). In the latter Richard Drozy the Dutch Orientalist (1820-1883) is quoted as maintaining that the Umayyads showed their antipathy to Islam when in the guise of the heirs of the Prophet, they set about desecrating much of what was sacred.
[38] For an account of Imam Husayn's life and the battle at Karbála see further al-Balagh Foundation (1990), *Imam Hussein and the Day of Ashura* (Tehran: Al-Balagh Foundation), or Rashid, A. (1993), *Imam Hussein: may Allah be pleased with him* (London: Ta-Ha).
[39] Enayat, H. (1982), *Modern Islamic Political Thought* (London: Macmillan Press), p. 19.
[40] Ibid., p.23.
[41] For a broad look at the divisions within Islam see further al-Baghdadi, `Abd al-Qahir ibn Tahir (1935), *Moslem schisms and sects: the history of the various philosophic systems developed in Islam* (London: Luzac).
[42] This claim has been made against 'The Muslim Brotherhood' in Egypt; see Enayat, H. (1982), p.7.
[43] See further Keddie, N. (Ed.) (1981), chapter entitled 'Religion and Society'.
[44] *Ulema* has often been translated to mean 'clergy', while this facilitates greater understanding, it is inaccurate. In Christianity the clergy are placed between man and God, while the *ulema* are not meant to intercede on man's behalf but are there to carry out other tasks, such as Islamic law and education. For an insight into other Farsi or Arabic terms/dates relevant to this research see further appendix IV.
[45] It is important to remember that as the fourth Caliph, Ali is as much revered by the Sunni's as by the Shia's. Many Sunni's view the Caliphate of the Umayyad's as being illegitimate and tyrannical and Ali's battle against them as being a just one.
[46] Keddie, N. (1981), p.7.
[47] Balyuzi, H.M. (1976), p. 236.
[48] The name Iran comes from the word 'Aryan', which was used to, described a group of Indo-European migrants who pass through the region in or around 1000 BC. Those called Iranians remained in Iran while the remainder the Aryans continued their journey on to the Indian sub-continent.
[49] For an insight into the pre-Islamic religious influence in Iran see further Shaked, S. (1994), *Dualism in transformation: varieties of religion in Sasanian Iran* (London: University of London).

[50] On the Zoroastrian faith see further Boyce, M. (1991), *A history of Zoroastrianism* (New York: Brill).
[51] See further Shaked, S. (1994).
[52] Ibid.
[53] For a more in depth look at the conflict between Safavid Iran and the Sultan of the Ottoman Empire, and the politicisation of the Shi'i faith under the Safavid rulers read Aubin, J. (1970), 'La Politique religieuse des Safavides', *Le Shi'ismamite*. Also interesting on this topic are Mazzaoui, M. (1972), *The Origins of the Safawids* (Wiesbaden: F. Steiner), or Grey, C. (1873), *A Narrative of Italian Travels in Persia, in the Fifteenth and Sixteenth Centuries* (London: Hakluyt Society).
[54] Shah Ismail Safavi was the founder of the Safavid dynasty that ruled Persia from 1501-1736. He lived from 1487-1524.
[55] Mazzaoui, M. (1972), p.19.
[56] Ibid., p.19.
[57] The Qajar dynasty was established in 1796 and last until their overthrow by Reza Khan in 1925.
[58] Keddie, N. (Ed.) (1983), *Religion and Politics in Iran, Shi'ism from Quietism to revolution* (New Haven: Yale University Press), p.17.
[59] See further Corbin, H. (1971), *En Islam Iranien* (Paris: Gallimard).
[60] Enayat, H. (1982), p.18.
[61] Ibid., p.18.
[62] Ibid., p.19.
[63] Ibid., p.20. The verses from the Quran used to justify this position were (6:116) (12:106) and (38:24).
[64] Ibid., p.20.
[65] Ibid., p.21.
[66] Ibid., p.27.
[67] Modern day examples of this would be Saudi Arabia, Qatar and most of the Persian Gulf Emirates.

Chapter 2
The Islamic Movement – in Resurgence or in Decline?

Religion made its re-emergence on the political stage in the 1970s. Following the Second World War the trend was towards the secularisation of the State. Religion became progressively a private matter and the division between the state and religion became the norm. Religion's role in society too was weakened. Technology appeared to have a greater influence on the direction of society and its values, than did any values associated with religious faith. Society was leaving behind the traditionalist religious institutions, which were viewed as being incompatible with modern society. This clash with modernity affected all of the major religions. The Catholic Church convened the Vatican II Ecumenical Council, which was in some ways an attempt to find points of commonality between Catholicism and modern society.[1] The church was trying to identify with the modern world and in many ways was striving to adopt some of its values, making itself part of the development process rather than solely a spectator. Similarly within the Muslim world, Islamic intellectuals were creating a discourse in which the concept of Islam and modernity were considered together, they attempted to define Islam in terms of modern society in much the same way that other religions were doing in this period.

By the mid-1970s society began to fear the excesses of modernity, and societal problems were increasingly being blamed on an alienated from God.[2] Political, cultural and even economic stagnation was being defined in terms of state and societal separation from religion. This religious revival occurred at a time when various other groups were challenging the status quo in society and the capitalist social order. Marxists, one of these groups, viewed the ills of society and the disintegration of its values as occurring out of the quest for consumerism, which capitalism encourages. These two movements, religious and Marxist, competed for adherents throughout the Middle East in the 1970s. Marxism and Islam have many parallels, not least the fact that both dogmas aspire to create societies based on the concept of equality. Many ideologues of the Islamic movement borrowed the concept of revolution, prevalent throughout Marxist thinking, and adapted to Islamic terminology, injecting a sense of radicalism to the movement in the latter part of the 1970s.[3]

The Islamisation of Social Outrage

Islamic activism was by far the most radical religious movement throughout the 1970s. Islamic agitation in Saudi Arabia, Egypt and Iran created headlines, which struck fear into the hearts of western governments.[4] That said, the Islamic Movement was never a cohesive organisation, it was as diverse in its goals as it was in its influences. The Islamic movement can be divided in a geographic sense, as well as an ideological sense. For example the Sunni Arab movement in Saudi Arabia and Egypt has little in common with the Sunni movement in South East Asia, while the Iranian Shia movement was again quite distinct from all of the others.[5] One reason for this was because the Islamic resurgence was less a result of religious belief than it was a product of the society from which it stemmed. Islam in the 1970s became a symbol of protest against the modern world, against a world many in the Muslim community could neither feel a part of nor could they associate with its values. This can be seen by the fact that militants in the Islamic movements were rarely from a clerical background and the advances in Islamic thought occurred more through Islamic scholars with secular education's than by those with traditional seminary backgrounds. In many cases the hotbed of Islamic activity was in the university campuses throughout the Muslim world, where Islamic activists rubbed shoulders with Marxist agitators. The resulting ideas that emerged possessed equal amounts of inspiration from both.

The Islamic Movement Misunderstood

The movement that developed in the 1970s was not a 'traditional' Islamic movement. The Islamic movement has been depicted in the West as an attempt to re-create the society and values from the time of the Prophet Muhammad. Nothing could be further from the truth. Far from trying to re-create the society of the 7th Century, the Islamic movement in the 1970s was trying to re-interpret Islam for the modern age. It is possibly for this reason that the main advocates of the 1970s movement were Islamic intellectuals and not members of the clergy. That said, the one Islamic movement led by a cleric developed a political framework which resulted in the installation of the first modern theocracy, that movement was in Iran and its ideologue was Ayatollah Khomeini.[6] As we will see in future chapters, Khomeini has been portrayed in the west as a religious fanatic with a desire to drag Iran back into the Middle Ages, as being a traditionalist in every sense of the word. The reality of the Iranian Islamic movement and of Khomeini's own ideals are almost the antithesis of these statements. If by traditional one means a strict adherence to the writings of the Quran, then Khomeini's views on the state and the clergy's role in politics is quite radical. Khomeini is better described as a populist leader of a social movement rather than as a fundamentalist leading a religious reformation. The Islamic movement was as much a social statement, as it was a religious assertion. The followers of the Islamic movement can be largely defined as city dwellers who were content with the trappings of modernity but who were discontented with their society which prevented them from attaining the additional benefits of modernity, such as social justice, that they craved. This means that agitation against corruption, economic stagnation and political imperialism which resulted in the social exclusion of vast segments of society, all found a voice in Islam which fought against tyranny, injustice and which attempted to create a society based on justice and equality.

It was through this endeavour to create a society based on equality that Islam and Marxism found adherents from similar backgrounds. Furthermore, the Islamic movement shared with Marxist movements, the desire to create a new society based on cultural norms and traditions prevalent in their society. Marxist movements from Mao Tse Tung in China to Colonel Gadaffi in Libya all re-interpreted Marxism to fit their unique societal experience. There is one major difference, however, between Islamic movements and Marxists movements of the post-1945 era. While Marxist movements from Cuba to Peru were largely rural based affairs, the Islamic movements of the 1970s were predominantly urban based. A further element of the Islamic movement was that it not only contained trappings of Marxism but it took on the garb of a third world movement, viewing Muslim society as being oppressed, in a political and economic sense, by the western world. The Islamic movement also shared a propensity for violence with other third world movements. The numerous terrorist hijackings in the early 1980s and the bloodletting following the Iranian revolution are all testament to that. But it was the anti-imperialist and anti-colonialist rhetoric of the Islamic movement in the 1970s that closely associated it with a third world movement.

Throughout the Arab Middle East, the three successive defeats at the hands of Israel seriously dented the legitimacy of the leadership of Arab nations.[7] The period particularly following the 1967 conflict led many Marxist movements throughout the region to believe that their time had come to instigate a Marxist revolt. However, the 1973 oil-crisis brought back the confidence that was lacking in the leadership of the Arab

Sheikdoms. Not only did the oil embargo and the increase in oil prices bring in large sums of petrodollars to these previously impoverished countries, but the leadership also found that with oil they had an even stronger weapon than war to make their views heard. A crucial by-product of the 1973 oil-crisis was an increase in funding for Islamic movements throughout the region. The vast gains in petrodollars bought oil rich countries, such as Saudi Arabia, a seat at the international table. They used their wealth not only to buy influence but also to propagate the faith, which they claimed as the cornerstone of their political legitimacy. Up until this time the Islamic movement was a largely impoverished venture. The cash gains from the oil crisis re-energised the movement and throughout the early 1970s we can see a decline in the support for Marxist organisations throughout the Middle East and an increase in these organisations oriented more towards Islam.

The Urban Disinherited[8] and the Student Movement

The Islamic movement also found a sympathetic audience amongst the socially 'disinherited' and the university population. A by-product of the 1973 cash windfall by the oil producing countries of OPEC[9] was the commencement of large capital projects that resulted in a sizeable migration from rural to urban areas. The rural youth that came to the urban areas to find their fortune were often disappointed and disillusioned with what was the reality of the oil price boom. Throughout the Middle East, a class of people was established on the outskirts of all the major cities and while the shantytowns may not have had shops or other facilities there inevitably was always a mosque through which the Islamic movement could proliferate its views, to an attentive audience.

While housing may not be status symbols the increased petrodollars enabled the governments of these countries to undertake large building projects, which often included the extension of university facilities. This resulted in many Middle Eastern governments opening up the university system to those who were previously excluded. This had different effects in the various countries of the Middle East but in almost all cases the university campuses became a recruiting ground for the Islamic movement. Furthermore, many governments perceived the rise of Islamic student movements as a counter balance to the increased influence of Marxist or Communist groups amongst the student population. In Iran following the 1973 influx of petrodollars, the government commenced numerous programmes that provided financing for post-graduate study in the West. Furthermore, the opening up of the Iranian University system to those from across the Iranian social strata provided universities with a cross section of students. Many from Islamic backgrounds took advantage of the government funded study abroad programme and it was these highly educated people who were to form the backbone of the government bureaucracy for the Islamic Republic following their return to Iran after the revolution. This point is not to be underestimated when it comes to analysing how the Islamic Republic survived the early, turbulent years following the 1979 revolution. If we are to look at most of the post-colonial societies throughout the Middle East, many of these regimes experiences great difficulty because of the lack of an educated elite to run the country following their independence. In addition, the development of the Islamic movement through the university campuses of the Middle East gave the movement an increasingly intellectual rather than religious edge. It is for this reason that we see the proliferation of many other philosophical ideas throughout the Islamic movement of the 1970s.

The Islamic Resurgence from Above and Below

Most, if not all, religious movements like revolutions are puritan in nature and the Islamic movement is no exception. In many ways it was a rejection of modernity while at the same time seeking to find a place for Islam in contemporary society. It is a sociological movement as much as a religious one. It is a return to values and beliefs that are at odds with modern society. The lack of these values in society is seen as the reason for the failures that are inherent in many developing countries inability to match modernity with social and economic stability. While being products of modernity, Islamists try to deconstruct the very society from which they sprung. They desire to re-direct society back towards a path with Islam as its ideological focus.
    There have been however two perspectives on how to achieve an Islamic society which have divided the Islamic movement from its inception. There are those who believe in revolutionary Islam, the political activists who believe in the overthrow of the apostate rulers and the Islamisation of society through the institutions of the state. The other side of the spectrum also uses political activism but in a persuasive, neofundamentalist manner tries to bring about an Islamic society by influencing society from the bottom up. The former Islamists, by taking control of the vestiges of the state, intend to impose an Islamic state from above. The Iranian Islamic movement was revolutionary in nature; its

intention was not the persuasion of the political order but the overthrow of that order and installation by force of an Islamic state.[10] Alternatively, an example of a neofundamentalist Islamic movement could be the Muslim Brotherhood in Jordan who actively work within the confines of the political system of that country. Similarly *Jamaat-i Islami* in Pakistan while being adamant in their goals of creating an Islamic state have always attempted to do so in a legal manner.

A question remains whether Islam is compatible with the modern national state and perhaps herein lays the problem facing the Islamic movement. It is said that Islam and politics in a Muslim society are synonymous. While this is true, it presents a serious dilemma to all Islamic states. Islamic thought and the Quran advocate the establishment of an Islamic state and specify how the individual should perform his family and societal duties. However neither provide much detail as to how society itself should be organised. While nobody would argue that politics is central to Islam, politics in this sense should be viewed as how one chooses to live ones life. Islam is not about *haute politique,* there is no mention of institutions or social structures in the Quran. The Quran solely deals with how the individual should organise his/her life in order to fulfil the criteria necessary to be a good Muslim. In many ways, Islam is political in a micro and not a macro sense. Islam is political in a personal sense but not when it comes to providing strict societal structures. Indeed, it could be argued that if a truly Islamic society were created, if that society's population were good Muslims, then there would not be any need for institutional structures to ensure the perpetual Islamisation of society. Such a view is not dissimilar to Khomeini's views of religion and society and will be examined in more detail in later chapters.

All advocates of the Islamic movement, no matter which side of the spectrum they come from, agree that political power is essential to achieve their goal of re-directing society back on an Islamic path.[11] Political power is necessary to ensure that every Muslim has the societal structure required for them to fulfil their Islamic duties and to be good Muslims. For this reason, Islamists often advocate that it is impossible for a Muslim to live under a non-Muslim government. While the reasons for this are evident, they are also based upon the life of the Prophet Muhammad, who rather than live under the control of a society unwilling to accept Islam, left Mecca (performing the *hijra*) to create an Islamic society in which he could live.[12] Therefore the creation of an Islamic society is a Muslim's life's endeavour even if that means having to overthrow an infidel government.[13] In Iran, religious life has become synonymous with the internal politics of the country and as one source pointed out, since the end of the war (the

Iran-Iraq war) and the increased opposition to the government's economic and social policies, the numbers attending religious services have steadily decreased.[14] Political protest against government policy, it would appear has taken the form of increased religious apathy, or at least apathy towards the outward participation in religious ceremonies.

The Islamic scholar Maududi confirms that the Quran does not lay down the political structures necessary to govern an Islamic state, 'Islam does not prescribe any definite form for the formation of the consultative body or bodies for the simple reason that it is a universal religion for all time and climes.'[15] While Khomeini believed that the confinements of the Quran could be overcome, the Sunni movement found the transition from a social to a political movement difficult. This was mainly due to their lack of a theoretical framework from which to create an Islamic state. Furthermore, the Sunni sect of Islam contains neither a centralised clergy nor a hierarchy from which they could possibly build a theocratic administration. Shi'ism on the other hand does have a hierarchy and is relatively centralised and perhaps this is why the Islamic revolution in Iran was the only segment of the Islamic movement from the 1970s to bear fruit.

Khomeini's Quranic Additions

This is not the sole area of difference between the Islamic movement in Iran and elsewhere. Iran's was the only movement in the 1970s that was guided by the clergy. While Iran did have its own Islamic intellectuals putting forward ideas that traversed Islamic and Marxist ideologies, the movement, which finally resulted in the establishment of the Islamic state, was the product of intense clerical activity. Khomeini and his clerical followers were by no means representative of the predominant views of the Iranian clergy, who were in favour of continuing their previous quietist approach to temporal leadership.[16] Khomeini, by supplementing the Quran, was able to develop 'Islamic' institutions[17] and thereby establish the first modern Islamic State, in a political as well as religious sense.[18] Khomeini believed that to create an Islamic society, one needed an Islamic State. In many ways it was a top-down approach to Islamising society. The Quran by itself was insufficient in providing the necessary structure to administer a modern state. That said, many within the Islamic clergy, both inside the Islamic movement in Iran and elsewhere, have strongly advocated against other movements taking similar initiatives when attempting to institutionalise Islam. For them, Islam is a universal religion, one that transcends ethnicity, class or any sense of citizenship. Therefore, the boundaries or structures that make up the modern state have no place in Islam.[19] As sovereignty lays with God alone, no man-made structures or boundaries carry any weight in Islam. Man can neither legislate nor create laws to govern, as God has already declared the law through the Prophet Muhammad, as stated in the Quran, it can neither be supplemented nor re-interpreted for the benefit of modern society, to do so is to pervert the true meaning of Islam.[20]

Ayatollah Montazeri, the highest-ranking cleric in Iran today, has stated that by adapting Islam to fit into the structure of the nation state, by enabling the clergy to take direct control of the political aspects of Iranian society, Khomeini was doing an injustice to Islam.[21] Politics is well known as a 'dirty game', the modern nation state divides rather than unites man; by intertwining Islam with such concepts it is argued that Khomeini has smeared Islam with the inevitable underhand political dealing necessary to ensure the survival of the State. As the clergy are in political control, they neither have the capacity or the objectivity, which they previously possessed, to act as the moral guide of society. When the economic situation in Iran suffered during and after the eight-year war it was the clergy who were in charge of economic affairs. It was the clergy and through them Islam that was blamed for the ills of society. Being tainted by political mismanagement the clergy brought Islam into disrepute and for this reason, the effectiveness of the top-down approach to Islamising society has to be called into question.

The Sunni Movement and the Problem of Institutionalising 'Virtue'

The situation amongst the Sunni movements was somewhat different. Apart from the Taleban in Afghanistan no Islamic movement of the Sunni sect ever got into a position of total political power. Furthermore Afghanistan is a unique case in Sunnism and has more in common with the Iranian revolution, as it believed in revolutionary Islam, than it does with any Sunni movement throughout the Muslim world. Sunnism with no hierarchy or clerical structure has little to utilise when attempting to outline the institutional structure of an Islamic state. For the Sunni scholar Maududi, the key to the establishment of an Islamic society is not the Muslim nature of the institutions, but the principles that guide them.[22] If neither governmental institution nor earthly person can be a source of law then why are institutions necessary for an Islamic society? It is for this reason that the Sunni Islamic movement, when discussing the necessary criterion of an Islamic state often get bogged down, not in discussions of institutional structures but on the type of person or virtues the country's leadership should possess. In an Islamic state the sole purpose of institutions should be to assist the believer in being a better Muslim, if they do not achieve this goal then they cannot be deemed Islamic institutions. Furthermore, we can presuppose that if a community is virtuous (i.e. the community is made up of good Muslims), then there is no need for institutions to guide them. 'The more virtuous a society is, the more the state withers away'.[23] Herein lies the problem with the Sunni Islamic movement; by trying to institutionalise virtue they are entering the realm of the impossible. Indeed, many might argue that such a feat is hopeless in the modern world, where politics is rarely used in the same context as virtue. With an international system based on the concept of the nation state, the Islamic movement has become dislocated from the realities of the modern world. The Sunni movement's preoccupation with a discussion on virtue and its unwillingness to deal with the practical implications of an Islamic state has prevented the Sunni movement from transcending the theoretical to achieve the practical manifestation of its goals.

For the Sunni movement, the non-separation of religion and politics meant their disregard of the political in search of the ideal religious (virtuous) state. The true Muslim state could only be created within oneself and no institutional structure would assist this. The difference between the Iranian and the other Islamic movements can be best described in terms of a top-down, bottom-up approach to creating an Islamic society. The Iranian model for an Islamic state entails the creation of a rigid institutional structure that is Islamic in nature and thereby would 'encourage' its citizens to be better Muslims. Whether Iran's particular Islamic structures encourage its citizens to be better Muslims is questionable. While it can be argued that some Islamic moral presence in the political life of a country, can have a positive effect on the Islamic nature of society, Khomeini's lifting of the ban on clergy holding political office[24] eventually lead to the monopolisation of political control by the Iranian clergy. Such an approach to Islamising society is inherently flawed, as any enforcement of certain behaviour, be it religious or otherwise, usually results in the manifestation of the very behaviour that it has attempted to prevent. Furthermore, throughout history, it has been shown that the mind and its beliefs cannot be controlled through state or religious institutionalisation. Iranian society has developed an outward façade to fulfil the obligations required by the institutionalisation of Islam. Male and female Iranians have an outward appearance,[25] which they don to obtain social and political acceptance, however this façade is a mere cloak to mask their true values and practices.

Ayatollah Khomeini firmly believed that a state should not merely have institutions Islamic in nature but these institutions should have Islam as their core belief. In other words they should be the creation of Islam itself. However the problem arises here that Islam or the Quran is not obviously forthcoming with any form of institutional structure. Khomeini filled this institutional void with the concept of *velayat-e faqih*.[26] The Shia faith already possesses a clerical hierarchy, which awaits the return of the hidden Imam. The position of the *velayat-e faqih* is intended to bridge the gap of uncertainty left by the hidden Imam. While there has always been a tradition of following a living *mujtahid* (grand ayatollah),[27] it was up to the faithful to choose which *mujtahid* they wished to follow. By choosing whom the leading religio-political figure was, Khomeini was attempting to institutionalise Islam, to give it a definite structure. Many argue that the very reason for Islam's survival throughout many turbulent centuries was the inherent lack of structure that it possessed. Structure and institutionalising Islam gives it a sense of inflexibility, something that Islam most certainly is not. The position of *velayat-e faqih* was imposing the choice of *mujtahid* whom the people should follow, running contrary to centuries of Shia practice that left such a decision up to the free will of the faithful. In many ways the position of *velayat-e faqih* would only work if the person chosen had the religious authority and credentials, to be the generally accepted ultimate living 'source of emulation'. While Khomeini was the undisputed Islamic leader of his time,[28] if his successors were not than the very legitimacy of the position of *velayat-e faqih* could easily be called into question.

By trying to create an Islamic society from above, the post-revolution government in Iran stifled the very inspiration of Islam that had made it such a vibrant religion. The Sunni movement on the other hand was attempting to create an Islamic society from the bottom up. By creating good Muslims, it was hoped that this would influence society at large to become more Islamic and as such would create an Islamic state. This is why the Sunni movement became preoccupied with creating a virtuous state; it was less an attempt at attaining political power than it was at influencing societal values. It is for this reason that the Islamic movement in Sunni countries failed on a political level, while it may have succeeded in heightening religious awareness, this did not automatically manifest itself politically. It is interesting to note at this stage that one is more likely to see manifestations of religiosity in countries like Bahrain or Saudi Arabia than one is in Iran. In fact, this was one of the first things that struck the author on his arrival in Iran. Islam has become so politicised that its true religious practice has now become a personal endeavour.

Both of these ideological perspectives on the implementation of an Islamic state have had some success, with the installation of an Islamic Republic in Iran and the participation of Islamic political parties in governments from Indonesia to Turkey. That said, neither type of Islamic movement has truly achieved their ultimate goal. The Iranian revolution has been continually beset by internal power struggles. The 'islamisation' of society has largely been cosmetic with the real emphasis being placed upon political and economic control. Similarly, Islamic groups from Sunni countries, that have followed the path of revolutionary Islam, have only succeeded in alienating their organisations from any position of influence within their society and political structure. In addition, the politically active groups who believed in re-Islamising society from below were also relatively unsuccessful. Their lack of focus on developing a possible alternative to the secular political structures in their countries meant that political power remained outside their grasp. Overall, it can be said that no amount of institutionalisation can undo modernity, which is largely responsible for directing the values of society today. Furthermore, the Islamic movement needs to re-assess its goals, if it is to create good Muslims and as such a Muslim society. In the long term, attempts to Islamise society from below may have had a greater impact on society, than those movement that have imposed rigid Islamic structures, as is the case in Iran.

Iran and the Problems of Ideologising Religion

The Islamic movement in Iran and elsewhere in the 1970s brought Islam into the sphere of political activity throughout the Middle East. The Iranian movement by giving Islam a definite political, legal and social form completed the use of Islam as an ideology. The word ideology rarely has a positive connotation; Napoleon used the term to describe day dreaming people who could not see reality for what it was.[29] Marx developed this theme to describe ideology, as the veil that cloaked and deceived people's minds so that they could not perceived reality in its true form.[30] The important thing here is that ideology is a creation used to give legitimacy to a certain way of thinking. It was by turning Marxism into an ideology that much of the structures and ideas about how society should function were developed. Marx also viewed religion in ideological terms, as an attempt to develop an understanding of society based on certain predetermined criteria, providing the infrastructure with which to create the 'perfect' society.[31]

The main problem with this is that religion, like all ideologies, is a direct reflection of how society was perceived at a specific time. The structures that the ideology creates are a similar reflection of society at a particular time, it views reality as a constant, which it is not. Therefore, as reality inevitably changes, the imposed structures and their ideologies are no longer representative of society. The above would be the product of viewing religion in the same terms as other ideologies, such as Marxism. Therefore the moment an idea becomes ideologised is the moment it becomes incapable of change or motion. As society and its values are not static, any state structure based on an ideology will inevitably become unrepresentative of the values of the society it serves. If a political structure does not reflect adequately the values of the society it serves, the more likely that society will rebel against those same structures.

Shariati takes a different approach to ideology, viewing ideology as superior to both science and philosophy; he views a man without ideology as being less than a man.[32] While both science and philosophy are attempts to describe or explain the world, ideology is a way to prescribe the world, not as it is but as it should be. Therefore, a person with no view as to how the world should be, in Shariati's perspective is an empty person, without a cause or reason for being. To overcome the idea of ideological stagnation, Shariati proposed the need for perpetual ideological motion. Taking such an idea would assist in overcoming the problem of a political structure based on a particular ideological standpoint becoming dislocated from the values of society. For such a scenario to succeed however, the political system must possess the ability to continuously evolve to meet the changing beliefs of its society. Herein lies the problem with the Islamic State in Iran. If we are to take Shariati's idea that ideology, and therefore in the Iranian sense religion, is of benefit to society as it prescribes how society should idealistically be, then there should be a general acceptance that the ideology should not produce structures that are so rigid so as not to have the ability of evolve. The question of whether Iran's current political ideology (i.e. Shia Islam or at least the Iranian interpretation of Shia Islam) manifests itself in rigid political structures will be dealt with in later chapters and will assess the ability of the current Iranian system to evolve and overcome the problems of having an ideologically based political system.

Iran's Islamic Movement and the Clergy

The Islamic movement in Iran throughout the 1960s and 1970s differed from its counterparts elsewhere. This was mainly because it was the only

Islamic movement where the clergy played both an active and a crucial role in the proliferation and success of the movement. Furthermore, it was the only movement that succeeded in creating, at least in name, an Islamic state. If we are to look for the reasons behind the success of the revolution in Iran, it is without doubt the alliance between the clergy and the intelligentsia. This alliance resulted in the movement being not only Islamic in nature but it also meant that it took on many of the characteristics of a Third World Movement. It was this mixture of the radical with the religious that ensured that the post revolutionary Islamisation of Iran would not take on the conservative characteristics of their counterparts in other countries, such as Pakistan and Saudi Arabia.

Depending on your perspective the proclamation of Shi'ism as the state religion by the Safavids in the sixteenth century[33] was either the best or the worst thing for Shi'ism as a religious and a political force. Shariati viewed this declaration as leading to the co-option of the faith.[34] The movement of Shi'ism from an outside to an inside force, severely reduced its capacity for change and misguided the faith from its true path and meaning. For Shariati it was the institutionalisation of the clergy in the aftermath of the Safavid's accent to power that striped Shi'ism of its cherished independence.[35] In contrast to Shariati's view, another perspective is that while the Shia *ulema* lost their religious independence under the Safavid's because of the latter's ability to impose their authority due to their religious legitimacy,[36] they regained much of their independence and influence under the subsequent Zand (1750-1794) and Qajar (1796-1925) dynasties. Furthermore, it was the previous institutionalisation of the clergy that was vital for the transformation of the clergy and Shi'ism into a political force in twentieth century Iran. Historically Shi'ism has its roots in the Arabian Peninsula, as we have seen in the last chapter, the rupture between Shi'ism and Sunnism occurred over the rights of succession to the Prophet. The Safavids were a tribal people of Turkoman ancestry, whose leaders were directly descended from the Prophet. Following their seizure of power, the installation of Twelver Shi'ism as the state religion was a way to make the differentiation between their territory and that of the Sunni Ottoman and Afghan lands. That is why the modern-day borders of Iran are not representative of any ethnic divide[37] but are more a religious divide between predominantly Shia and Sunni lands.

The Safavid's declaration of Shi'ism as the state religion had two serious consequences; the first was that by becoming the state religion Shi'ism became increasingly institutionalised. In addition, Shi'ism began to be identified as an Iranian phenomenon. Shi'ism began a process of

Iranianisation, the Shia clergy was increasingly of Iranian origin or had strong ties to Iranian seminaries. That said, the Shia clergy were historically quietist, as we shall see in subsequent chapters, even Khomeini was a quietist for most of his life. While the clergy's independence was severely curtailed during the Safavid period, in fact their relationship with the State was akin to their Sunni brethren. During the subsequent Zand and Qajar dynasties, who did not possess the religious legitimacy of the Safavids, the ulema began to reassert its independence. The ulema's ability to reassert themselves within society is one of the main reasons why it could evolve into a political force in the twentieth century. Two occurrences in the eighteenth century greatly facilitated the ulema's increased independence from the Iranian State. Following the Afghan invasion in 1722 the Shia clergy no longer felt wholly secure on Iranian soil. This, therefore, began a tradition of the high Shia clergy settling in Najaf, in modern day Iraq. This extra-territoriality accorded to the Shia ulema by the Ottoman Empire enabled the Shia clergy to remain largely outside the control of the Iranian political leadership.[38] A further rift within Shi'ism enabled the Iranian ulema to remain financially independent. This occurred out of a theological debate that developed in the eighteenth century surrounding the right of *ijtihid* (or interpretation) of the holy texts. The Iranian ulema almost wholly believed the right of interpretation remained with the Shia clergy. The other group, known as the traditionalists, believed that the right of interpretation had ended with the disappearance of the twelfth Imam. Their interpretation of *ijtihid* is close to that of Sunnism and therefore the Iranian ulema's position marked not only their independence within the Shia clergy but also within Islam itself. The resolution of this debate also brought financial independence to the Shia ulema in Iran. With the right of *ijtihad* given to the most senior clergy (those of the rank of *mujtahid*), it was the tradition that each of the faithful pay their Islamic tax directly to their chosen *mujtahid* and not to the state. With their financial and geographic independence, the nineteenth century saw the establishment of a hierarchical structure within the Shia clergy. It was these three components that differentiated the Shia from the Sunni clergy. The financial and political independence enabled the Iranian ulema to place itself, at times, in opposition to the government.[39] The hierarchical structure within the Iranian clergy enabled Khomeini to develop the idea of *velayat-e faqih* into a form of political hierarchy and facilitated the establishment of an Islamic form of government that worked in tandem with the modern idea of the nation state.

While much of Shariati's writings can be perceived as being anti-clerical, the vast majority of those involved in the Islamic movement in Iran had strong ties to the clergy. While Iran's Islamic movement shared many points of similarity with other movements, it was this alliance between the Islamic intellectuals and the clergy that makes the Iranian experience unique. Twice in the early part the twentieth century; this alliance resulted in drastic changes to Iranian government policy. It was not, however, until Khomeini and his followers that the clergy considered moving from a position of perpetual opposition to that of possible power brokers. Khomeini was in many ways the catalyst for this movement within the ranks of the Iranian clergy, towards direct clerical control. His unconventional views on Islam and the State meant that he acted as a bridge between the intellectuals and the religious classes. In fact, Khomeini shared a mistrust of the clergy with Shariati, which could explain his initial reluctance to openly criticise Shariati's views.[40] Khomeini believed that the clergy, as an institution, were unwilling to change and feared to question the status quo. It is for that reason that Khomeini sought support for his ideas on Islamic government amongst Islamic intellectuals and junior clergy. In fact, when Khomeini's ideas on *velayat-e faqih* were published, they were rejected by all of the grand ayatollahs, except for Montazeri who was a student of Khomeini's and his designated heir.[41] Some of the senior clergy came out and directly attacked Khomeini and his ideology,[42] while others continued their quietist approach to politics even in the aftermath of the establishment of the Islamic Republic. In many ways the Iranian revolution did not result in the 'reign of the Ayatollah's'[43] as depicted by some authors, but rather was a movement by junior clergy for greater political activism within the religious leadership.

Has Islam as a Political Force Failed?

The Islamic movement that swept through the Middle East in the 1970s and 1980s, promising a restoration of the 'Golden Age' of Islam and promising the creation of a new society with the principles of Islam as its guiding force, has failed to live up to these lofty expectations. There are a number of reasons for this; not least because its vision of society was incompatible with the precepts of modernity and the structure of the international system. A rejection of modernity whilst attempting to hold position in the international system is impossible. The Islamic movement with its Third World Movement rhetoric could not reconcile its ideology with the necessity to participate in the international economic order. Ideology means little when your people demand the trappings that modernity can provide. Furthermore, modernity is a process that has already begun; it is a

Pandora's box that cannot be re-sealed. No amount of institutionalisation can prevent the encroachment of modernity, even into the most traditional societies.[44] Therefore, structures that promise to reverse modernity are bound to fail. Islam and modernity whilst not being fully compatible can find an accommodation and it is this ground that the Islamic movement should be seeking to find.

The western perception of the Islamic movement as a continuing threat to its ideology and way of life is unfounded. The Islamic movement is not homogenous, each movement from Algeria to the Philippines, has adapted its goals and aspirations to their particular society. This is a sign that the movement is as much a sociological statement, as it is a religious declaration. Furthermore Iran, the sole Islamic movement that has succeed in gaining political control, has overtime adapted its goals to meet the political reality of the international order. Therefore, the Islamic movement is less a movement in a universalist sense and more of a re-discovery of Islamic values by various political and social movements throughout the Muslim world.[45] In most cases, Iran included, while the Islamic movement espoused an anti-western tone, it inevitably took on the garb of a western system.

Individually each movement developed its own perspective on how to Islamise society. Some such as Iran have taken a top-down approach, concentrating on creating societal structure that would ensure its population's adherence to Islamic values. Others such as the Islamic movements in Jordan or Pakistan have concentrated on creating good Muslims; have taken a bottom-up approach to creating an Islamic state. Both modes of Islamising society have failed due to the problems of institutionalising virtue and the problems resulting from ideologising religion. For this reason the Islamic movement as a political force is spent.

Arguing that Islam as a political force is spent, especially in the aftermath of the 11th of September attacks in the US can be difficult. However, it is important to differentiate between legitimate and the illegitimate use of Islam. There are those who highlighting the need for Islam to play a role in Muslim society, and those who utilise Islam as a tool to blame western society for the social ills prevalent throughout the developing and Muslim worlds. Therefore, it is important to understand the reasons for the resurgence of Islam over the past number of decades. As argued earlier, these reasons have mainly developed through the social alienation of vast sections of society, who for whatever reasons are unable to attain the benefits of modernity or are unable to reconcile modernity with their individual cultural values. The social problems that have resulted in the proliferation of groups manipulating Islam as a means of attacking the international order have not decreased over the past number of decades. It is for this reason that the methods used to combat these problems must change and while Islam has a role to play, the Islamic movement must adapt its tactics in order to successfully achieve its ultimate goal. One possible vehicle through which the Islamic movement can continue to remain a positive and effective force in society is through President Khatami's concept of 'Dialogue Amongst Civilisations'. This unique idea was introduced during the 8th Islamic summit of the Organisation of the Islamic Countries (OIC)^{46} held in Tehran in 1998. Taking dialogue amongst civilisations in its most simple form, it represented a bridge between Islam and the West, increasing the understanding and acceptance of Islam in modern society. Potentially, it is much more than an attempt to cultivate an environment for discursive communication and facilitating understanding between various cultures.^{47} If properly utilised, it could revolutionise foreign policy as we know it and provide a platform for the pro-active development of the Islamic movement.^{48} Dialogue amongst civilisations is less about the practice of *haute politque* and is concentrated more in the arena of twin track politics, meaning that it is about cultural understanding and dialogue rather than the institutionalisation of a particular perspective or viewpoint. Instead of Islamising from above or below, dialogue amongst civilisations would be more a horizontal movement towards creating societies that understand and fully accept Islam, its principles and practices. The Islamic movement has always maintained that a Muslim cannot live under a non-Muslim government. Furthermore, some segments of the Islamic movement believed that Islamic institutions must be created if society was to be Islamic in nature and to enable the faithful to practice their beliefs. Through the active participation of the Islamic movement in 'dialogue amongst civilisations' the environment of cultural and religious understanding can be created that would enable the Islamic movement to achieve their ultimate goal of creating a society in which the faithful can practice and be 'good Muslims'. Rather than redefining Islam for the modern age, dialogue amongst civilisation has the capacity to create the understanding necessary to redefine modernity, towards greater understanding of Islam and its practices.

Notes

[1] Kepel, G. (1995), *The Revenge of God* (Cambridge: Polity Press), p.1.
[2] Ibid., p.2.
[3] Roy, O. (1994), *The Failure of Political Islam* (London: I.B. Tauris), p.3.

[4] Such as the storming of the Great Mosque in Mecca in 1979, the assassination of Egyptian President Anwar Sadat in 1981, the Iranian revolution and the ensuing hostage crisis which begun in 1979 and the Mujahedin movement in Afghanistan against the Soviet invasion.

[5] See further Lapidus, I. (1983), *Contemporary Islamic movements in historical perspective* (Berkeley: Institute of International Studies) or for a comparative analysis see Hussain, A. (1983), *Islamic movements in Egypt, Pakistan and Iran* (London: Mansell), for an overview of the ideas and thinking behind the movement see Mawdudi, Abu l-A'la (1984), *The Islamic movement: dynamics of values, power and change* (London: Islamic Foundation).

[6] For a truly in-depth look at the man who became the main ideologue of the Islamic Republic see further Moin, B. (1999), *Khomein: life of the Ayatollah* (London: I.B. Tauris), and Nu'mani, M. (1988), *Khomeini, Iranian revolution and the Shiite faith* (London: Furqan).

[7] For an overview of the Arab-Israeli wars and their aftermath see further Herzog, C. (1988), *The Arab-Israeli wars: war and peace in the Middle East from the War of Independence to Lebanon 2nd ed* (London: Arms and Armour), for the effect that the Arab defeat had on the incumbent administrations of the region see Ibrahim, S. (1993: Spring), 'Crises, elites, and democratization in the Arab world', *Middle East Journal 47*, pp.292-303.

[8] This expression is used by Kepel, G. (1995), *The Revenge of God* (Cambridge: Polity Press), to describe the people who moved from the countryside to the cities, across the Middle East following the oil price boom. Their governments left them to live in temporary and inadequate housing on society's periphery, largely forgotten by the governments that promised them so much.

[9] OPEC – Organisation for Petroleum Exporting Countries. The eleven (eight of which are Arab/Middle Eastern) countries that make up the Organisation of Petroleum Exporting Countries (OPEC) produce about forty percent of the world's oil and hold more than 77% of the world's proved oil reserves. OPEC also contains nearly all of the world's excess oil production capacity (see further http://www.la.utexas.edu/misc/porc/msg00020.html).

[10] It is important to note here that the Islamic movement in Iran was not always revolutionary in nature, it was for most part of the last century quietist in nature, preferring to work with the ruling establishment and only entering the political sphere only twice during the Tobacco Protest (1892) and the Constitutional Revolution (1906). Khomeini also initially advocated a quietist approach, however when the very foundations of Islam were threatened, in his view it was legitimate to seek to overthrow the ruling regime.

[11] If one goes to any Friday prayers throughout Iran, but especially in the main Friday prayer meeting in Tehran University, there are signs a plenty emphasising that 'Participation in Friday Prayers is a Social -Political Statement'. Friday prayers are as much a political rally, as they are a time of worship. The government use the prayer meetings throughout the country as a means to mobilise the masses in favour of socio-political policies.

[12] It should be noted here however that Mecca at the time took on a decidedly anti-Islamic demeanour and did not take a neutral position as regards the practice of the faith.

[13] Remembering that while Muhammad left Mecca because of his wish not to live under a government that was polytheist and unreceptive to Islam, he returned to Mecca some eight years later with his Muslim army and took control of the city to establish his Islamic society.

[14] Source: interview carried out September 1999.

[15] Maududi, A. (1980), *The Islamic Law and Constitution* (Lahore: Islamic Publications) p.260.

[16] See further, Keddie, N. (Ed.) (1983), *Religion and Politics in Iran: Shi'ism from quietism to revolution* (New Haven: Yale University Press).

[17] Khomeini's main addition is the creation of the position of *velayat-e faqih*, or supreme religio-political leader. This is dealt with in more detail in chapter 5.

[18] Here other Islamic states such as Saudi Arabia, Pakistan and Sudan are discounted, as the clergy are not in direct control of the political as well as the religious life of these societies.
[19] Interview with a Shirazi cleric April 1999.
[20] Ibid.
[21] Ayatollah Montazeri's memoirs have recently been published on the internet however the Iranian government has since had them removed, as they contain revelations concerning the early excesses of the revolution together with details of clerical impropriety.
[22] Maududi, A. (1980), *The Islamic Law and Constitution* (Lahore: Islamic Publications) p.260.
[23] Roy, O. (1994), *The Failure of Political Islam* (London: I.B. Tauris), p.63.
[24] This occurred following the removal of Bani-Sadr from the Iranian Presidency and Khomeini's withdrawal of support for the democratic process. It was during this period that Khomeini came under the influence of conservative clergy from the Haggani Seminary in Qom (source: interview with a member of the Iranian administration February 2000) who encourage Khomeini to allow the clergy to take total control of the Iranian administration, fearing the loss of power to democratic elements within the opposition coalition, Khomeini agreed. This is covered in more detail in chapter seven.
[25] Such as the practice of the male growing the requisite beard or the female wearing the traditional *chador*.
[26] See further Khomeini, R. (1981), *Hokumateh Eslami* (Islamic Government) (Tehran: Bozorg Bookshop) and Khomeini, R. (1981), *Islam and the Revolution: Writings and Declarations of Imam Khomeini*, translated by Hamid Algar (Berkeley: Mizan Press).
[27] *Mujtahid* translated means 'source of emulation'. It is the practice that each Shia chose a living *mujtahid* whom they are to look to for spiritual and social guidance. Their religious taxes can be paid straight to the *mujtahid* or his representatives. For more details of religious terms see further appendix IV.
[28] Although Ayatollah Khomeini was not the most senior cleric in Shi'ism at the time of the revolution, his religious credentials and revolutionary background gave him a special standing in Iran. Ayatollah al-Khu'i was more senior and had an extended following even amongst the Shia faithful in the Lebanon, however he resided in Najaf (in modern Iraq) and so we can say that Ayatollah Khomeini was the most senior cleric in Iran at the time of the revolution.
[29] Soroush, A. (2000: Summer), 'More Robust than Ideology', *Discourse Vol. 2, 1*, p.82.
[30] See further Marx, K. (1983), *Karl Marx and Fredrick Engels, Selected Works, Vol. 1* (Moscow: Progress Publishers).
[31] Soroush, A. (2000: Summer), p.83.
[32] For an overview of Shariati's thought on religion and ideology see further Shariati, A. (1988), *School of thought and action* (Tehran: Kazi Publications), or (1980), *Marxism and other Western fallacies: an Islamic critique* (Berkeley: Mizan Press). There are also a number of websites that have extracts from Shariati's writings and speeches, see further www.wco.com/~altaf/shariati.html or www.ioanufind.com.
[33] For an comprehensive look at the Safavid period and the role of Islam see further Melville, C. (Ed.) (1993), *Safavid Persia: the history and politics of an Islamic society* (London: I.B. Tauris) or Savory, R.M. (1980), *Iran under the Safavids* (Cambridge: Cambridge University Press).
[34] See further Shariati, Ali (undated), *Tashiiyeh Alavi va tashiiyeh Safavi* (Tehran: Hoseinieyeh Ershad Publications).
[35] Ibid.
[36] As the Safavid's were able to trace their lineage to the House of the Prophet, this gave them much religious credibility.

[37] In fact modern day Iran is a mixture of a number of ethnicities and languages, the common denominator of the Iranian people is their religion.
[38] Roy, O. (1994), p.170.
[39] In many cases the Sunni *ulema* were/are employees of the state and therefore found themselves in a difficult position when it came to opposing certain government policies.
[40] It was only when Shariati's ideas were gaining adherents from within the Islamic movements ranks that Khomeini openly criticised Shariati.
[41] Source: Interview with an Islamic intellectual September 1999. It should also be noted that Ayatollah Montazeri was subsequently deposed as Khomeini's heir for criticising the excesses of the Islamic State and for questioning the very concept that he had helped impose. He is currently under house arrest in Qom and is an advocate for greater political and religious freedom in the Islamic Republic.
[42] For example Ayatollah's Al-Khu'i and Shariat Madai openly opposed Khomeini's thesis on *velayat-e faqih*. While other senior clergy such as Ayatollah's Gulpaygani, al-Qummi, al-Shirazi and al-Najafi al-Mar'ashi continued their quietist approach to politics and refused posts in the new administrations. See further Roy, O. (1994), p.173.
[43] This phrase was taken from the title of a book by the same name, see further Bakhash, S. (1990), *Reign of the Ayatollahs - Iran and the Islamic Revolution* (New York, Basic Books).
[44] A prime example of this is in the proliferation of modernity through various modes of communication. In Iran no amount of government control or threat of punishment prevents the ordinary people from having satellite dishes. These dishes bring modernity and its trappings into view while the political system ensures that they remain agonisingly outside their grasp.
[45] These movements may not necessarily be opposition movement, Saudi Arabia for example can be said to have experienced an Islamic revival in the 1970s but this was a product of a government-sponsored endeavour to further legitimise their rule.
[46] The OIC – The Organisation of the Islamic Conference 'is an international organisation grouping fifty six states which have decided to pool their resources together, combine their efforts and speak with one voice, to safeguard the interests and secure the progress and well being of their people and all of the Muslims in the world' – (taken from organisations mission statement). See further www.oic-un.org. It was established in September 1969.
[47] It is the contention of this work that Dialogue Amongst Civilisations can also be used to bridge the political gap within the Iran today however this will be dealt with more in later chapters.
[48] See further Downes, M. and Keane, R. (2000: Spring), 'Dialogue Amongst Civilisations – the road to deconstructing unipolarity', *Iranian Journal of International Studies*, Keane, R. (2000: February), *Dialogue amongst civilisations, creating an institutional framework* (Tehran: IPIS Conference Paper).

Chapter 3
Revolution in Review

> When I read that looting TV sets from neighbourhood stores is an act of revolutionary violence, I wonder whether politics and theatre are not converging - to the detriment of both.
>
> Robert Dahl[1]

While there is much written material covering the advent and causes of a revolution, a universally acceptable definition of what a revolution represents has never been formulated. This is perhaps because of the multifaceted nature of a revolution, and disagreement as to how and why a revolution occurs. Revolution as theoretical concept, is an inherent part of this current body of work because it is only through an understanding of the progress and evolution of a revolutionary situation that we can begin to understand Iranian political and social developments post-1979. Furthermore, an understanding of the causes leading to the Iranian revolution together with the role played by the actors of the revolution, both foreign and domestic, is vital in comprehending the philosophy of the current regime and their relations with the international community. While this chapter hopes to provide understanding of the Islamic revolution through a systematic analysis of the current body of knowledge on the subject, it will also endeavour to challenge the current academic discourse on revolution by focusing on the effects of revolution rather than the causes.

It is the contention of this work that contrary to the current thinking on the subject a revolution is actually an evolutionary phenomenon. To state that the Chinese revolution occurred in 1949 or that the Iranian revolution was complete following the fall of the Shah is to misrepresent the idea of what a revolution is. Revolutions occur over a longer time span than is generally accepted. Furthermore they often can, as in the case of Iran, be side-tracked for a number of years before the true ideals which precipitated the revolution are achieved. The process of revolutionary change is a delicate one; a society in the process of re-structuring the state apparatus can easily be manipulated by an organised elite, resulting in a totalitarian or autocratic regime. This is what will be argued was the case in Russia following the assent of Stalin to power and in Iran following the fall of Bani Sadr;[2] in both of these cases the true ideals of the revolutionary endeavour, liberty and freedom, remained illusive for many years. In the case of Russia, these ideals were attained in a limited fashion only after 1989, after some seventy years and the dismantling of the authoritarian machinery of the Soviet Union. In Iran the process continues with the attempts at reform by the current administration of President Khatami.

It is the contention of this work that revolution is part of an evolutionary process. With the realisation of man's insatiable desire to be free[3] and to control his own destiny marking the end of the process. It is here that this book's definition of revolution will differ from the current body of knowledge, as this work will be focusing on the results of a revolution rather than the causes. The following chapter will build upon this idea, arguing that a revolution can only be completed when the binary opposition between the state and the electorate is diminished as far as possible. More often than not, revolutions to date have merely meant the reallocation of power and the changing of the elite within the political structure. It is a further contention of this work that only through an understanding of the 'revolutionary process', can the post-revolutionary history of Iran be put into its correct perspective. Central to the Iranian revolution is Ayatollah Khomeini and his vision of Islamic government. As with many revolutions it is the revolutionaries and their ideas that decide the direction and focus of the most important period in any social upheaval which is the transition period of a revolution. This is why in subsequent chapters; we will be looking at Ayatollah Khomeini and his ideology, evaluating his role and his legacy to the Iranian revolution. Through fully understanding Khomeini's role throughout the revolutionary period in Iran and placing this in the context of our theory on revolution, only then can we fully understand the power struggles that have engrossed Iran over the past two decades. In turn this will allow us to see through the inaccurate titles and labels that have been attached to the 1979 upheaval. Terms like 'Islamic revolution' or 'Islamic government' have led to the interpretation of the contemporary Iranian history as a conflict defined in terms of a secular monarchy against a clerical movement. While this aptly defines a segment of the Iranian revolution it is misleading and gives the revolution in Iran too narrow a focus, leading to a misinterpretation of the ideals and objectives behind the social upheaval that overthrew the Shah and his government. Through conceptualising revolution as a process rather than a *fait accompli*, the conflict and discord within the political arena of Iran today can be better comprehended within its historical context.

Revolution – an Overview

The main question that needs to be asked in this section is how, why and what is necessary for a revolution to occur? It is only when this question can be adequately answered that a theoretical framework on revolution may be formulated. While this endeavour may appear straightforward, the current body of knowledge is conflicting, at times contradictory, with no set principles established. Most theories attempt to answer the questions 'how' and 'why' revolutions occur and even though there is a plethora of reasons given by theorists, they rarely, if ever, agree. Whilst there are many theories to choose from, most can find their origins in either the Marxist or the Functionalist Schools of revolutionary thought.

The Marxist perspective argues that revolution is a normal product of the inequality that is inherent in the makeup of our society and is therefore inevitable. This view of society had been adapted many times by other theorists; both Lenin and Mao have based their theories on this basic concept and have put their adapted theories into practice in their respective countries. The main area where Leninism and Maoism differ from the Marxist theory is 'where' and 'when' revolutions are most likely to take place. In contrast, Functionalism focuses on the commonalties, which enable societies to persist over time. The Functionalist would agree with the Marxist view that conflict is an endemic feature of our society. However, the point of contention between both would be in relation to the source of that conflict. In saying that revolution is inherent in society, the Marxist believes that it is inevitable and unavoidable. The Functionalist by contrast believes that conflict is indeed avoidable, if one is to study the components of societal persistence. In fact, while Marx welcomes revolution as a means of societal development from one era to another, Functionalists perceive revolution as being counter-productive and therefore should be avoided at all costs.

A third perspective on revolution, which is linked to the functionalist approach, is the Theory of Mass Society. The exponents of this theory put forward the view that there are certain structural characteristics in society and it is only when these structures are endangered that there is the possibility of mass social upheaval. Therefore, social conflict is avoidable, if these structures can be maintained. The Functionalist and the Mass Society Theorists, therefore, do not agree with the Marxist view that there are 'natural' inequalities in the social structure that lead to conflict. In fact, their belief is that it is only by adhering to the traditional structure and ensuring mass support of this structure, that social conflict can be avoided. The mass society theorist also believes that the consequences of revolutionary movements are totalitarian regimes, because only a totalitarian regime can provide the security that was previously provided by the traditional structures in society.

Other non-Marxist theories attempt to explain the nature and reasons behind societal upheaval, giving psychological explanations for the occurrence of revolution. This group generally disagrees with the inevitability concept put forward by Marx and can be divided into a number of groups. The first believes that revolution occurs only when the general population is oppressed and perceives their present situation as being untenable. Only if the population believes that their present situation is unbearable, will society be prone to rising up against their perceived oppressors. A further argument postulates that when a population is aware of the basics that the state should be providing (this knowledge usually stems from a comparison of one's own situation with other societies), the possibility of social unrest is increased when the dichotomy between what is perceived to be the basic necessities and the reality is viewed as being excessive, in such a situation the population is more prone to rise up *en masse*. This idea can be expanded to include an economic dimension; here the possibility of social unrest is augmented if a period of protracted economic growth and social progress is followed by a sharp economic decline. The theory of rising expectations argues that when the expectations of society have been falsely increased and there is a general unwillingness to accept the current situation, responsibility is placed at the feet of the ruling establishment. A further dimension of the psychological school of thought deals with what motivates a person to become a revolutionary. While this group would generally agree that there are revolutionary personalities, it would further accede that revolutions may only occur when revolutionary personalities, clash with a revolutionary situation. The personality does not necessarily create the situation but utilises the available disquiet in society to fulfil their revolutionary ambitions.

The Roots of Revolution

There has been much debate concerning what exactly constitutes a revolution. The term has been used to describe many varied and different situations. Some theorists have used it to describe societal developments, such as industrialisation, urbanisation or advances in technology or science. In many respects the term revolution has become overused in our society, with many varying types of social changes being termed 'revolutionary'. This has confused attempts to find a generally accepted definition of revolution. It is important for the purposes of this work that our definition of revolution will concentrate solely on the political science perspective concerning revolution. Whilst within this area there are still a plethora of opinions, their interpretations mainly vary in respect of the amount of social and political change that has occurred together with the degree or level of violence involved. Many theorists have concentrated on the level of violence associated with the overthrow of a state's ruling establishment. Others have concentrated on revolution as being the radical alteration of values within a community.[4] These two concepts of violence and value alteration are the core components in many of the theoretical definitions of revolution. The weight and emphasis placed on each of these concepts can vary enormously. Furthermore, the difficulty associated with empirically measuring both of these concepts makes finding a generally accepted definition an exceedingly difficult task.

So what is a revolution? Accepting that no two societies are similar and no two societies develop along the same continuum of change, it is safe to say that obtaining a generally acceptable definition of revolution will be difficult, if not, impossible task. As Amann points out 'there is no "true" definition of an abstraction: such a term is a semantic device which may or may not be useful, not a reflection of some absolute Platonic prototype'.[5] While both of the above statements are true it is still necessary for political scientists to overcome definitional ambiguity, because if this is not possible the results of any study cannot be deemed to be anywhere near conclusive.

In essence, an understanding of the theories on revolution would lean towards a division into two broad theoretical groups. The first group would constitute what has been called the 'Great Revolutions', which would include the French and American Revolution of the 18th Century and the Russian and Chinese revolutions of the 20th century.[6] This group, it will be argued, could also include the 1979 revolution in Iran, where Pettee's description of a revolution as 'a reconstitution of the state'[7] would appear valid. In this case the social structure of the state has been changed to such an extent to be almost unrecognisable in comparison to the original system that existed before the revolution. Arendt has proposed the view that the 'modern concept of revolution' has become 'inextricably bound up with the notion that the course of history suddenly begins anew, that an entirely new story never known or told before is about to unfold'.[8] Such structural or fundamental changes could include a change in the ruling establishment and the political institutions, the prevalent political philosophy or structures.

The second major group, would provide a broader definition, incorporating those who are part of the first but would expand the definition to include all forms of power transfer within a state which are illegal or achieved through violent means.[9] Therefore, added to the previous list of revolutions would be the numerous *coup d'états* and forcible takeover of power such as the military coup in the Ivory Coast in 1999 or the overthrow of Milosevic in Yugoslavia in October 2000. Excluded from such a definition would be a transfer of power, which though dramatic, was achieved through either peaceful or legitimate means. An example of this would be the Spanish transition to democracy after the death of Franco, even though this period dramatically changed the political landscape in Spain, it was achieved peacefully and therefore could not be termed a revolution under this definition. This school of thought is exclusively concerned with how the change was achieved, not with the extent of the change attained. Theorists from this group would generally define a revolution as an illegal, violent transfer of power.

The 'Great Revolution' school of thought would be of the view that monumental social change is necessary if an *époque* is to be considered revolutionary. This school of thought is essentially concerned with how this change is achieved. While all of the theorists from this school of thought would accept that revolutions are basically illegal acts, their concern is centred on the various facets of revolutionary change. These facets of change would include social and structural change, alteration in the political institutions and a change in the values of society, as well as the change in the role and personality of the ruling elite. Incorporated into this would be how the change was achieved; however this would account for just one of a number of facets of change. Within this school of thought the main difference amongst the theorists concern the weight and importance they place upon each of the facets of change mentioned above. Most would agree, however, that it is the alternation of societal values that is of utmost importance in the study of revolution. For example, Pettee has defined a great revolution as 'one in which the reconstitution of the state association is coincident with the substitution of one myth for another as the main integrating guide in the culture'.[10] Huntington considers a revolution to be 'a rapid, fundamental, and violent domestic change in the dominant values and myths of a society'.[11] While Neumann too termed revolution as 'a sweeping fundamental change ... in the predominant myth of the social order'.[12] Myth in this sense would refer to the social/political values of the society. The idea that revolution is based upon a new beginning and the establishment of new ideas is fundamental to the 'great revolution' theory. While conceptually this is easy to accept, it is almost impossible to quantify. Even to ascertain the general values of any 'stable' society is a difficult enough task, however to quantify the values of a society in transition would be almost impossible.

Within the Functionalist school of thought, value alteration is the primary tool used to measure a revolutionary scenario. Others concentrate on violence and personnel change, such as Kuhn who suggests that political revolutions occur because the parties to the revolution 'differ about the institutional matrix within which political change is to be achieved and evaluated'.[13] Therefore, as a result of diverging opinions within society about the role, goals or development of that society, one ruling elite is overthrown by another. An example of this would be the Reformation in Europe which began in the 16th century, where both the Lutheran movement in Germany and later the Tudor monarchy in England, shifted away from the traditional ruling authority of the Church of Rome. Here again we are left with a concept that is extremely difficult to measure. Therefore, very little empirical work has been carried out in this area. Measuring value change in a society is easier with hindsight but also when measured in conjunction with other aspects of social change such as change in the political structure and the political elite. Here change is more apparent and there are fewer generalisations.

Changes in the structure of society have been categorised as a major facet of revolutionary change. Marx's theory of revolution revolves around this idea of the alteration in the structure of society. For Marx revolution denotes the movement from one epoch to another. Each epoch is further defined through the mode of production utilised at that particular time. The reason for this is that the relationship between the various classes in society changes, as the mode of production develops, as society moves from a feudal to a capitalist society. Marx views the situation of the proletarian, 'the exploited class', as deteriorating throughout this process of development. At each stage of development revolution occurs when a class of men see no other way out of their misery other than through revolution. In Marx's view, the final stage of this evolutionary process occurs with the elimination of class conflict. During this period the structures of the state will wither away, as they will be no longer needed due to the fact that a social structure, or the state, is the mechanism used by the dominant class in each epoch to control society and fulfil their interests. Marx was by no means the only theorist to focus on social structures. It is Neumann's opinion that changes in both the social structure and in the control of the economy is what denotes a revolution. While their focus may vary, almost all theorists acknowledge that a revolution results in some manner of change to the social structure that previously existed.

For political scientists, power is core to their understanding of any society. Since Plato,[14] political scientists have pondered how power should be distributed in society. This theme of power, its distribution, and the abuse of the same, has played a central, though unacknowledged role in many modern day theories of revolution and societal change. What constitutes power, once again is a difficult question that must be answered. For many, power in society rests within the confines of its political institutions; therefore it is a change in the control of or in the structure of these institutions, which constitutes a revolution. Moore, for example has defined revolution as being change which 'engages a considerable portion of the population and results in a change in the structure of government'.[15] The Islamic revolution in Iran, led to sweeping institutional changes, with the movement of government from a monarchy to an Islamic Republic. Other forms of institutional change could include the abolition of one arm of the legislature or merely the redefinition of its powers under the new regime. In the case of the Islamic revolution in Iran, institutional change can be perceived as a reflection of the change in the values of that society. The monarchy in Iran was a secular leaning institution, while the institutions of the Islamic Republic were designed in an attempt to represent the dominant values and beliefs that the society held in Islam and more specifically the belief in Shia Islam. The change in the values of society over time can be gauged effectively by the changes that occur in the institutions of that country. As Cohan points out, 'by examining the change in institutions we are actually measuring the degree to which values have been altered in the community'.[16] It must be said, however, that the opposite may also be true – that the institutions of a society may be changed to encourage or enforce a change in the values of that society; this can be well illustrated through the example of the Iranian revolution. Was the Iranian revolution Islamic or one based upon ideals such as freedom and liberty? While we will delve into this question in more detail in later chapters, suffice to say at this stage that the dominant values in Iranian society may not have been reflected adequately in the institutions that were constructed after the revolution. However, the leadership at the time, which was predominantly of a clerical background, built institutions that they believed represented their objectives and the ideals that they held for society. While both the elite's and the institutions changed, power still remained a minority of Iranian society. Therefore, the use of elite and institutional change can be questioned, as to whether it represents a true change in the values of society, or whether the change is purely cosmetic in nature.

An easier change to gauge following any social upheaval is that of the governing elite. Here again, however, there is disagreement as to the extent of change that is necessary in the elite for the changes to be deemed revolutionary. Tanter and Midlarsky are of the opinion that 'a revolution may be said to exist where a group of insurgents illegally and/or forcefully challenges the governmental elite for the occupancy of roles in the structure of political authority. A successful revolution occurs where, as a result of a challenge to the governmental elite, insurgents are eventually able to occupy principal roles within the structure of political authority'.[17] From the various definitions utilising elite change as a facet of revolution, it is clear that elite change by itself is not sufficient for a scenario to be deemed revolutionary. For a revolution to be declared, it would appear that elite change has to occur through either violent or illegal means and result also in social or institutional change. So while elite change is useful in defining a revolution, it cannot be the sole component. Others argue that elite change in a revolutionary sense means that the new elite should not come from the same class as the previous regime. If we were to accept this definition, it would discount for example, the numerous military coups that have occurred from Turkey to Pakistan. This in a sense is a valid argument, as the change of the elite from the same class, would appear to be merely a personnel change and would not result in resounding changes in either the social values or the political institutions.

If a government has lost its 'moral right' to rule, is a rebellion against this government illegal? Also can the transfer of power through legal means be considered a revolution? Dunn is of the opinion that 'there can be no revolutions, however abortive, except where the previous regime has lost the right to rule'.[18] Therefore if a government has lost the moral right to rule, a revolution in one sense could not be deemed illegal as the laws by which the incumbent government rule would be deemed illegal or immoral by the majority of the population. In the aftermath of a revolution that results in majority rule, it would only be the previous government who would claim that the act of rebellion was illegal.[19] As Edwards points out 'in a revolution one system of legality is substituted by another'.[20] The question of whether a revolution is a legal or illegal act can be quite a subjective one.

That said, most theorists would agree that a legal transfer of power could not be termed a revolution. This would include any change of power through constitutional or legislative means. If this were not the case then every change of government in Western Europe could be deemed revolutionary. For example the introduction of the political party *Clann Na Poblacht* into government in Ireland in 1946 with its republican/socialist philosophy led to sizeable changes in government policy. However such ideological transition cannot be considered a revolution. This change led to the declaration of a 'Republic' in Ireland,[21] together with its exit from the British Commonwealth of States. While many, especially republicans may have seen this as a monumental change in Irish society, it was achieved through wholly legal and constitutional means and hence reflects an evolution of power rather than a revolution.

Violence is one of the most contentious facets of revolution, with few theorists agreeing whether or not a revolution should involve some form of violence. Remembering that we are looking at revolution from the political science perspective, Edwards is probably the most notable theorist who claims that revolution need not necessarily occur as a result of a violent act. While Dunn, Huntington and Marx[22] all attribute some form of violent act to the revolutionary process, they note that violence may accrue either from the regime in power or from the opposition. The amount of force utilised by the government will normally depend on whether they have lost the legitimacy to rule in the eyes of the population. If this is the case, the force necessary to quell any uprising will increase significantly. If the government still holds the support of the majority only minimal force will be necessary. While most non-Marxist theorists, such as Calvert,[23] view violence as stemming from the revolutionaries, for Marx the initial violent act that precipitates a revolution, occurs on the part of the state through its repressive policies. For Marx the state, which is the instrument of the ruling class, wields its power in a manner that leaves the proletarian with no alternative but to revolt. When they do so, it is solely in response to the state's policies and, therefore, they are not the initial instigators of violence, they are merely responding in kind. Calvert on the other hand, states that revolution is 'simply a form of governmental change through violence'.[24] He is not from the Marxist school of thought and is in effect making violence the core of his definition of revolution. Mao took a similar approach and viewed violence as a natural part of the revolutionary process, 'a revolution is an insurrection, an act of violence by which one class overthrows another'.[25]

While it is apparent that violence is a facet of revolution, defining revolution solely through violence is insufficient. The reason for this is that it is not the act of revolution that is most important but the outcome. Johnson puts forward the idea that the act of violence could be displayed on a continuum. He believes that one way of looking at 'the concept of revolution is to view it as a form of violence'.[26] The idea could be developed, as Cohan has, by putting social change also along a continuum.[27] By doing this and contrasting it with the level of violence present throughout the period of social change, we may than be able to develop a viable definition of revolution. Figure 1 is an attempt to elaborate on this idea and outline various possibilities regarding the variations available through the interaction of violence and social change.

HIGH VIOLENCE

Revolution, examples would be the French, Russian and Iranian revolutions. Where one political system is overthrown in favour of another. Where the state, its structures, social values and philosophy are altered, so that the previous system of governance is almost unrecognisable.

Failed attempt at revolution/ Social uprising. Where a social uprising is put down by the government or where they make concessions to the revolutionaries, thereby preventing the rebellion from becoming a revolution. An example would be the 1905 Russian Uprising or the 1906 Constitutional Revolution in Iran.

← MAXIMUM   SOCIAL | CHANGE   MINIMUM →

Occurs when change in societal values have occurred prior to institutional change. An example would be the Indian Independence movement or the civil rights movement in the US in the 1960s. These are usually termed *Mass non-violent movements.*

Coup d'etat, change of political elite but institution remains essentially the same. Elite change, however, is more of a personnel change as the elite's of both regimes are from the same class in society, examples would be the numerous military take-overs in Latin America, Turkey or the palace coup in Qatar 1995

LOW VIOLENCE

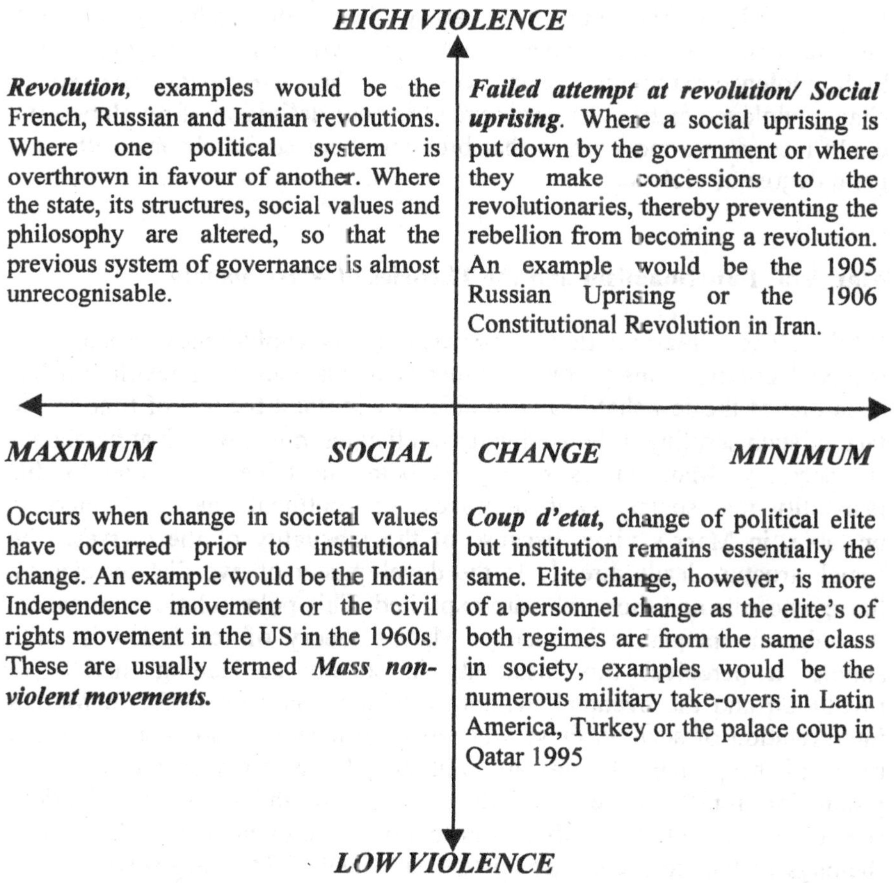

Figure 1: Using Violence and Social Change, in Defining Revolutionary Change

This model appears to work for the low violence, minimum social changes scenarios. There is some difficulty however, when differentiating between events with maximum social changes and high to low violence. Can non-violent social movements be deemed revolutionary? Taking the example of the Indian independence movement led by Mahatma Gandhi, can this movement advocating non-violence be simultaneously deemed revolutionary? While it could be argued that the Indian independence movement adhered to the philosophy of non-violence, the British government was not as accommodating. There was violence but not on the scale or magnitude of the Russian or Iranian revolutions. It is a matter of scale as to whether a scenario is violent enough to be deemed a revolution. There are those theorists such as Johnson who, for the above reasons, would remove both Gandhi's independence movement and Martin Luther King's civil rights movement away from the category of low violence/maximum social change, into the revolutionary category of the high violence/maximum social change. Therefore using the social change/violence matrix as measurement for our definition of revolution we could incorporate movements that brought about social change without a great degree of violence.

Marxism; Functionalism and the Theories of Mass Society

While Marx's interpretation of society and its evolutionary process has received criticism, his theory together with his views on revolution has been one of the few that has been able to withstand the test of time in the face of such scrutiny. It is for this reason that an in-depth look at his theory is necessary. Marx views society as being unstable. It is due to this instability that society is in a process of continual change. Society is unstable, in Marx's view, because of the inequality of the classes. The social structure leads directly to the development of two distinct classes, those who rule and those who are exploited. This polar relationship causes the inherent inequality in society. Marx's theory of revolution is quite simple; it perceives this instability in society as leading directly to revolution and the eventual overthrow of the dominant class. In Marx's interpretation of society, those who own the means of production are the rulers of the society, the rest are exploited, forced to work the means of production for the benefit of others. They are the proletariat. Modern society, Marx contests, is divided in this way. He explains that the worker 'belongs neither to the owner nor the land, but eight, ten, twelve, fifteen hours of his daily life belongs to him who buys them'.[28] When members of the proletariat become aware of their exploitation, they are drawn together by what Marx calls class-consciousness. The class-consciousness leads the exploited class to revolt and to overthrow the ruling class. Therefore, we can say that Marx's whole perspective of society is as an evolutionary process, where each stage in this process is defined in terms of its mode of production. The history of society is a history of revolutionary change, with Communism being the ultimate goal. Revolution for Marx is a change in the mode of production, which has inevitable knock-on effects for the structure of society, its political institutions and ruling elite. For Marx, everything, even the state which he holds as a mere reflection of the economic structure of society, could be defined with regard to the modes of production and the economic relations that result.

One of the major problems with Marx's theory is that it does not specify when exactly revolutions occur. Marx was relatively ambiguous about the transition from one epoch to another. He was of the opinion that the transition between epochs (i.e. the revolution) could only occur if the conditions were right. The correct conditions, in Marx's view, would only exist if the mode of production had developed to its full capacity. It is necessary for this to occur in order to create the intensity of relations (between the rulers and the ruled) that would spark the revolutionary zeal of the exploited class. Certain other criteria can be identified in Marx's writings that outline the conditions that are necessary for a revolutionary situation to exist; these are alienation and class-consciousness. Marx identified alienation as a major step towards the advent of a revolution. Cohen describes alienation as 'that process by which members of the working class find themselves to be nothing more than commodities in the general scheme of things'.[29] With the worker growing more disenchanted with his situation he looks for others who share his plight, leading to a growth of class-consciousness. Class-consciousness is necessary for the exploited class to articulate their alienation; only then can common goals be developed. After class-consciousness is developed, it is a short step to revolutionary consciousness. Marx himself never discusses how this occurs. Following the final revolution from capitalism to communism, there maybe a period of dictatorship of the proletarian, which is necessary to rid society of class divide. While Marx's theory of revolution has been the most enduring of all the theories available, the expectation that revolutions would stem from technologically advanced countries was incorrect. Rather, it took place in less economically advanced counties than he anticipated.

In many ways Khomeini's revolutionary ideology shares many similarities with Marxist thinkers, even though such an analogy would not be welcomed in Iran. As discussed in chapter three, the Islamic movement of the 1960s and 1970s shared a common platform, belief in equality and view of society, as Marxists of that time. Khomeini too, while being effective in mobilising the masses, did not feel it necessary to consult them further following his successful installation in power. He believed in a classless society and even saw the need for governmental structure withering away following the creation of a truly Islamic society.[30] He shared other similarities with Marxist thinkers, such as Lenin, who believed in the creation of an elite, whose role it was to guide society politically, socially and in Iran's case, spiritually. Khomeini was wary of the ability of the clergy, as an institution, to act as the guide for society and therefore set about creating his own 'party' which he established mainly from amongst his former students and junior clergy. It was to this group that Khomeini turned following the installation of the Islamic Republic. Also, Mao's idea of adapting revolutionary theory to the circumstances and culture of each society was mirrored in Iran. While basic similarities exist between the causes of Iran's revolution and revolutions elsewhere, the Iranian revolution also possessed cultural aspects that were unique to Iranian society.

Most non-Marxist theories of revolution refute the notion that all revolutions stem from the desire to alter class structure in society. Functionalists refute Marx's perspective on society and believe that there are a multitude of causes of revolution. In addition, they dispute the notion that a revolution is necessary for social development. Functionalists view revolution as being counterproductive; they view society as being consensual in nature and would oppose the idea that society is unstable due to some inherent social contradictions. In many respects functionalism is the only available theory to counter the Marxist notion of revolution. Two of the main figures in the functionalist school of revolutionary change are Parsons and Johnson.[31] Parsons did little work on the theory of revolution; his work dealt with understanding the social system and has been used by many others in the development of a functionalist theory of revolutionary change, not least by Johnson who has become synonymous with functionalism. Society for Parsons has the potential for conflict, unlike Marx however; he does not see this conflict as being inevitable. Indeed society is and has been able to solve its differences without resorting to conflict. Where conflict does arise, it is not, as Marx outlines, between the exploited and the exploiters, but because there is a general economic scarcity.

Rather than focusing on class antagonism, functionalists look for the causes of conflict in social structures or values. Functionalism is more inclined to believe that a society will be in danger of a conflict situation, if the values of that society do not correspond adequately to the environment. However, once the values of society are re-oriented to the new environment, the possibility of conflict is reduced. Under the functionalist perspective there is no clear path of change in society. Society adapts itself when the need arises and as different societies have different values, each society would develop in a different manner. Johnson, who developed the main functionalist model of revolution based on Parson's initial interpretation of society, states that 'revolutions must be studied in the context of the social systems in which they occur'.[32] The main necessity of a society from a functionalist approach is balance, or equilibrium. When the environment becomes imbalanced it denotes a need for change; the answer is not conflict but compromise. If the ruling class is unwilling to compromise, if they are unwilling to respond to environmental needs, there is the possibility that the government or regime could become dislocated from the population and thus be seen as illegitimate in the eyes of the larger populous. If a regime is deemed to be illegitimate by the population, this leads to what Johnson calls a loss of authority and power deflation. This forms the basis of elite intransigence, which Johnson has used as the basis for his model. In brief, Cohan has simplified Johnson's model,[33] as follows:

Multiple dysfunction + Elite Intransigence + X = Revolution

The 'X' factor in this equation relates to the inability of the elite to reduce their loss of authority by coercion or their inability to maintain the support of the armed forces to crack-down on opposition activity. Unfortunately this model does not bring us much closer to understanding why revolutions occur and for this reason the Marxist theory of revolution and its offspring, holds much more theoretical value.

That is not to say that the functional approach to revolution does not have its benefits. Its interpretation of society is interesting and provides the only viable alternative to Marxism. It's understanding of environmental change, its effects on values and roles in society, together with the propensity for conflict that this may cause, is useful when dealing with how a regime may counteract a revolutionary movement. Indeed, in defining and categorising societal change, functionalist theorists have also been helpful. Neumann, for example defines revolution as being 'a sweeping, fundamental change in political organisation, social structure, economic property control and the predominant myth of a social order, thus indicating a major break in the continuity of development'.[34] Here Neumann, would appear to negate the possibility of a rebellion or a *coup d'etat* being considered as a revolution. In addition, Neumann makes the point that a seizure of power must be successful if it is to be viewed as a revolution. Johnson, on the other hand, differed greatly from Neumann's view. He viewed revolution as any attempt to overthrow a government or ruling elite, whether successful or not. Johnson also considers revolutionary activity as being deviant behaviour and does not consider the question of whether revolutionary behaviour is still deviant in a society where the ruling elite has lost their legitimacy and the moral right to rule. Furthermore, Johnson consistently viewed revolution in a negative light, as something that can and should be avoided at all costs.

The theory of mass society is an attempt to explain the mass movements of the early twentieth century. Major theorists such as Arendt and Kornhauser; have developed their theories looking specifically at the rise of Nazism in Germany throughout the 1930s.[35] Unlike Marxism, which was developed years before the movements it inspired, the theory of mass society is largely a retrospective theory attempting to understand past events. It provides us with an insight and understanding of the causes and outcomes of mass movements. Through their analysis, Arendt and Kornhauser relate mass movements to the development of totalitarianism in society. Basically what the mass society theorists argue is that following the breakdown of class structure and social barriers, there is a period in which the population, unable to rely on the previous social structure, feels isolated and threatened. In such a state they are open to manipulation by an organised elite intent on mass mobilisation. Individuals in society are willing to accept the new ideology provided by this elite, as it replaces both the structure and security that were previously lost. It is through this manipulation by the elite of mass mobilisation that the threat of totalitarianism surfaces. As Arendt points out 'the truth is that the masses grew out of the fragments of a highly atomised society whose competitive structure and concomitant loneliness of the individual had been held in check only through membership of a class'.[36]

A final theory associated with the Mass Society school of thought takes a psychological perspective in understanding how revolutions occur and how revolutionaries are born. Possibly the most interesting of these approaches from our attempt to understanding the Iranian revolution is the Theory of Rising Expectations. De Tocqueville[37] first put his theory forward during this study of the causes behind the French revolution, however, it has been developed further by many other theorists and has led to a greater understanding of revolution in general. A further hypothesis related to the above, is the theory of the repression of instincts. Sorokin,[38] is one of the leading figures proposing this theory and defines revolution as 'a comparatively sudden, rapid, and violent change to the obsolete official law of the group, or of the institutions and system of values which it represents'.[39] The basic concept of this theory is that there is a system of values in a society, which is no longer representative of the society or its environment. Sorokin is a functionalist from the point of view that he believed revolutions are to be avoided, the idea being that they inevitably led to greater oppression than that which was the original cause of the social unrest. Sorokin, coming from a sociological background, based his theory largely on his study of the human psyche. He describes man as having two aspects to his nature: man as an emotional creature, including violent emotions; and man as a social animal living within a society of peers. For this society to exist, certain rules must be developed to resolve disputes, so that they do not end in violent, anti-social behaviour. A revolutionary period, for Sorokin, is when these rules are perceived to be no longer credible and when the inherent violent aspects of man's nature find their true expression. A revolution ends, when these or other rules are restored and are representative of society and bring society back to order.

Sorokin is of the view that a regime can avoid a revolutionary situation if after a demand by the population to reduce the regime's repression; it is curtailed leading to an orderly change in the values of that society. If the demands of the population are not adhered to, the possibility of revolution is decidedly increased. However during a revolution, due to the lack of any social order the primary nature of man results in increased violence, death and disorder. The population *en masse* suffers to a greater extent directly following the overthrow of a regime than they did beforehand. For this reason, Sorokin is of the opinion that revolutions are undesirable and that a progressive level of development is preferable to the rapid development which may accrue due to a revolution, but which will inevitably result in increased human suffering. Iran, while not a part of Sorokin's original analysis is a prime example that can be used to substantiate his theory. The Shah had many opportunities to adhere to the opposition's demands for change. Rather than making significant concessions, that could have acutely deflated opposition demands, the Shah met any sign of opposition activity with increased oppression. Furthermore, in the direct aftermath of the overthrow of the Shah's regime, the level of bloodletting far exceeded that which the opposition were attempting to curtail. That said however, the attempts of the current reformist government to implement change on a gradual rather than a sudden, explosive basis, shows that the lessons of the negative effects of revolution on society have been learnt in Iran. President Khatami's attempts to incrementally re-align the values of the current regime with those held by society at large, is a difficult and precarious task, but a necessary endeavour to prevent the re-rupturing of Iranian society along lines similar to that which occurred in 1979.

The theory of rising expectations is based upon the premise that it is not always the case that the greater the oppression in a society, the greater the chance there is of revolution. Therefore, oppression is not the sole reason societies rebel. This is evidenced by the fact that some societies have experienced incredible levels of oppression yet they have not revolted, while others in comparison have experienced relatively little oppression, yet that society has attempted to overthrow the incumbent regime. This phenomenon is explained by the hypothesis that 'revolutions are most likely to occur when a prolonged period of objective economic and social development is followed by a period of sharp reversal'.[40] An earlier version of this theory put forward by de Tocqueville surmised that people are less likely to revolt when society is being oppressed, due to their necessity to concentrate on survival. The potential for revolt in an oppressive regime occurs only when the regime begins to loosen their control upon society. This perceived weakness encourages those who wish to overthrow the regime. The evidence provided by the Iranian revolution substantiates both elements of this theory. More details will be given of this period in later chapters, suffice to say at this stage that during the period 1973-1975, following the oil crisis and the quadrupling of Iran's oil revenue's, the Iranian economy experienced an unprecedented boom period. However, due to a mixture of mismanagement, corruption and the state of the international markets this period was followed by a serious recession. The boom period increased the expectations of the working classes who suffered the most under the recession. Following Davies interpretation of the theory of rising expectations, this scenario made the Iranian working class ripe for a revolution. In addition, this coincided with the election of President Carter in the United States, who 'encouraged' the Shah to implement a variety of changes that considerably weakened his hold on society. This in turn provided the opposition with the space and encouragement they needed to manoeuvre the population into revolt.

Brinton also put forward the opinion that in the economic sphere, a revolution is more likely to occur because of 'a feeling on the part of some of the chief enterprising groups that their opportunities for getting on in this world are unduly limited by political arrangements'.[41] He uses both the French and Russian revolutions to substantiate this assertion. Prior to the period of revolution in both of these countries, their populations experienced a period of intense hardship and famine, while the population rioted there was little evidence of their desire to revolt. Revolutions occurred, however, during a period of relative economic well-being. Evidence in support of this theory can also be obtained from the Iranian experience. One less acknowledged reason for the success of the Iranian revolution was the support and financial assistance given by the *bazaari* (merchant class) to the revolutionary movement of Ayatollah Khomeini. The main reasons for their support can be traced to their inability to compete for a variety of state contracts due to the corrupt nature of the Shah's regime, where his family monopolised the economy and the Shah's policies favoured foreign enterprise. Therefore, believing that their economic development was constrained by the policies and politics of the Shah, they lavishly financed the revolution in the hope that this situation might change and their prominent position within the Iranian economy might be returned.

A newcomer to the Mass Society school of thought is the theory of relative deprivation. Much of the work on this theory is centred on the social unrest in the United States during the 1960s. One of the leading protagonists of this theory is Gurr who proposes that the propensity for revolution be based on a perceived inequality and frustration within society.[42] The more frustrated a group is within society, due to the values or the environment of that society, the more inclined they are toward violent opposition, with anger being directed towards the dominant values or ruling elite of that society. Gurr, also points out, however, that civil strife or revolution does not always achieve it's objective and may worsen a society's situation. In many cases revolutions result in civil war, worsening economic and social conditions and in extreme cases result in the advent of a totalitarian regime. While this theory is largely based upon the primary data of the civil unrest in the United States during the 1960s, Gurr's findings have failed to find an exact correlation between the causes and resultant effects of a revolutionary scenario. The basic concept whereby if people perceive inequality they will be more prone to addresses this injustice has, however, been shown to be true. The degree of civil unrest or inequality necessary to provoke a revolution has, on the other hand, not adequately been answered.

The final area covered under the psychological theory of revolution relates to the studies of what makes a revolutionary. This is perhaps the most tenuous of all the psychological theories. Taking the leaders of the 'Great Revolutions' this theory attempts to generalise on what characteristics of childhood experience assisted in the creation of a revolutionary personality. This is achieved by highlighting the similarities in both upbringing and experiences of the chosen revolutionaries. While there are many similarities, the only result from this endeavour is to show that there is a multitude of potential revolutionary leaders within society. The question whether revolutionaries would have become leaders if the environment were not fertile for their revolutionary ideologies, remains outside the scope of this work.

Developments in Revolutionary Theory – Post-1989

There are some difficulties in classifying recent events, especially the events across Eastern Europe in 1989 leading to the fall of communism, as revolutions. Tilly is the only theorist to have analysed these difficulties.[43] In the aftermath of these events he defined revolution as 'a forcible transfer of power over a state in the course of which at least two distinct blocs of contenders make incompatible claims to control the state, and some significant portion of the population subject to the state's jurisdiction acquiesces in the claims of each bloc'.[44] While this definition appears to have been developed specifically to understand the events of 1989, Tilly makes an interesting distinction between a revolutionary situation and a revolutionary outcome. A revolutionary situation is discernible by the presence of 'multiple sovereignty' within a state. This is where two or more blocs make effective and incompatible claims to control the state or to be the state. Therefore, in Tilly's opinion, there are three causes of a revolutionary situation:

1) Two or more opposing elements in society make competing claims to control the state or a segment of the state apparatus;
2) there is a commitment to these claims by a significant segment of the citizenry; and
3) there is a incapacity or an unwillingness of the rulers to suppress the alternative coalitions, furthermore there is an unwillingness to agree with the oppositions claims.

A revolutionary situation can be turned into a revolution if the above coincides with one or more of the following:

1) there is a significant defection of polity members;
2) there is acquisition of actual force by the revolutionary coalition or the neutralisation or defection of the regime's armed forces; or
3) the control of the state apparatus is taken by members of the revolutionary coalition.

The above analysis by Tilly is interesting for our understanding of how socio-political unrest can develop into a revolutionary situation and how such a situation can succeed in toppling an incumbent regime. Furthermore, Tilly applies Tarrow's analysis of protest politics[45] to argue that waves of revolutionary situations are often discernible, whereby one group of citizens are encouraged by the achievements of another, perhaps in another country. This analysis facilitates our understanding of one aspect of the outcome of revolution, that being that revolutionary behaviour can be exported abroad. It explains the wave of revolutionary activity that swept across Central and Eastern Europe in the aftermath of the fall of the Berlin Wall, together with the Shia uprisings in many of the states of the Persian Gulf following the establishment of the Islamic Republic in Iran. That said Tilly's analysis does not further our understanding of how to measure the propensity for socio-political unrest in society. The following chapter is an attempt to use the experience of the Iranian revolution to redefine revolution in terms of the re-distribution of power in society and to measure the socio-political unrest in society through an analysis of the binary opposition inherent in a country's political system.

Notes

[1] Dahl, R. (1970), *After the Revolution* (New Haven: Yale University Press), p.105.
[2] Bani-Sadr was the first democratically elected President of the Islamic Republic, who was impeached by a clerical dominated *majlis*, resulting in the exclusion of democratic forces from government and the centralisation of power in the hands of the clerical minority. He current lives in exile in France.
[3] See further Rousseau, J. (1987), *Social Contract* (Harmonsworth: Penguin).
[4] Cohan, A.S. (1975), *Theories of Revolution* (London: Nelson), p.10.
[5] Amann, P. (1962), 'Revolution: a Redefinition', *Political Science Quarterly*, 77, p.36.
[6] Theorists who follow this definition would include Pettee, Neumann and Marx. See further Pettee, G. (1971), *The Process of Revolution* (New York: Harper), Neumann, S. (1948-49), 'The International Civil War', *World Politics*, 1 and Marx, K. (1983), *Karl Marx and Fredrick Engels, Selected Works, Vol. 1* (Moscow: Progress Publishers).
[7] Pettee, G. (1971), p.3.
[8] Arendt, H. (1986), *The Origins of Totalitarianism* (London: Deutch), p.21.
[9] Theorists who follow this definition would include Johnson and Davies. See further Johnson, C. (1982), *Revolutionary Change* (London: Longman), and Davies, J. (1971), *When men revolt and why: a reader in political violence and revolution* (London: Collier-Macmillan).
[10] Pettee, G. (1971), p.22.
[11] Huntington, S.P. (1968), *Political order in Changing Societies* (New Haven: Yale University Press), p.264.
[12] Neumann, S. (1948-49), 'The International Civil War', *World Politics*, 1, pp.333-334.
[13] Kuhn, T. (1962), *The Structure of Scientific Revolutions* (Chicago: University of Chicago), p.93.
[14] On Plato's ideas see further Plato (1966), *Plato's Republic* (Cambridge: Cambridge University Press).
[15] Moore, W. (1963), *Social Change* (London: Prentice-Hall), p.132.
[16] Cohan, A.S. (1975), p.20.
[17] Tanter and Midlarsky in Cohan (1975), p.21.
[18] Dunn, J. (1989), *Modern Revolutions, an introduction to the analysis of a political phenomenon* (Cambridge: Cambridge University Press), p.13.

[19] Such a situation was recently seen during the overthrow of the Milosevic regime in Yugoslavia. Claims that those involved in the opposition were guilty of treason, having illegally attempted to undermine the government, were changed to heroic accolades following the success of the October 2000 revolution there. Showing that legality is subjective and is dependant on who is in power at the time. Although the people of Yugoslavia prefer to call the October 5th events as 'transition' rather than a revolution, the idea of legality still holds true.

[20] Edwards, L. (1965), *The Natural History of Revolution* (New York: New York: Russell & Russell), p.2.

[21] As opposed to its previous title as a 'Free State', which enabled Ireland to be autonomous but kept the Queen of England as the official head of State.

[22] See further Dunn, J. (1989), *Modern Revolutions 2nd Ed.* (Cambridge: Cambridge University Press), Huntington, S.P. (1968), *Political order in Changing Societies* (New Haven: Yale University Press), Marx, K. (1983), *Karl Marx and Fredrick Engels, Selected Works, Vol. 1* (Moscow: Progress Publishers).

[23] See further Calvert, P. (1967), 'Revolution: the Politics of Violence', *Political Studies, 15*.

[24] Ibid., p.2.

[25] Mao Tse-Tung (1967), 'Report on an investigation of the peasant movement in Hunan', *Selected Works of Mao Tse-Tung, Vol. I* (Peking: Foreign Language Press), p.28.

[26] Johnson, C. (1966), *Revolutionary Change* (London: Longman), p.7.

[27] Cohan, A.S. (1975), p.27.

[28] Karl Marx (1962), 'Wage, Labour and Capital', *Karl Marx and Fredrick Engels, Selected Works*, Vol. 1 (Moscow: Progress Publishers), p.83.

[29] Cohan, A.S. (1975), p.63.

[30] See further Chapter 6 for an in-depth analysis of Khomeini's views of society and government.

[31] See further Parsons, T. (1966), *Societies: Evolutionary and Comparative Perspectives* (Englewood Cliffs: Prentice Hall); Johnson, C. (1982), *Revolutionary Change* (London: Longman).

[32] Johnson, C. (1966), p.3.

[33] Cohan, A.S. (1975), p.128.

[34] Neumann, S. (1948-49), 'The International Civil War', *World Politics, 1*, p.2, in Cohan (1975), p.129.

[35] See further Arendt, H. (1986), *The Origins of Totalitarianism* (London: Deutch), and Kornhauser, W. (1960), *The Politics of Mass Society* (London: Routledge & Kegan Paul).

[36] Arendt, H. (1986), p.317.

[37] See further Tocqueville, A. (1980), *Alexis de Tocqueville on democracy, revolution, and society: selected writings* (Chicago: University of Chicago Press).

[38] See further Sorokin, P. (1969), *Society, Culture and Personality* (New York: Cooper Square).

[39] Sorokin, P. (1969), p.189.

[40] Davies, J. (1962), 'Toward a Theory of Revolution', *American Sociological Review, 27*, p.6, in Cohan (1975), p.195.

[41] Brinton, C. (1960), *The Anatomy of Revolution* (Englewood Cliffs: Prentice Hall), p.35.

[42] See further Gurr, R. (1970), *Why Men Rebel* (Princeton: Princeton University Press).

[43] See further Tilly, A. (1993), *European Revolutions 1492-1993* (Oxford: Blackwell).

[44] Ibid., p.8.

[45] See further Tarrow, S. (1989), *Struggle, Politics and Reform* (Ithaca: Cornell University).

Chapter 4
Revolution, Power and Binary Opposition

Iran – A 'Great' Revolution

The social unrest in Iran in 1979 culminated in the creation of a new and original political system. Iran's current system of government is unique in that it is an attempt to create an Islamic government that is compatible with the modern age. In essence, it is a practical manifestation of Khomeini's interpretation of Islamic thought. Whether we consider the result of this new venture a success, is not my focus here, neither is the question of whether the Islamic government is a true reflection of the values espoused by the revolutionaries in 1979, this will be covered in the later chapters. The purpose of this chapter is to evaluate the tangible results of the Iranian social movement of 1979 and its implications for the theory of revolution. This will be achieved primarily by proposing the idea that the Iranian revolutionary process is still not complete and therefore the true product of Iran's revolution cannot be yet known. This idea that Iran is still in a position of revolutionary flux is substantiated by the use of a binary opposition analysis to evaluate the extent of political change that has occurred in the post 1979 period. Through using the above analysis, the tangible changes that have occurred in Iran's political system, together with its implication for electorate empowerment, will be highlighted. Using the criteria established by Pettee and his contemporaries, we can say with certainty that Iran was a 'Great' revolution of the 20th Century. 'A re-constitution of the State',[1] did occur in the post 1979 period in Iran, with the socio-political changes possessing similarities with both the French and the Russian revolutions.

In the previous chapter a review of the current literature available on revolution, its theory and consequences was outlined. Based on this review we can see that what occurred in Iran in 1979 fits well into the criteria of revolutionary change. That said, the previous review also highlighted some of the inadequacies of the current literature in quantifying revolutionary change and in anticipating potential revolutionary situations. For instance, the 'great' revolution theory attempts to quantify the changes in society based on the value structure or the myths that guide society.

These changes are then used to ascertain whether a revolution has occurred. While such an endeavour is valuable in understanding the causes of revolution, it is difficult if not impossible to quantify. Furthermore, the functionalist school of thought while also utilising value alteration as the basis of their definition of revolution, employ other aspects of social and political change, such as elite alteration and/or violence, here again there are problems of quantification. Moreover, as was shown in the previous chapter, using the case of Iran it can be proven that both elite and institutional change can give the perception of value change in society, yet such change may not be reflective of the true values of the society that the institutions serve. While it is accepted that violence inevitably occurs in tandem with revolutionary change, there are again problems with quantification but also there is the problem of relating the violent act to the changes that have occurred in society.

Figure 1, in the previous chapter, did assist in the development of a workable categorisation of social and political change. That said, the changes in social structure and level of violence required for change to be termed revolutionary, are arguably subjective matters. Indeed, due to their subjectivity and ambiguity, the empirical measurement of revolution and its aftermath, using the current literature, is not possible. Furthermore, it fails to incorporate the idea that revolution is a process; that the changes involved in revolution may occur over time. Nor does it make any correlation between the main causes of revolutionary activity and the outcomes of a revolutionary process. Therefore, while figure one provides a valid basis for categorising potentially 'revolutionary' scenarios, a more in-depth evaluation is needed to fully understand revolution, especially for us to understand what occurred in Iran over the decades, since the events of 1979. In addition, none of the theories mentioned previously can specify when revolutions are likely to occur. That said, the need for the values of society to correspond to the social and political structures, as proposed by Johnson, can be accepted, together with the idea that the path of development of each society varies as the values of each society also varies. The functionalist interpretation of society is enlightened; its understanding of social/environmental change is also useful. Furthermore, the functionalist approach to counteracting a revolutionary movement through changes in the political structures of the ruling regime to correspond to the changes that occur in society's values, interacts well with our attempts to understand revolutionary change in terms of the direct relationship between the state and the population.

Possibly the best explanation of the events of 1979 is the theory of rising expectations. With the oil price increases of the early 1970s and the ambitious development plans that followed, the expectations of Iranian society were increased unsustainably. The economic recession that followed in the mid-1970s severely hampered the realisation of these development plans; this together with the government's inability to fulfil previous expectations made Iranian society ripe for revolutionary activity. That said, it would be difficult to say that Iran was economically oppressed in the 1970s and this was the reason for the revolution. Like most great revolutions, the revolutionary activity was not economically motivated[2] nor did it occur during a period of heightened economic and social oppression. Rather it occurred at a time of substantial change in society, where the ruling regime loosened its grip on society. Therefore, while the theory of rising expectations assists our understanding of the events that occurred in Iran throughout the 1970s, it does not encompass all of the factors that eventually precipitated the overthrow of the Shah. The causes of the Iranian revolution cannot solely be found in the sphere of economics, also included should be the level of political oppression by the Shah's administration and the desire for greater empowerment by the Iranian people.[3]

In the aftermath of 1979, Iran experienced all of the post-revolution criteria outlined in the previous chapter from elite change to value alteration. So if one was to follow the current thinking on the subject, Iran has fulfilled the criteria necessary for a revolution to have occurred. While this work does not contend that Iran failed to experience all the changes necessary for the advent of a revolution, it argues that these changes were not wholly representative of the causes of the revolutionary process in Iran and therefore the complete *raison d'etre* of Iranian revolution remains unknown. It is further contended that the revolutionary process in Iran was diverted from its true course by a series of events subsequent to Khomeini's return from exile, which enabled an organised elite to re-institutionalise political power in the hands of a minority. Therefore, the revolutionary process in favour of greater political pluralism was replaced by a regime and political structure that failed to fulfil the original goals of the revolutionary process. Through our analysis of the Iranian revolution and its aftermath, the author intends to substantiate the argument in favour of viewing revolution as a process rather than an event in time. Iranian history over the past two decades provides us with a unique insight into the evolution of a revolutionary situation. For that reason, while the current literature is relevant to the Iranian situation, it is also inadequate. Iran today is a product of a revolutionary process that is still continuing, however contemporary theories on revolution do not assist our understanding of the evolutionary nature of the revolutionary process in Iran. It is for this reason that a new definition of revolution needs to be developed, integrating a number of ideas from previous theories, but viewing revolution as an open ended process. Furthermore, a concrete connection has to be made between the initial goals of a revolution and the final outcome, even though the true outcome of the whole process may not be apparent for some time. At the very heart of this new definition is the acceptance of the Marxist view that society is involved in a evolutionary process, however where it differs is that this evolution is not viewed in terms of economics, as Marx does, but rather in terms of the political organisation of society. In many ways the new definition mixes Marx's idea's on societal evolution with Aristotle's ideas on political systems, viewing society in motion from one political system where power is maintained in the hands of a few to a political system with pluralism and electoral participation as its guiding principles. Therefore, while not challenging the criteria established by previous theories, this chapter will attempt to overcome the problems of quantification highlighted earlier. This will be achieved by viewing change in terms of the redistribution of power and by defining the relationship between the state and the people in terms of the binary opposition in society. While this chapter will concentrate solely on Iran and its pre- and post-1979 political system, analysing Iranian society's potential for socio-political unrest based on the binary opposition inherent in its political system, it is the contention of this work that this model is adaptable to other societies and other potentially revolutionary scenarios.

Redefining Revolution

It would appear that revolution is a multi-faceted phenomenon, providing the political scientist with a myriad of difficulties when attempting to conclusively define it. In essence, a revolution should alter in some way the values of its society, its social structure and its political institutions. It should change the leadership of the state and the new leadership should not be from the same class as the previous regime. The transfer of power should be illegal, although it is accepted that legality is a subjective matter. In addition, the transfer of power should incorporate some form of violence, either from the revolutionaries or the state, who may use violence in their attempt to dissuade the revolutionaries from their demands.

Definitions that are currently available usually consider most, if not all, of the above and merely differ in the degree of emphasis placed on each dimension of revolution. There is, however, a further misunderstanding that should be highlighted. Many theorists use violence as the backbone of their definitions and such emphasis gives the impression that a revolution is an event in time, which is quite misleading. While the violent event might be the highlight of the revolutionary process, focusing solely on this event neglects possibly years of revolutionary activity. In addition, it is often difficult to evaluate the violence of a revolution with changes in the social values, institutions and political actors. In order to find some consensus amongst the other theories mentioned so far, we could define a revolution as either a reconstitution of the state, as proposed by Pettee or a radical mutation in the social structure of a society, which occurs over time, through both violent and illegal means. Changes in the social structure in this context are defined as a fundamental change in the state philosophy, including institutional and elite alteration.

Taking the above definition of revolution would greatly facilitate our understanding of revolution and would assist our categorisation of what is or is not a revolution. A problem arises, however, with how we should categorise social change, with its the multiple dimensions, so that we could say a sufficient amount of social change occurred for the movement to be seen as a revolution. The answer to this question can be found by incorporating binary opposition into our analysis of social and political change. However, before this is done some consensus on what constitutes political and social change must be achieved.

As political scientists, one method of measuring change is through the re-allocation of power in society. Morgenthau[4] puts forward the idea that all politics, including international politics is about power and therefore one of the main determinants of state behaviour is the quest for power. Power is the core of political activity with the ultimate political activity being the fight for revolutionary change. The purpose of such mass participation in politics has always been to right a perceived injustice, whether real or imagined. The perceived injustice in all cases of 'great' revolutions, have been to right a political imbalance of power, in favour of the masses as opposed to the political elite, where the political elite are dependant solely on a class structure or economic superiority to maintain such an imbalance. All of the changes we have discussed previously changes in the political elite, political institutions and even social values can be viewed in terms of power. The purpose of changing political institutions, for example, would be to reallocate the power to make or enact legislation, or to increase the representation of the population. Similarly, changes in the political elite have the same purpose, to provide a more equitable political representation in society. Even changes in social values, while being slightly more ambiguous, can be viewed in terms of power. Taking the example of Iran, following the 1979 upheaval there was a concerted effort on the part of the government to define society in terms of the Shia faith. In essence, what the government was attempting do was to reinforce a certain set of social values and by doing so fortify their power/political support base. A change in social values could, therefore, be viewed in terms of a change, or attempted change, in the allocation of power in society.

When Aristotle dealt with revolution, his ideas included several possible classifications for viewing the political structure of a state, two of those being democracy and oligarchy.[5] Democracy is a political system where power is possessed and the rule is by the many, whereas in an oligarchy rule is by a minority of the population. Following Aristotle's model there were two possible types of revolutions, the first is where there is an attempt to re-constitute the state, in essence, 'when men seek to change from an existing form (of government) into some other, for example, from democracy to oligarchy, and from oligarchy into democracy, or from either of them into constitutional government or aristocracy, and conversely'.[6] The second form of revolution is a change in political personnel, when one revolutionary group tries to take over the leadership of the state administration. Both of these revolutionary scenarios stemmed from the same cause, inequality. How do we define inequality? Perhaps it is easier and more productive to define its antithesis, equality. Equality, in a political sense, can be defined as a situation where each and every citizen of the state has the same voice in the decision making process of that state. Inequality, therefore, is the opposite where the voice of each citizen in the decision making process is not equal.

A revolution, therefore, occurs due to an inequality in society. Marx would have defined this inequality in terms of economics. While Aristotle makes the point that wealth is the basis of power in an oligarchy, while freedom is the basis of power in a democracy. Adding Aristotle's interpretation of society to our previous discussion on the components of a revolution brings forward some interesting results. Firstly, we can discount the revolutionary scenario in figure one, where revolution is defined as a change in the personnel of the political elite, as this is not compatible with the current literature on what constitutes a revolution; this is termed a *coup d'état* instead. Taking Aristotle's view that revolution is a motion from one type of political structure to another, in search for greater political freedom by the masses, and marrying this to Pettee's idea of revolution as a 'the reconstitution of the state', we can view revolution as a form of motion or a political evolution in much the same way as Marx does, instead this time it is a motion towards political empowerment. If revolution is viewed as a motion from one political structure to another, which provides greater political empowerment of the masses, then we can understand better the reason for the apparent dismantling of the Soviet Union some seventy years after the Russian revolution. Furthermore, we can understand the continuing political friction within Iranian politics today, over twenty years after the declared end of the Iranian revolution. The reason for both of the above is that the causes of the revolution remained unfulfilled, whether through misrepresentation of the true ideals of the revolution or through the re-institutionalisation of power in the hands of a few. How, therefore, can we measure whether society has changed sufficiently for a revolution to be deemed complete? Through viewing political and social change in terms of power and the goal of revolution as being the re-allocation of power in favour of the masses, some light can be shed on this issue. Furthermore, by understanding the dynamics of a state's political structure in terms of the binary opposition within the state, we have a means of measuring the amount of 'real' change that has occurred through the socio-political upheaval. Binary opposition in this sense is meant as a reflection of the relationship between the state and the populace. It is, therefore, argued that the only manner in which to define the re-constitution of the state is in terms of the change in the relationship between the people and the state apparatus. If the binary opposition within the political structure does not change, for example, if there is merely a *coup d'état* within a military regime or if there is a move from an oligarchy to an autocracy, then it is argued that the state has not been re-constituted and a revolution did not occur.

A change within the political elite and/or the renaming of institutions can be viewed as merely variations upon the former political structure and, therefore, such change cannot be deemed revolutionary, no matter the amount of violence that is associated with it. Only when the very relationship between the state and the people is altered significantly can we say that there was true political evolution. How can we therefore measure the change in the binary opposition within society? This is a difficult task, as it cannot be measured in terms of economics or a new political structure but can only be achieved through an analysis of the change in the political participation of the population. In other words, it is a measurement of the extent to which a person can influence the political structure or the policies of their government; this is what is representative of the change in binary opposition within society. Binary opposition in this respect is viewed as the distance between two poles, representing the state and the people. The defining factor in this respect is the political system or more specifically the facets of the political system that define the state/population relationship. A diagrammatic representation of this idea can be seen in figure 2 in the next section. When the people gain more political empowerment the difference between them and the state structure decreases and visa versa. When the difference between the state structure and the people is minimised as far as is possible, society can be said to be in a state of relative equilibrium. The further society is from a state of relative equilibrium, the greater is the possibility of social unrest.

The problem remains, however, as to what amount of change in the binary opposition within society is significant enough for us to deem that the revolutionary process is complete. This is a difficult question and is again a matter of degree. For example, during the 1979 social unrest in Iran the political system changed from a monarchy to an Islamic Republic. If we gauge the populaces' involvement or influence in the political system before and after this event we can see that there is a change in the binary opposition, but is it significant enough for the revolution to be deemed complete? Prior to 1979 the populace's influence in the political system can be said to be negligible, especially after the creation of the *Rastakhiz* Party[7] in 1975. This effectively created a one party state and coupled with the Shah's rule by decree meant that the Iranian people had little say in the policies of their government.[8] After the installation of the Islamic Republic, we see that the binary opposition between the state and the people has changed, but not to a similar value as in other democracies. While Iran, especially in recent years, can be said to have free and open elections, which significantly decreased the binary opposition in society, there are still areas such as open political expression and selection of candidates that maintains a certain amount of political discontent within society.[9] Just to clarify this point, there will always be some amount of political discontent within society, as government policy may not reflect all views held by that society, however, if one has a significant voice in the political process the level of discontent is vastly decreased. In Iran this is not always so, there is still the suppression of some political ideas and groups and the overall ability of the current structure to move with the political will of the majority is still in doubt. Therefore, while there has been some movement in the binary opposition between the state and the people, we can say that there remains a significant level of tension in society due to a high level of binary opposition. A total reduction in the binary opposition between the state and society will never occur, however, once the cleft remains minimal so will the urge to revolt.

Measuring Binary Opposition

The inevitable question that will be asked when using binary opposition to explain the phenomenon of revolution is how can it be measured. One possible method is given as a diagrammatic representation in figure 2. Here the two poles of the vertical axis represent the state and the population. The horizontal axis represents the political system; each type of political system can be placed along the horizontal axis, while the system with the least level of public participation is fulcrumed at the greatest distance from the point of intersection of both axes. For example, a monarchy, dictatorship or oligarchy could be represented by point C and a liberal democracy would more likely be in the area around point B. The distance between ACA and ABA would be representative of the binary opposition within that state/political system. The line DD is the point before which the tensions inherent in society are such that the binary opposition does not lead to social unrest. After the line DD the possibility of revolution or socio-political unrest is incrementally increased.

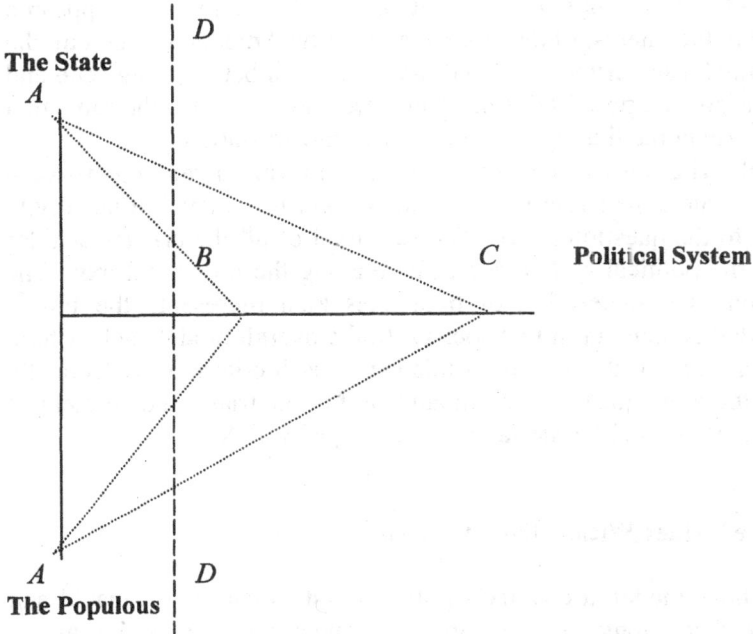

Figure 2: Measuring Binary Opposition, State: Population Power Distribution

What determines where each country's political system is placed along the horizontal axis? This can be achieved by breaking down the criteria that will determine the level of a population's participation, freedom and influence in the political process and giving it a numeric value. Such criteria could include the following:

- **Elections** – are they fair and free from manipulation?
- **Political institutions** – do they balance and limit political power within society?
- **Political association** – is there freedom of political association, with all the other freedoms that this implies?
- **Electoral systems** – how representative is the electoral system of minority views?
- **The political systems capacity for change** – can the system change to reflect the views of society, as society's values change?

The above criteria are viewed as the major issues effecting the interaction of the population in a political system, therefore it appeared most useful in the interest of developing a theoretical model to ascertain the degree to which each criteria affected the interaction between the state and the populous pre and post 1979 Iran. The used above are also the same that the OSCE[10] use in facilitating the process of democratisation.[11]

Each criterion can be broken down into values ranging between zero and ten, where the larger the value the greater is the level of negativity in response to the question posed. The sum total of all the criteria enables us to place the political system somewhere along the horizontal axis. The distance from the intersection of both axes then represents the binary opposition that is inherent in that society. In the overall model each criteria is given equal weight, the reason for this is that each criteria is dialectically related and therefore must develop in tandem. For the true empowerment of the electorate to occur, all criteria must carry equal weight.

Defining the Values Within Each Criteria

Using the above model, a country's political system can be evaluated and placed somewhere along the horizontal axis. The criteria are used to assess the level of political participation/influence experienced by the general population. This is necessary as it is the contention of this work that the greater the binary opposition in society the greater the possibility of socio-political unrest. Binary opposition is being used in this sense as a measurement of the population's role and influence in the political system. Taking the above model the distance from the state to the population is dependent on the analysis of the political system and signifies the level of binary opposition inherent in that society. The larger the binary opposition, the more prone that society is to social unrest, as the population does not feel a part of the political process, leading to the political system losing legitimacy in the eyes of the public.

How do we calculate the value to be placed on a 'political system'? Using the criteria developed earlier, each criterion should be broken down into a numeric value between one and ten, then each political system should be given a value within this range. The higher the numeric value the lower the populations' level of influence. These values are added together, giving a total sum that can be placed along the horizontal access. While the numeric values attributed are arguably subjective, I have concentrated on developing a flexible model that attempts to incorporate the complexities of these particular aspects of a population's involvement in their political system. Admittedly the values selected for each criterion are personal but it is suggested that the values below are the most appropriate means of explaining the diversity within each criterion.

A) Elections
Value 1 – Elections are free and fair, with adequate election information, ease of voter registration and no apparent voter intimidation.
Value 3 – Elections are free and fair, election information is limited and, voter registration has difficulties. There is no apparent voter intimidation.
Value 5 – Some doubts remain as to the validity of the election results; however, there was not widespread intimidation. Election information is available but is biased in favour of the incumbent government. Voter choice may also be limited.
Value 7 – Elections are held but are used solely as a reflection of current government's level of popular support. Serious doubts hang over the election results and election information is biased. Some voter intimidation was present and voter choice was limited.
Value 9 – No elections are held or if elections are held they are amongst the political elites with little or no consultation with the larger electorate.

B) Political Institutions
Value 1 – Election results directly reflect the balance of political power within the state. Furthermore there is a balance of power amongst the three arms of government (the executive, the legislature and the judiciary). Each arm of government is independent and free from intimidation from any outside source or each other.
Value 3 – Election results do not always reflect the balance of political power, with some key positions within the political system outside of

electoral influence. The independence and integrity of the arms of government are not under question and there is a balance of power of sorts that allows review/public debate of political decisions prior to their implementation.

Value 5 – While technically there is a division and a balance of power, the practical application of this results in one institution possessing a worrying amount of political power. If used incorrectly, this power could result in the move away from an open and democratic form of government.

Value 7 – The balance of power is uncertain, the independence of the judiciary is called into question and a review of political decisions prior to implementation rarely occurs. Institutions have the capacity to turn into fiefdoms and open political debate is curtailed or stifled.

Value 9 – Political position is not dependent on elections. Rule is arbitrary, held by a few key personnel, there is no balance of power per se, no review or public debate of political decisions occurs.

C) Political Association

Value 1 – All forms of political affiliation are legal and no particular party has state funding in excess of its representation.

Value 3 – While all forms of political affiliation are legal, some political ideologies are openly discouraged. Furthermore, through either the use of political or economic monopolies an increase in the number of parties contesting ballots is curtailed.

Value 5 – While believing in political pluralism, this political system has legally banned some ideological groups, leaving adherents to this philosophy without direct political representation.

Value 7 – Party or political organisations are limited, with those organisations allowed reflecting the ideology of the incumbent government. All other forms of political persuasion are discouraged or banned outright.

Value 9 – No political expression or association is allowed and the population's participation in the political process is discouraged.

D) The Electoral System

The test for the electoral system is largely based on the level of disproportionality resulting from within the electoral system.[12] This will measure the ability of minority views to participate in the political system. Here there is a difference made between countries using the main types of electoral systems, namely proportional representation systems and plurality systems. Furthermore values should also be available which represent countries that have an electoral system that does not allow any form of opposition representation.

Value 1 – The electoral system in place facilitates the participation of minority views in the political process. This type of system usually has large multi-seat constituencies and results in coalition governments. An example here would be proportional representation.

Value 3 – This electoral system also facilitates the participation of minority views, the electorate is offered lists of candidates, there are large multi seat constituencies and the threshold for election is low enough for minority participation in the political institutions. An example of this system might be the list system.

Value 5 – This electoral system might discriminate against minority participation in the political process. This system would usually favour larger parties, being based on 'a winner takes all' philosophy and normally results in single party majority government. An example here would be the pluralist system or the first past the post electoral system.

Value 7 – This electoral system discriminates against certain parties, minority groups or persons, through direct government policy. This is achieved either through electoral funding, electoral information and/or criterion necessary for candidate selection.

Value 9 – No apparent electoral system is in place, or if one is officially professed it is rarely adhered to. Elections are merely used to confirm a continuation of the current regime; the election outcome is not always a true reflection of the political views of the electorate.

E) The Political Systems Capacity for Change

Value 1 – The political system is a product of a constitution, therefore, any change in the political system requires a change of the constitution. For this to be achieved a referendum must be held so as to obtain the views of the electorate, who directly decide on whether changes are warranted. Furthermore, the electorate can demand a referendum without the direct approval by the executive or legislature.

Value 2 – The political environment is wholly dependent on the outcome of the electoral process. There may or may not be a constitution, however, changes to political institutions/system can be achieved purely through legislation.

Value 7 – The political environment is fluid, and while there my be a constitution, a plurality of political sources makes it difficult, not only, to control changes in the political system but also to know if and when those changes have taken place.

Value 9 – Changes to the political environment/system can easily be made by the ruling elite without consultation with or responsibility to the electorate.

Here again it is important to stress that values are arbitrarily determined. Furthermore, it remains outside the scope of this work to correlate a specific value with a specific numeric weight. The values were developed through the primary research carried out for this work, and are intended to operationalise the theoretical model.

Defining the Zone of Relative Equilibrium

The area between the point of intersection of both axes and the line DD, is intended to represent the area of relative equilibrium, or what Marx might call 'the zone of least alienation'. A truly democratic form of government does not exist in practice, at least presently. Therefore there is a point before which the population's dislocation from the state structure will not lead to socio-political unrest, this is represented by the area of relative equilibrium. For the purpose of theoretically developing this model, the sum value of three for each criterion is arbitrarily taken to represent the point of relative equilibrium. The value of three is taken, as it is believed to be a realistic reflection of a stable and well functioning liberal democracy. The value of three represents not a perfect value but one after which society would be likely to actively pursue a change in this criterion. In this sense it is argued that most liberal democratic states would reside within the zone of zero to fifteen, the latter point represents the sum total of three for each criterion.

Binary Opposition in Practice

An evaluation of the political system pre and post 1979 was carried out (as can be seen in Table 1), so that the political development as a result of the Iranian revolution could be observed.

On the issue of political development, it is noted that a country's revolutionary movement should, theoretically, cease once they reach the area of relative equilibrium, or at least the possibility of socio-political unrest should incrementally decrease the closer any country's political system gets to this zone. Using the above table and figure 2 in the previous section, a new diagram can be developed (see figure 3) that would show the development of Iran's political system toward the area of relative equilibrium over the past two decades.

CRITERIA	A	B	C	D	E	Total
Iran under the Shah	7	9	9	9	8	**42**
The Islamic Republic of Iran today	5	3	6	7	7	**28**

Table 1: Binary Opposition Analysis of Iranian Political Systems Pre- and Post-1979

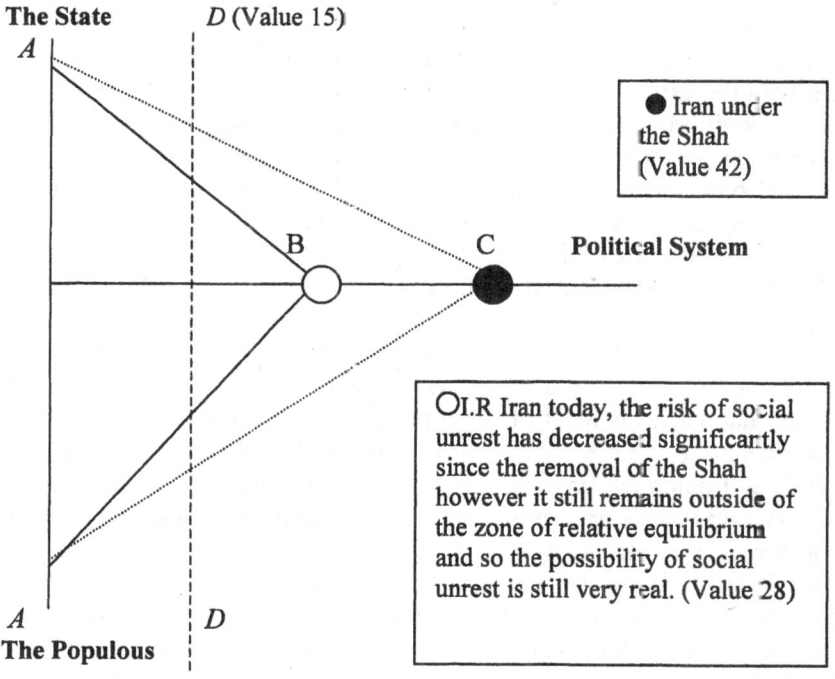

Figure 3: Binary Opposition in Practice – the Case of the Iranian Political System Pre- and Post-1979

The Binary Opposition Analysis of Pre- and Post-1979 Iran

Taking the overall analysis of revolution carried out in this and the previous chapter, we can re-draw many conclusions on the evolution of a revolution, its causes and when revolution is to be deemed complete. A revolution can be said to have occurred only if there is a significant change in the level of binary opposition in society. Furthermore, revolutions are not events in time but are rather processes, which may take months or even years to achieve their results. Viewing revolution in this way enables us to take a more holistic view of revolutionary movements and their consequences. By viewing revolution as an evolutionary process, from a political system where power is maintained in the hands of an organised elite for their own personal benefit (autocracy or oligarchy) towards one where power is firmly maintained by the masses. Therefore, it can be surmised that the core cause of this political evolution or revolution is the desire for empowerment by a population. Furthermore, successful revolutions occur when the population is content with the extent of their empowerment and when society is in a state of relative equilibrium. This means that when the population is involved, or at least perceives that it is involved, in the political system and has a role in policy development, it is less likely to partake in socio-political unrest. In addition, it is noted that the process of a revolution may take many years before the final outcome of the process is known.

Using the analysis described in this chapter, the line DD (in figure 1) was found to have a numeric value of 15, while the pre-1979 political system in Iran had a value of 48. Therefore, taking into account the autocratic nature of the political system under the Shah, it was not surprising that a serious level of socio-political unrest developed. Bringing this analysis up to the present day; Iran's political system still maintains a high degree of potential for socio-political unrest (value 28). While the new political system established under the leadership of Ayatollah Khomeini did provide for greater participation of the population in the decision making process, it still leaves the population somewhat alienated, feeling the political structure is unrepresentative of the true values of Iranian society.

Furthermore, the analysis carried out in table 1 can be used to highlight the areas within the political system causing the most population/state dislocation. The Islamic Republic's political system scores high in the criteria C, D and E, the result of which means that Iranian society is still prone to a certain level of socio-political unrest. The main areas of contention relate to the selection of candidates, the right of political association and the perceived ability of the political system to change in order to reflect the values of society. These findings are substantiated in the following chapters when a contemporary analysis of the political environment in Iran under President Khatami is undertaken. However, before we go on to analyse the contemporary political situation in Iran, perhaps it would be of relevance to introduce Moore's ideas on the outcome of revolutionary situations.[13] He has developed the idea that revolutions either developed from above or below and in many ways this is similar to the debate on the development of the Islamic movement that was outlined in chapter three. Moore puts forward the idea that revolutions from above are those where the bourgeois impetus was weak while the peasant solidarity is strong. These types of revolution inevitably result in one of two types of regime, either fascist or communist, here he gives the example of Germany, Japan or Russia. In contrast, if the role of the bourgeois is strong then the revolutions will developed from below, examples of these type of revolution include England, France and the United States. In the latter's case the resultant effect is usually a system based on greater freedom and emancipation. What is interesting from this theory is not only its possible similarity with the progress of the Islamic movement, but also the fact it may also shed some light on the outcome of the Iranian revolution if we can ascertain the role of the bourgeoisie and the trajectory of the revolution.

Notes

[1] See further Pettee, G. (1971), p.3.
[2] This was substantiated by an interview with a 1979 revolutionary, who pointed out that the individual income in Iran today was 25% of that earned in the years leading up to 1979. Interview carried out September 1999.
[3] See further Downes, M. (2000: Autumn), 'The Islamic Resurgence: the case of Iran', History Studies 2.
[4] See further Morgenthau, H. (1993), *Politics Among Nations: The Struggle for Power and Peace* (New York: McGraw Hill College).
[5] See further Aristotle (1999), *Politics: books V and VI*, translated by David Keyt (Oxford: Clarendon).
[6] Aristotle, 'The Politics' in Cohan, M. & Fermon, N. (Eds) (1996), *Princeton Readings in Political Thought* (Princeton: Princeton University Press), p.123.
[7] In 1975 the Shah announced at all legal political parties would now be merged into a new single party entitled the *Rastakhiz* (resurgence) Party, effectively creating a one party State.
[8] A full analysis of the pre- and post-1979 political systems in Iran is carried out and can be seen in section 5.5.
[9] See further Chapter Seven and Appendix Two.
[10] OSCE – Organisation for Security and Co-operation in Europe.
[11] See further Keane, R. (2000), *Creating space in which to live; deconstructing binary opposition – The case of Bosnia and Herzegovina* (Limerick: University of Limerick), chapter 8.
[12] The values for disproportionality is based on analysis of the disporportionality of electoral systems in Western Europe, see Gallagher, Laver and Mair (2001), *Representative Government in Modern Europe – institutions, parties and governments* 3rd edition (London: McGraw Hill), chapter 11.
[13] See further Moore, B. (1991), *Social Origins of Dictatorship and Democracy: lord and peasant in the making of the modern* (London: Penguin).

Chapter 5
Ideologies of the Iranian Revolution; the Rise of Khomeinism

> He came to symbolise everything the West found incomprehensible and baffling about the East: his intense, ascetic spirituality and air of other worldly detachment; his medieval, theocratic mindset, which drew its parallels and precedents from the Islamic world of the 7th Century, the mystical certitude that he spoke in the name of God, his country and Muslims everywhere
>
> *Time* Magazine,
> June 12th 1989, a commentary on the death of Ayatollah Khomeini

Leaving aside the question of whether the Iranian revolution can be termed an Islamic revolt or a search for greater political and social freedom, this chapter will delve into the numerous influences, ideologies and characters that shaped the revolt that toppled the Shah and saw the establishment of an Islamic Republic. While the opposition to the Shah had a distinctly Islamic flavour, it was not the sole ideology that was professed by the masses.[1] Every ideology from Islamic Marxism, to outright communism, from liberal democracy to secular constitutionalism, found a voice within the opposition movement. There were many leaders within the movement, who represented one or many of these different shades of political expression. However it is safe to say that one of the most profound and unquestioned influences on the opposition movement in Iran was Ayatollah Khomeini. While prior to the revolution, due to the fact of his exile, he may not have been as widely known amongst the young revolutionaries; upon his return to Iran in February 1979 he became the unquestioned leader of the opposition movement and the leading architect of Iran's political future.

    Ayatollah Khomeini symbolised many things to many people; opinions about him are as diverse as they are conflicting. To some he is a fanatic, a fundamentalist; to others he is a patriot, a leader, a savior. Even within the confines of the Shia clergy, views on Khomeini differ. Some saw his views on Islam as being enlightened, to others his views are near heretical. No matter how one views Khomeini, few could argue that his influence on the political and social life in Iran today is profound. He was not the sole representative of this diverse movement. While the opposition easily united behind this ageing revolutionary, his voice and his philosophy was not the only one heard. The purpose of this chapter is to investigate the variety of personages and opinions that prevailed in pre-revolutionary Iran. Since Khomeini has played such an important role in post-revolutionary Iran, much of this chapter will be taken up with his ideas and his philosophy. That said, the influential Islamic theorists from this period, such as Shariati and Soroush,[2] together with political visionaries such as Bazargan, Hanifnejad[3] and the many who transcend these labels will also be discussed in some detail.

Khomeini – First and Foremost a Populist Leader?

Khomeini was a man as diverse as the opinions that were held about him. He has been depicted in many ways as a fundamentalist, an Islamic traditionalist and as a man unwilling to compromise on his beliefs. What made him feared so much by the West and worshipped by others in all corners of the globe? What was his philosophy, his ideology and his theory of clerical rule? Orientalists who believed that he perfectly represented a Muslim world, incapable and unwilling to enter into the modern age, often scorn him.

Khomeini was, at the same time, all and none of the above. Khomeini was not an Islamic traditionalist in the true meaning of the word; he forged his theory of government and society upon a *mélange* of socialism, mysticism, utopianism and Shia Islamic beliefs. He was militant whilst being pragmatic; he was at times contradictory, being populist whilst at other times stringently sticking to his beliefs. He was overall a revolutionary leader and tactician whose movement mobilised intellectuals, socialists, parliamentary democrats and Islamic militants alike. His outlook and interpretation of Islamic texts are at times visionary, at times radical. He has become synonymous, in western eyes, with the revival of Islamic activism throughout the world from Sudan to Indonesia. He developed a 'third-way' in international politics,[4] espousing a policy of 'Neither East nor West', providing an alternative philosophy in the realist defined bi-polar world that represented the latter half of this century. His unwillingness to play by the rules that were not of his creation and his constant austere visage has made him the focus of unobjective western antagonism. Ayatollah Khomeini was not a fundamentalist, for fundamentalism by its very definition denotes ideological inflexibility, political traditionalism and a puritanical approach to religion. Abrahamian's description of Khomeini as a populist is far more apt.[5] For populism fuses both, 'ideological adaptability, intellectual flexibility, with political protests against the established order, and with socio-economic issues that fuel mass opposition to the status quo'.[6] The term fundamentalism fits the description portraying Khomeini as a man intent on dragging his country back to the time of the Prophet Muhammad, while in fact he attempted to bring Iran into the family of nations', not as a subordinated power but as an equal. His creation of a political system, which fuses both religious beliefs from the 7th century with political structures of the modern age, should be considered in tandem with his unwillingness to compromise on social and economic inequality. At times his ideology takes on a more Marxist perspective than his allies would acknowledge, his views on the Islamic faith and its role in society have been compared to the development of Protestantism within the world of Christendom.

Khomeini's outline of Islamic government shows him and his ideology to be innovative and would seriously question the use of the label 'fundamentalist' to describe him. Fundamentalism has been a label that has been attached to Khomeini and the revival of political Islam, which he inspired. This is a misunderstanding; fundamentalism implies a sense of rigidity, a rejection of the modern world and a strict adherence to tradition. In a religious context fundamentalism would mean a return to the words of the only true (i.e. Quranic) texts and a rejection of any modern interpretation of their meaning. It would mean the rejection of modernity, which in a political sense means, a rejection of the nation state. Abrahamian compares the movement that Khomeini led, to the populist movements, which swept across Latin America.[7] By a populist movement he means a movement aimed at the lower classes of society, the less educated who are easily swayed by rhetoric, personal charisma and imagery. Populist movements have less a plan for economic and social development and rely more upon a charismatic individual espousing the woes of foreign ideologies while emphasising national and cultural superiority. It is true that Khomeini did much to promote pan-Islamism and at times even gave the impression that he did not care about the Iranian nation-state, but rather Iran's spiritual well being. Probably his most famous statement in this regard was made during his return journey from exile. A reporter on the plane, asked Khomeini the question, 'we are now over Iranian territory, what are your emotions after so many years in exile?', his response was '*Hichi*', meaning 'Nothing'.[8] This gave the impression that he cared nothing for his country, which was in a state of bloody flux. However, the true intention of this statement was to highlight that to care for anything other than God was to show a lack of religious conviction and portrays Khomeini's true guiding principle. Moin's work on

Khomeini gives the impression that Khomeini was a man who felt it necessary to put on this persona of impregnable religious fervour in order to add legitimacy to his position.[9] Zubaida further argues that Khomeini did not reject the concept of the nation state.[10] Whilst he frequently argued against such topics as imperialism, both physical and cultural, from an Islamic centred perspective, through his words and actions he recognised and supported the idea of the nation state. This can be especially seen in his early speeches when he espoused both Islamic and nationalistic ideals, evoking themes of patriotism and the Iranian nation. In the aftermath of the success of the revolution, his belief in the supremacy of the nation-state became even more evident. A year before his death in 1988, for example, he issued a *fatwa* ruling that the Islamic Republic was superior to Islam, stating that 'if necessary even the seven pillars of Islam – including fasting, praying and the *Hajj* pilgrimage – could be suspended in the interest of the state'.[11]

In the direct aftermath of the revolution, one could be led to believe that with Islam's position in Iranian society now secure, the emphasise would shift to the restoration of the state. Furthermore, clerics were initially forbidden to run for elected office, which appeared to condone state-religious separation. Khomeini even went as far as to disqualify one of his close supporters, the frontrunner during the 1980 Presidential campaign, Jalal ad-Din Farsi because his father was an Afghan and the new constitution demanded that the President be Iranian by birth. This action appears to value Iranian citizenship higher than the Islamic faith in the post revolution governmental structure. Islam and nationalism have always been a cause of friction in Iranian society. Khomeini however, managed to bridge this gap. Perhaps his apparent nationalism was a rouse to create broad-based support for the new regime. That said, this apparent contradiction between Khomeini's apparent nationalism and his pan-Islamic views continued side-by-side well into the first decade of the revolution.

Much of what is the Islamic Republic of Iran today, from its institutions, constitution and social structure were developed from a blueprint of Ayatollah Khomeini's views on government and society. Rarely, if ever, has a revolutionary leader had such a carte blanche in creating a post-revolutionary society, as Khomeini had in Iran. Khomeini, his influence, philosophy and ideology are therefore of paramount importance to our understanding of the revolution and its aftermath. It is the purpose of the proceeding pages to see through both the western misconception of Khomeini and the over zealous Iranian portrayal of

Khomeini as the Imam, the chosen one to lead the Iranian people to true justice, to see him as the architect and icon behind the Islamic Republic.

Khomeini is often portrayed within the Islamic Republic in an almost saint like manner, born to humble unprivileged surroundings. In reality Khomeini was, in fact, born to what could be termed a middle class family in Khomein, a small town in the semi-arid central province of Golpayegan. Both of his parent's came from clerical families, his mother was the daughter of a well-respected *mujtahid* from Esfahan.[12] Khomeini's father, Sayyid Mostafa, was himself a cleric having studied in both Esfahan and Najaf.[13] Khomeini begun his theological studies under the guidance and tutelage of Shaykh Abdul-Karim Ha'eri, one of the leading senior clerics of the time. In fact, Ha'eri was to become one of the main influences in Khomeini's life over the next fifteen years. When Ha'eri was invited to move his school to Qom,[14] to assist in the revival of this once famous seat of religious learning, Khomeini too moved with his teacher.

Ha'eri was a quietist, he believed that the clergy should not be involved in politics and went to great lengths to live by this belief, including moving to Najaf (that was part of the Ottoman Empire at the time) during the 1906 Constitutional Revolution in Iran. A period in which both the influence of religion and the clergy in society was seriously undermined. No longer was the mullah the central figure in society who would perform a wide variety of duties from prayer leader, to judge, to teacher and advisor. With the victory of the constitutionalists, a path was set towards what they termed modernity. Their view of modernity was generally based on the French enlightenment, which leaned increasingly towards secularism. While the changes successfully implemented by the constitutionalists would not include a viable democracy or an open society, it did manage to remove many of the traditional roles of the clergy and replace them with state sponsored bureaucrats. In the immediate aftermath of this period the clergy went through a serious transition; some clergy continued their administrative work, exchanging their clerical garb for state positions. Others became more active in trying to redress what they viewed as this serious attack to the people's faith. For this reason many within the clergy supported the re-installation of the Shah, who was perceived to be the lesser of two evils and more favorable to the ulema's continued high profile role within the community. In such a charged and polarised atmosphere Ha'eri's quietist position was almost unique. Ha'eri's move to re-establish Qom as a leading center of learning coincided with the beginning of the meteoric rise of the Cossack officer Reza Khan. A dedicated secularist, he in many ways accelerated the process of secularism, even though he courted the clergy in the early days of his reign.

An ambitious man, whose sights were set on obtaining the ultimate power in Iran, he was at pains to undermine the constitutionalists and those who envisaged their struggle leading to the establishment of any form of democracy in Iran.[15]

During Khomeini's years in the seminary, followed by his time teaching in Qom, it would haven been difficult to envisage his leading role in the overthrow of the existing state structure. While Khomeini became a popular teacher, a well-respected cleric and author,[16] he followed Ha'eri's view of remaining outside of the political fray. When Ha'eri died in 1937, Ayatollah Mohammad Hosayn Borujerdi filled his place as the leader of the Shia faithful and the person whom Khomeini ideologically followed.[17] Borujerdi was also a quietist, and preached the need for the clergy to remain apolitical. Following the abdication of Reza Shah, Borujerdi came to an understanding with the new Shah and his administration. In return for Borujerdi's attempt to contain the movement within the ranks of the clergy calling for a more political stance of the religious leadership, the young Shah agreed to retract some of the more severe and anti-clerical policies of his father, which included the prohibition of the Islamic veil.

While Khomeini was extremely close to Borujerdi,[18] his views on the clergy could not have been more diametrically opposed to those held by his mentor. Borujerdi was not without his dissenters either; there was a growing number of clergy who viewed him as a conservative and a traditionalist. They believed that Borujerdi was indirectly supporting the status quo and, therefore, the Shah's regime. Khomeini for the most part concentrated on his teaching and writing during his early years in Qom. He largely remained apolitical, with the exception of one publication in 1943, from which we can begin to see the development of his views on secularism. The book entitled *Kashf Al-Asrar* (The Discovery of Secrets), indirectly attacked the apolitical clergy and was written in response to a book *Asrar-e Hazar Saleh* (Thousand Year Secrets), which he deemed as an attacked on Shi'ism and a sign of the growing influence of secularists in society.[19] This was Khomeini's first foray into the political scene and shows to some extent his early views on the role of the clergy and politics. It was only when he considered that the very fabric of Shi'ism in Iran was under attack, did he feel it correct to speak out. After publishing the above manuscript, Khomeini returned to relative obscurity within the confines of the seminaries of Qom. He was not enticed back into commenting on the political situation of Iran, even during what would have been seen as an obvious opportunity provided by the Mossadeq[20] government of the early 1950s. Mossadeq was supported by some of the clergy, the most senior and notable being Ayatollah Kashani.[21] Mossadeq's unwillingness, however, to include Kashani in his cabinet in 1951 would have a fundamental effect on the course of the 1979 revolution. It would be used following the revolution, as a sign that the democrats too had a secularist agenda, which should be defended against with the same zeal with which the religious classes opposed the Shah.

Khomeini's time as a quietist cleric came to an end following the death of Borujerdi, releasing Khomeini from his loyalty to his mentor and ideological leader. For clerical leaders like Borujerdi, support of the Shah enabled them to continue in their work of securing the future of the faith. Khomeini also believed that Islam should be protected at all costs, however, he also believed that the faith should never be compromised by acquiescing with secularists or those who were unbelievers. For the Shah, the clergy had served their purpose, during the Mossadeq crisis the support of prominent clergy and their mobilisation of the masses enabled him to regain control of the government. However, his détente with the clergy soon outlived its usefulness and he returned to his development plans that included modelling Iran on contemporary French secular society.

In later years, Khomeini in an attempt to explain his years of silence towards the Shah's regime compared his stance to that of Imam Ali, who sacrificed his right to become Caliph in order to maintain unity amongst the Muslim faithful. He told one congregation that 'Ali co-operated with the caliphs because they appeared to be acting according to the rules of religion. When Mu'áwíyah turned the Caliphate into a monarchy which was contrary to Islam, there was no other choice for him but to incite resistance and uprising'.[22] All at once Khomeini was condemning the totalitarianism of the Shah's regime as being anti-Islamic and comparing his defence of Islam to that of Imam Ali against the usurper Mu'áwíyah. This was an early signal of the depth of Khomeini's belief in his holy mission and should have signalled to the government that he would be an opponent who would be increasingly difficult to silence. Khomeini's unwavering stance would also put him at odds with his fellow clergy, many of who believed he was endangering the very faith he claimed to represent. Khomeini was as hard in his condemnation of those clergy who were in favour of maintaining the status quo as he was against the regime. He compared them to those who advised Ali against opposing Mo'awiyah (i.e. cowards). By evoking the images associated with the Imamate of Ali, Khomeini was able to appeal to the emotions of the faithful and by placing himself in the position of Ali; he was able to imply his superiority to the other clergy.

The launch of the next stage of the Shah's development program in 1963 gave Khomeini the opportunity to test his level of support amongst the people and to examine the resolve of the regime. The Shah for his part attempted to undermine the clergy and their appeal to the masses, by putting his policy changes and, in effect, his right to rule directly to the people in a plebiscite. The Shah's six-point reform plan, which he referred to as the 'White Revolution of the Shah and his people', was an attempt to implement some land reform. In addition, it also incorporated some aspects of electoral reform that enabled women, for the first time, to vote. Khomeini made a declaration claiming that the Shah's electoral change was anti-Islamic and his referendum was unconstitutional, while at the same time warning the clergy in general that these reforms would further weaken their position within Iranian society. Khomeini's declaration added to the rising tide of opposition to the Shah and his reforms.[23] By utilising the argument that the Shah's referendum was unconstitutional Khomeini was able to appeal to the secularist opposition. Since the overthrow of the Mossedeq government and his subsequent internal exile and house arrest, the center-left secularist opposition was without its previous charismatic leadership. Khomeini, was a visible and ardent opponent to the injustices of the Shah's regime and as such gained many secular, as well as, lay Islamic constitutionalist followers. Many might have re-thought their support of Khomeini had they known his true views concerning the constitution, 'if we talk of about the constitution, it is because the government uses it to justify its existence, and we want to beat them at their own game. We neither care about the constitution nor want anything to do with it. Our constitution is the law of Islam'.[24] Being the pragmatist, Khomeini realized that the secular opposition could be useful and so he, by and large, kept his arguments against the Shah as general and as populist as possible.

When dialogue failed to dissuade the Shah from his proposed reforms the stage was set for confrontation, there were skirmishes between the Shah's security forces and seminaries during the annual No Ruz[25] pilgrimage in Qom. It resulted in a number of deaths on both sides, increasing the tension and entrenching the positions of all concerned. The Shah believed that his reforms were imperative to maintain the support of his population, while Khomeini who was convinced that the Shah attacked the very principles of Islam was becoming more active in his opposition. When all else failed to quell the rising tensions, the Shah sent an envoy to Khomeini to ascertain his demands. Far from finding a solution, Khomeini's response resulted in him being targeted as one of the main causes of unrest and dissent.

Islamic mythology mixed with reality created powerful images in the Iranian psyche. It is for this reason that the upcoming (1963) *Muharram* celebrations were to take on such an important role, providing an occasion for open dissent. *Ashura* is the tenth day of the mourning month of *Muharram*. It holds particular significance for Shia's, as *Ashúrá* is the day when the Shia faithful remembers the martyrdom of Imam Husayn and his small band of followers, who fought a gallant but fatal battle against the overwhelming army of the tyrannical Caliph Yazíd. Holding the moral high ground, while being surrounded by injustice and tyranny, has been an image continually evoked by Shia leaders. Throughout the revolutionary period the emotions evoked by such celebrations would be utilised effectively by the clergy to mobilise the emotions of the masses. The Shah would continually be depicted in the role of the tyrannical and unjust Caliph Yazid, while Khomeini's supporters would portray him in the role of Imam Husayn.

The 15th of Khordad – the Birth of Khomeini's Revolutionary Movement

The *Ashura* procession in June 1963 turned into an open display of protest against the regime. Many pinpoint this date, the 15th of *Khordad*,[26] as representing the birth of Khomeini's revolutionary movement. Crowds assembled in Qom to hear Khomeini as he compared Husayn's defense of Islam to their current opposition to the Shah. Repeating Husayn's words as he went into battle in Karabala, 'If the religion of Muhammad cannot be restored except with my blood, may the sword take me …' Khomeini brought moral and religious justification to their current plight. Crowds in Tehran and elsewhere were whipped up into a similar frenzy, where mourning processions became occasions for open decent. Crowds shouting 'Death to the Shah, Death to Dictatorship … Long Live Khomeini', made their way through the streets of the capital. During a repeat demonstration the following day, there were mass arrests in Tehran. Two days after his own fiery anti-Shah sermon, Khomeini was arrested.
    Word of Khomeini's arrest resulted in protests that soon engulfed Qom, Tehran, Mashad, Esfahan and Shiraz. In each of these cities crowds attacked police stations and other symbols of the regime. In an attempt to regain control, soldiers were order to open fire; the resultant loss of life was significant. While the protests appeared to have a semblance of spontaneity, it was not so. With the growth of Khomeini's opposition movement, he encouraged a number of *bazaari* merchants to establish what became known as the Coalition of Islamic Societies, in 1962. While the Coalition was originally founded by a small group of Tehrani merchants, Khomeini placed his closest students and allies to supervise its development. Many of

the post revolutionary leaders of Iran can trace their political roots to the Coalition and their role in disseminating Khomeini's word. The Coalition grew and its influence spread to other cities and other *bazaars*. In the years that followed, the Coalition became an indispensable tool for mobilising the masses, for disseminating information and for accumulating the financial resources necessary to fund the course of Khomeini's revolutionary activities. Khomeini, the pragmatic strategist, knew that he needed not only the support of the secular masses, but also the financial support of the traditional *bazaaris*. On the morning of June 5th 1963, the Coalition was quick to organise demonstrations against Khomeini's arrest. In the chaotic atmosphere that followed, it was only the shoot to kill order that enabled the Shah's forces to maintain any semblance of stability. With the Shah, his government and his forces taken by surprise and having underestimated the potential of the religious threat, they had little option but to impose martial law.

With Khomeini out of circulation, the government's propaganda machine went into overdrive in an attempt to discredit the clerical opposition. These actions together with the strict control over the population's movement, through martial law, enabled the government to regain the initiative. Although opposition continued underneath the surface, there was an end to the mass street demonstrations that marked Khomeini's arrest. The government held Khomeini for two months; his eventual release was treated as a celebration in Qom. Upon his release, it was insinuated by a government publication that the clergy had agreed to remain outside of the political fray.[27] However, less than a year later, Khomeini was again openly denouncing the Shah's policies.

In the autumn session of 1964, the Iranian parliament passed a bill that would effectively give immunity to American personnel living and working in Iran. In essence, it placed all American personnel outside the jurisdiction of the Iranian judicial system, no matter what crimes may be committed, neither the Iranian courts nor the Iranian people could find redress. While agreements such as these are normal, when the military personnel of one country are placed in another, in the highly charged atmosphere of Iran where the memory of foreign domination was all too recent such a bill was bound to cause consternation. Khomeini once again chose his time and manner of reply effectively. The anniversary of the birthday of Fatemah, the daughter of the Prophet Muhammad, is a time of pilgrimage and celebration. In his sermon to the pilgrims who visited Qom, Khomeini took a tone not of celebration but of mourning. In the speech that followed Khomeini criticised the passing of the bill, depicting it as a treacherous sellout of Iranian sovereignty and independence. Through depicting his opposition in a religious setting, whilst also speaking out in defence of Iranian independence, Khomeini was at the same time appealing to the faithful and the secularists alike. Khomeini's speech was the most severe attack ever made against the Shah and his policies, it left little doubt concerning his views, and furthermore it did not permit the possibility of a negotiated settlement to his opposition. His terms were clear and unequivocal, the Shah and his polices were a direct attack on Islam and in such a situation there should be no compromise. In certain sections of this speech it is evident that Khomeini was calling for the overthrow of the government, the Shah and the monarchy.[28] His unwavering opposition to the Shah's regime and his inflammatory denunciations of the government's policies led the regime to single out Khomeini as the focal point of anti-government sentiment. Something would have to be done to reduce this ever-increasing threat to government stability. Some within the administration wanted to have Khomeini arrested and executed for his anti-government behaviour, others however feared making him into a martyr and argued that an alternative solution had to be found. It was obvious that mere imprisonment was insufficient to silence Khomeini's rhetoric, therefore it was decided that removing Khomeini from his audience, would be the most effective method to neutralise his influence. Therefore, on the morning of November 4th 1964, Khomeini was again arrested and flown to exile in Turkey.

While it is evident that before Khomeini's exile he had decided that only the overthrow of the Shah could safeguard Islam, it was his time in exile that fine-tuned Khomeini's philosophy and hardened his resolve for the task ahead. Khomeini moved from Turkey to the Shia holy city of Najaf in Iraq where he was to spend the next thirteen years. Initially he concentrated in teaching Islamic law and continued his academic writings. It was during this time that he developed his version of Islamic government. After six years in exile, he unveiled his plan in a series of seventeen lectures given in the main mosque in the Najaf bazaar. The speeches were, at the same time, an attack on the apolitical clergy who were too willing to compromise in the face of government confrontation (in both Iran and Iraq), while also laying out his vision for Islamic governance. The contents of these lectures were circulated throughout Iran under the title *Velayat-e Faqih: Hokumat-e Islami* (which literally means, The Jurist Guardianship: Islamic Government). This book contained the crude outline of the system of government that would unfold in the aftermath of the revolution; it contained his views of the relationship between man, the state and God and was a culmination of his work as a teacher, philosopher and Islamic scholar.

Khomeini and Iran's Pre-Revolutionary Islamic Influences

Khomeini was a religious revolutionary; but the term orthodox could rarely be used to describe his interpretation of Shia Islam. Not many clergy initially followed Khomeini's ideas on the role of religion in politics. While the clergy, or rather the religious establishment, were crucial in mobilising the masses against the Shah, the ulema remained deeply divided throughout the 1960s and 1970s as to the role that the clergy should play in society. Many believed that in order to preserve the religion of Islam, the clergy should remain outside the political fray, remain independent, aloof from any political situation that might embroil the establishment and lead to its possible destruction. Khomeini too, as we have seen, remained a quietist throughout most of his adult life, concentrating on his studies rather then getting involved in opposition politics. As stated earlier in this chapter, he was later to justify this by saying that Imam Ali too remained silent until the future of Islam was at stake. That said not everyone agreed, as Khomeini did, that the fate of Islam was such that the clergy should take an active role in the overthrow of the State. Let us remember that the Shia faith had survived thus far through a number of different and sometimes brutal regimes' by always reaching an accommodation with the terrestrial leaders.

Khomeini – the Mystic, the Marxist, the Warrior of God

Khomeini's early influences as we have seen were the clerics Ha'eri' and Bourujerdi, both of whom believed in a division between politics and the clergy. However, even under the guidance of these men, Khomeini showed his individuality of thought by studying mysticism. Especially as many within the clergy believed the study of mysticism to be heresy. We can see the influence of mysticism in his writings on *velayat-e faqih*. His blueprint for Islamic government and his ideological leanings have other influences as well. One such influence was the writer Jalal Al Ahmed, who coined the term *qarbzadegi*, or what became known as westoxification.[29] The opposition movement was as divided in terms of its ideology, as the clergy were in terms of their role. The dubious coalition that helped topple the Shah comprised a wide spectrum of views, from the Communist *Tudeh* party,[30] to the Marxist- *Feda'iyan-e Islam*,[31] the secular National Front and the militant Islamic *Mujahedin-e Khalq*.[32] Many writers of the time, concentrated on the decline of Iranian culture as a sign of a general malaise effecting society at large, others favoured to the clergy's perspective that it was a decline in society's moral values or distance from Islam that was at fault. Al-Ahmed's writings against the negative influence of western culture captured the imagination of intellectuals and the opposition movement alike. Al-Ahmed was part of a new brand of Iranian intellectual that espoused Islamic ideals, while at the same time championing the cause of underdevelopment and modernity. His writings capture successfully the ideals of a generation of educated men and women who enabled the revolution to succeed. These men and women were willing to put their fate in the hands of the clergy, believing that they had the moral independence necessary to guide society through this vital stage of development. It was also believed that the clergy, as was their position historically, did not have the will to participate in the actual running of the country. Al-Ahmed viewed the clergy as being in a prime position to exact political change. Shi'ism sees the clergy as the vice-regents of the Imam and as such entitled to claim the right to replace the rulers of their time. The clergy by their very position and the nature of their faith represented an alternative to the government.[33] The clergy's apparent objectivity and quest for the equality and justice that unpins the Islamic faith, made them in Al-Ahmed's view a buffer through which society could be protected against the negative aspects of imperialist western culture. While Islamic tradition was the figurative sword, which the clergy could wield in defence of Iranian society, it also represented the main argument for the clergy not to be entrusted with political leadership. The clergy he noted, were defendants of tradition. He surmised that they therefore, 'oppose all change, progression and revision. This is why they are called the opiate of the masses. Since protection of tradition is a retrograde process, we observe that the clergy not even protect the present situation'.[34] While Al-Ahmed was correct that the clergy's view of society would curtail the progress of the apparent collective will of the revolutionary movement, they would be a major force for change in the lead up to the revolution and in it's aftermath. Al-Ahmed's writings, struck a cord with Khomeini's own views on imperialism and this can be seen as one of the influences on Khomeini's final blueprint for Islamic government.

Shariati – the Luther of the Islamic Reformation

Ali Shariati, another influential writer of the time, took up Al-Ahmed's theme of *westoxification*, but instead of chastised the clergy for their inactivity in the defence of Islam,[35] he depicted the role that the clergy should play in society, as being that akin to a resistance movement. He pinpoints the sixteenth century as a turning point for the clergy in Iran. It was under the Safavid Empire, as we have seen, that Shi'ism became the official religion of Iran. Shariati saw this as the institutionalisation of the faith and the main cause of its ruin. He perceived this to be a watershed, after which the clergy could no longer claim to be the representatives of the ideals of the Imams who protected the oppressed and fought against injustice, especially as the state was largely the cause of oppression and injustice.

Before the Safavids, Shi'ism was a faith continuously under threat, marginalised and constantly having to fight for its survival. It was therefore ideologically representative of those alienated in society, the economically and politically oppressed. During the early years of Shi'ism, especially after the death of Imam Husayn, the Shia clergy were seen as reactionary. This contrasts significantly with the Sunni clergy, who have always been paid by the government and therefore seen merely as employees of the State. In the Sunni tradition there was never a division between the temporal rulers and the clergy. This has at times led to accusations against the Sunni clergy for being merely an instrument of government. However, in Shi'ism this division of powers between the state and the clergy provided society with a way to counter-balance government policy. Indeed, as we have seen during both the Tobacco Protests of 1892 and the Constitutional crisis of 1906, when the clergy wanted to exert its influence, it could still exact substantial change in government policy. This independence enabled the clergy to be a voice against injustice and gave them the credibility to be a force that the temporal leaders would disregarded at their peril. However, when the Safavid's adopted Shi'ism as the state religion, the clergy merely became a method by which the government of the day could proselytise its policies. Indeed one of the reasons behind making Shi'ism the state religion was an attempt by the government to reign in and control the reactionary clergy. As Shariati aptly noted, 'from the moment that Shi'ism succeeded in gaining formal recognition, from that moment it was vanquished ... from the moment that the powers that had been ranged against it began to accommodate it, they absorbed it, it ceased to be a dynamic movement, it became a powerful ruling institution'.[36] This alliance between the Iranian clergy and the state has throughout the modern history of Iran been an uneasy relationship. While the clergy had at various times attempted to exert their influence, they largely stayed outside of the political fray, this is especially true following the establishment of the Pahlavi regime. While Reza Shah initially used the clergy to consolidate his position against the ousted Qajars, his secularism and outright anti-clericalism eventually defined his reign. The clergy feared the possible outcome of a confrontation with the government; instead they retreated to their seminaries and followed a quietist approach to political activity. This, argues Shariati, was against Shia tradition and the clergy by their very silence were effectively supporting the status quo and the incumbent regime.

Shariati also argues that another, even greater change occurred in Shi'ism under the Safavids, which struck at the heart of Shi'ism as a revolutionary religion. He points out that the adoption of western practices, incorporated into the religion under the Safavids, robbed Shi'ism of its true purpose and direction. He speaks here of the Safavids emissaries to Europe, who returned to Iran with the western religious practices of mourning and passion plays, which they incorporated into Shia tradition. Indeed, it was during the initial period of the Safavid Empire that much of modern writings and traditions of Shi'ism were developed. Shariati argues, quite convincingly, that these new practices transformed Shi'ism from a revolutionary religion (which he depicts as red) to one of mourning and sorrow (which he terms black Shi'ism). 'The Safavids bewitched Shi'ism, they altered the nature of red Shi'ism – which is its eternal colour from Ali till eternity (having begun with his martyrdom) – to black Shi'ism which is the garment of death which in the name of mourning the Safavids have clothed it with ... making Ashura a form of opium for the Iranians ...'.[37] By the 1970s, the clergy in Iran were almost a closed society unto themselves. The clergy had strong links to the *bazaari* classes and were significant landowners. While this gave the *ulema* financial independence, it had the effect of distancing the clergy from the very people they were to represent; it made them in many ways immune to the suffering of their society.

Khomeini and Shariati, Polar Views on the Role of the Clergy

While it is difficult to say whether Khomeini agreed with Shariati on his interpretation of the decline of the clergy. It is true to say, however, that Khomeini did echo the general themes of clergy intransigence used by Shariati. It was when Shariati argued that Islam was meant to be pluralistic, that faith is a question between God and man, that the clergy had no right to claim the role of intermediary; it was here that Shariati's views met with vehement disagreement from Khomeini. While the *ulema* generally condemned Shariati and his views openly, Khomeini initially refused to do so.[38] It was only after Ayatollah Mottahari, Khomeini's main contact in the Coalition of Islamic Societies, informed him that Shariati's views were beginning to influence the student community and his prestige was even heralded amongst seminary students, only then did Khomeini change his position to open hostility against Shariati's views.

By taking the basic theme of the clergy losing touch with its true power base and becoming a part of the economic and political establishment, Khomeini consistently argued and urged the clergy out of its cosy détente with the state. Khomeini was able to effectively turn the clergy into a political force in its own right. For example, contrary to Shariati's belief that passion plays, such as the procession for *Ashúrá*, drained the people of emotions thereby taking the revolutionary zeal from the masses, Khomeini turned such events into an effective method of mobilising the masses and inspiring them towards revolt. Whereas Shariati saw the clergy's participation in politics as undesirable, from both a spiritual point of view and as regards the type of society that would result, Khomeini saw little difference between political and religious life. Many followers of Shariati's work believed that the clergy did have an important role to play in the post-revolutionary era, but as a moral guide for society, not as the political leadership.

Islamic Intellectuals – the Pawns of Khomeini?

Al-Ahmed and his contemporaries through their writings inspired many intellectuals and lay opposition activists to believe that the clergy had an important role to play in the drive for the overthrow of the Shah's regime. Khomeini soon realised the potential of this group. It was these Islamic intellectuals who would unwittingly eventually assist him in the creation of his version of Islamic government. The Islamic intellectuals saw in Khomeini the epitome of clerical opposition and revolutionary zeal, as espoused by both Al-Ahmed and Shariati, but failed to see the political strategist and leader that lurked below the clerical garb. Many realised too late that the clergy desired to be more than just a moral guide for society. Few took heed from Shariati's prophecy that the rise of a political clergy would result in what he called 'the despotism of the clergy' and which he potentially viewed as 'the worst and the most oppressive form of despotism possible in human society'.[39] As a result, the Islamic intellectuals were to pay a severe price, in the aftermath of the revolution, for this lack of foresight. However for now, they flocked to Khomeini's side, providing him with the intellectual and pluralist credentials through which he could address a much wider audience both at home and abroad, and convince them of the righteousness of his crusade.

Khomeini's Template for an Islamic State

Khomeini's *velayat-e faqih* was an idea that had evolved over a long period of time. In 1970 when Khomeini unveiled his life's work in a series of lectures in Najaf, he was sixty eighty years old. He had already completed a long and fruitful career as a teacher of Islamic law and ethics. He had spent a great amount of time studying Islam's great mystical and philosophical traditions of *erfan* and *hekmat*,[40] and had a formidable following amongst his many students. Indeed, Khomeini was a famous teacher and as many of his students had now returned to their hometowns throughout Iran, Khomeini's influence and teaching was significantly more widespread than just the academic and clerical circles of Qom. Others students had remained close to the Ayatollah and as we have seen were instrumental in the establishment and effective running of the Coalition of Islamic Societies. It is through this network of former students, that Khomeini spread his word throughout Iran. His student's writings were also influential on Islamic thought of the time, Ayatollah Mottahari[41] was also a prominent Islamic theorist of the time and one of Khomeini's closest students. Khomeini influenced many of Mottahari's views, we therefore can learn much about Khomeini's thoughts on the role of Islam in society through the writings of his former students and disciples.

Unlike many intellectuals of the day, Mottahari rejected outright any connection between Islam and Marxism. He argues that man was not created equal, that each has their role to play in society,[42] dependant on the aptitudes and strengths that were bestowed by God. He substantiated his argument by use of the Quranic verse, 'Do they divide the wealth and kindness of the creator. We have given them material and moral means, so that some have supremacy over others in aptitude, so that some conquer others. The benevolence of the Almighty is greater than all that they gather.'[43]

The above is central to Mottahari and Khomeini's belief that the clergy were the only ones in society with the depth of understanding of the Quran necessary to guide society effectively. Mottahari was an ardent anti-Marxist, arguing extensively against the incorporation of other foreign ideologies into Islamic thought, seeing Islam as being sufficient for the functioning of any society.[44] Mottahari did not see a role for intellectuals in the rule of society, viewing only the clergy as being capable of just leadership. Mottahari's interpretation of Islamic rule did not encompass the concept of *velayat-e faqih*, when he envisaged clerical rule it was more on a basis of consensus amongst the most learned of clergy. Mottahari goes as far as to reveal who he would choose to be a part of the clerical leadership, while it is representative of a broad spectrum of views amongst the clergy, there is no room for Islamic intellectuals or constitutionalists. In fact, he chastises the clergy in Iran for their failure to push the Islamic agenda to its final conclusion. Pin-pointing those who participated in the 1905 constitutional movement, he argues that the clergy should see the conclusion of the Islamic movement as being the establishment of an Islamic government. Instead, they handed over control of the government to intellectuals and they in turn betrayed the faithful, returning Iran to tyrannical rule. For those who followed the line of Khomeini the lesson was clear, this time they would not quietly return to their mosques and expect the intellectuals to protect the faith. This time the clergy would not only participate in the revolution, but they would take control of the post-revolution environment to ensure the creation of a truly Islamic government. What form that government would take was not largely discussed in the pre-revolutionary period, Khomeini and his followers, however, had the advantages of a well-developed structure already under review.

Khomeini was initially quite vague about his proposals for Islamic government and there were many valid reasons for this. The most important was that he believed it was too early before the revolution to outline his proposals and he did not want to alienate the many secularists who supported him. If one looks at the texts of his speeches from Najaf, however, one instantly recognises that the theory outlined by Khomeini was far from the practice that eventually became the political structure of Iran. Perhaps Khomeini did not fully elaborate in his speeches about the structure of government which he envisaged, or perhaps Khomeini was a utopian and his ideals were surpassed by the realities of a revolutionary situation. Khomeini's *velayat-e faqih*, which translates as government of the jurisconsult, tended towards the rule by a group of clergy rather than by one. In this his views are not dissimilar to Mottahari's, when he refers to the *foqaha* or religious jurisconsults who would be the natural leaders in an Islamic government. He stated that '... it is only the just *foqaha* who may correctly implement the laws of Islam and firmly establishes institutions, executing the penal provisions of Islamic Law'.[45] The *foqaha* received this right to rule as the guardians of the word of the Prophet as passed down by the twelve Imams. 'The *foqaha*, the religious leaders, are the trustees of the Prophet, [that means that] all tasks entrusted to the Prophet must also be fulfilled by the *foqaha*, religious leaders, as a matter of duty ... No one can doubt that the Imam (peace be upon him) designated the *foqaha*, religious leaders, to exercise the functions of government and judgeship.'[46]

More importantly Khomeini seemingly did not envisage the position of a Supreme Leader, as defined under the new Islamic constitution. He did not see the situation where one religious leader would take supremacy over the others, 'There is no hierarchy ranking one *faqih*, religious leader, higher than another or endowing one with more authority than another.'[47] Instead, his arguments in favour of Islamic government centred on the rule of the *foqaha* rather than the *faqih*. He takes a rather utopic opinion of how this government will function and did not even envisage the need for legislative elections. From Khomeini's initial perspective, society would be ruled in a manner not unlike the 'Golden Era' of the Prophet Muhammad or the reign of Imam Ali, where the leader's goal was the creation of a just society rather than political structures to control the population.

It was probably inevitable then that his vision of a naturally evolving just society based upon the benign rule by a council of religious leaders did not come to pass. The pressures facing a modern and divided society meant that in the aftermath of the revolution, the clergy were left with little alternative but to impose their rule and vision of society. Khomeini did outline a situation when a single leader could take control of the government. Possibly envisaging himself in the position he stated, 'When a *mujtahid*, religious leader, who is just and learned struggles for and succeed(s) in establishing an Islamic government, he will have the same rights and authority in the affairs of society, that were enjoyed by the Prophet. It will be the duty of the people to listen and obey this *faqih*. He will hold the supreme power in the government and management and control of social and political lives of the people in the same way as the Prophet and Ali.'[48] While not being the main thrust of Khomeini's plan for Islamic government, this was the eventual product of revolution.

Concerning other functions of government, Khomeini also had similar utopist views. He foresaw that in a truly Islamic society there would be no need for either the official judiciary or a formal system of State finance. These institutions would be of little use in an Islamic society and would cease to be necessary. 'Superfluous administrative organisations and the administrative method accompanied by fabrication of files and bureaucracy which are alien to Islam, have imposed expenses on the state budget, which are inadvisable ... this administration system is remote from Islam.'[49] Government taxes would be replaced by religious dues, which would fulfil the financial needs of the Islamic State. In a state that was willing to obey the word of God, there would be no need for a judiciary, as the majority of people would follow the tenets of Islam, the clergy would, when necessary, be there to settle disputes based upon the word of the

Koran. He argues that the official judiciary was cumbersome without being effective, while all the rules necessary for the functioning of society were present in the Quran.

Khomeini's vision of Islamic government, especially when we consider the division within Iranian society in the lead up to the revolution is unrealistic to say the least. His view that a modern state could function merely through the goodwill of the people is difficult to envisage. A society guided by the clergy to whom the population would submit was also an unlikely situation, even in the most devout of Islamic societies. Democracy does not appear to have a role in the society that Khomeini has outlined. The people do not elect the clergy, their position in the *foqaha* is not determined by consensus but by leading clerics or *marja'taqlid* who are elevated to the position by their peers. Taking into account how much of a closed society the clergy was in Iran in the 1970s,[50] it could be argued that it would result in the replacement of one autocracy by another. Not only would the idea of elections be contrary to Khomeini's vision but participation of women in the rule of society was also viewed as implausible. Women, under Islamic law, were not entitled to become the guardian of their children, therefore argued Khomeini how could they be expected to look after a whole society. Using this argument, Khomeini and his contemporaries dictated that a woman could never reach a significant position in society, that she could never join the *foqaha* or the judiciary that guide society. Democracy and democratic values, it could be argued are against Islamic principles, as a follower of Islam has only one duty and that is submission to the law of God as outlined by Muhammad. Therefore, in Islamic terms, Khomeini's vision of society can be adequately justified, however it should also be noted that Khomeini's interpretation of Islam is not universal. We have seen that Shariati argued that modern Shi'ism has lost the true course of Islam. He advocates a personal approach to Islam; it is sufficient for the individual to submit to God's word, with the relationship between man and God being categorised as a personal one. In his view there is no need for an intermediary between man and God, neither the clergy nor a *velayat-e faqih*, as outlined by Khomeini.

Khomeini's vision of Islamic government can be questioned in addition for other reasons, especially in its proposed application. It gave little attention to the political realities of the Iranian situation nor to the level of political and social development that had already occurred throughout the latter part of the twentieth century. It is for these reasons that when the revolution occurred, Khomeini's ideology was radically altered, some changes were made for pragmatic reasons, such as the role of women in society. It was changed in other ways too, so as to ensure its acceptance by the general population. In reality, however, Khomeini's theoretical *velayat-e faqih*, bore little resemblance to the Islamic Republic that was the outcome of the revolution.

Notes

[1] For an overview of the causes of the Iranian revolution and the immediate history of pre-1979 Iran see further Downes, M. (2000: Autumn), 'The Islamic Resurgence: the case of Iran', *History Studies*, 2.

[2] See further Rahnema, A. (1996), *An Islamic utopian: a political biography of Ali Shari'ati* (London: I.B. Tauris) and Vakili, V. (1996), *Debating religion and politics in Iran: the political thought of Abdolkarim Soroush* (New York: Council on Foreign Relations).

[3] See further Omid, H. (1994), *Islam and the Post Revolutionary State in Iran* (London: Macmillian Press Ltd).

[4] See further Haroon, S. (1984: August), 'Khomeini's crusade: an emerging global "third force"', *World Press Review; 31*, pp.29-31.

[5] Abrahamian, E. (1998), *Khomeinism* (London: I.B. Tauris), p.2.

[6] Ibid., p.2.

[7] See further Abrahamian, E. (1998), *Khomeinism* (London: I.B. Tauris).

[8] For an eye witness account of this interview, and the scenes surrounding the return of Ayatollah Khomeini to Iranian soil see Simpson, J. (1998), *Strange Places, Questionable People* (London: Macmillan), p.233 and (1998), *Behind Iranian Lines* (London: Robinson Books), by the same author.

[9] Moin, B. (1999), *Khomeini, Life of the Ayatollah* (London: I.B. Tauris), chapter 8.

[10] For a further insight into this argument read Zubaida, S. (1989), *Islam, the People and the State* (London: Routledge), chapter 1.

[11] Wright, R. (2000), *The Last Great Revolution* (New York: Random House), p.181.

[12] Esfahan was the former capital of the Safavid period (1501-1742).

[13] Najaf is situated in modern day Iraq, but during this period was part of the Ottoman Empire. Being the burial place of Imam Husayn, it is one of the holiest sites of the Shia faith.

[14] Qom is a town to the south of Tehran and today is the cleric center of learning in Iran and one of the leading seminaries of the Shia world.

[15] For an overview of the Pahlavi dynasty and the reign of Muhammad Reza Shah see further Ghani, S. (1998), *Iran and the rise of Reza Shah: from Qajar collapse to Pahlavi rule* (London: I.B. Tauris).

[16] Some of his early publications included *Misbah al-Hidaya* (Book of Guidance), *Shahar Do'ay al Sahar* (Interpretation of the Dawn Prayers), *Shahar Arbe'en* (Hadith Explanations), *Adab al Salat* (Prayer Literature), all of these books were published in Arabic and highlight Khomeini's growing knowledge and interest in mysticism.

[17] Ayatollah Mohammad Hosayn Borujerdi emerged in late 1946 as highest-ranking Shia clergy in Iran (after the death of Ayatollah Hossein Qomi). He was also of the belief that the clergy should remain out of politics, however the fact that he maintained an amiable relationship with the state led many to believe that he supported the *status quo* in Iranian politics.

[18] In fact Khomeini was Borujerdi's teaching assistance and Khomeini's daughter married into the latter's family.

[19] Abrahamian, E. (1998), *Khomeinism* (London: I.B. Tauris), p.9 and Moin, B. (1999), *Khomeini, Life of the Ayatollah* (London: I.B. Tauris), p.60.

[20] Mossadeq was the founder and leader of the National front, who became Prime Minister in the early 1950s creating a nationalist government, his governments popularity led the Shah to attempt to have him removed, when public support gathered around Mossadeq and his government, the Shah fled the country. Mossadeq's government policy of nationalization of the oil industry led many in the west to demonize Mossadeq as a threat to western security. After the coup that overthrew his government in 1953, he was placed under house arrest and remained outside Iranian politics until his death. For further reading on the period of Mossadeq's sojourn in power, its aftermath and the role Western powers played in his government's overthrow see further Elm, M. (1992), *Oil, power, and principle: Iran's oil nationalization and its aftermath* (Syracuse: Syracuse University Press); and Haykal, M. (1983), *The return of the Ayatollah: the Iranian revolution from Mossadeq to Khomeini* (London: Deutsch).

[21] Ayatollah Kashani was the religious leader in the *majlis* in the early 1950s; his initial support enabled the National Front government to survive following the opposition of the Shah and his administration. While having a good working relationship with Mohammed Mossadegh of the National Front, he also had connections with a growing number of small fundamentalist Islamic terrorist groups, one of which was the *Feda'iyan-e Islam*, which was founded in 1945.

[22] Khomeini, *Sahifeh-ye Nur*, vol.1 page 16, Tehran 1361/1982, in Moin (1999), p.82.

[23] Khomeini's declaration in opposition to the referendum can be seen in the text, *Nahzat-e Imam Khomein* (Imam Khomeini's Movement) (Tehran: Imam's Way Press) (1984, Vol. 1), pp.230-31. This text is a collection of all of Khomeini's declaration, decrees and *fatwa's* leading up to and during the revolution.

[24] Khomeini (1361/1982) *Sahifeh-ye Nur* vol.1, p.17, in Moin (1999), p.82.

[25] No-Roz is the Persian New Year, which takes place over a two-week period in March. It is a time of celebration, holidays and for many a pilgrimage to holy sites.

[26] In the year 1963 the date corresponded in the western calendar to the 3rd of June.

[27] Interview with an Iranian historian April 1999.

[28] See further Moin, B. (1999), p.104.

[29] See further Al Ahmed, J. (1962), *Qarbzadegi* (translated means Westoxification) (Tehran: n.p).

[30] An Islamic Marxist organisation became increasingly popular during the 1950s in university campuses throughout Iran. Their ideology finds similarities between the Marxist sense of social equality and justice with similar ideals inherent in the Islamic faith.

[31] *Feda'iyan-e Islam* or the *Devotees of Islam* was established shortly after WWII and led by a young cleric Nawab Safawi. It was formed with the aim of representing the growing discontent with the modernisation reforms of Reza Shah. Initially established as a forum for clerical opposition to the sidelining of Islamic law, it grew into an organisation that represented the discontent amongst the bazaari's and the poorer segments of society, left behind by Iran's modernisation programme. It became a radical organisation in the 1950s and 1960s, with alleged responsibility for a number of assassinations of government officials, including the Prime Minister Hassan Ali Mansour in 1965.

[32] *Mujahedin-e Khalq* or Holy Warriors of the People represent the radical left wing of Muslim organisations founded in the early 1970s. The group openly confronted pro-Khomeini forces in the late 1970s and early 1980s and has always alleged the arrest, torture and execution of is members under the Islamic Republic. In 1981 became a founding member of the National Council of Resistance (NCR), which is dedicated to the overthrow of the Islamic Republic.

[33] Al Ahmed, J. (1978), *Dar Khedmat va Khianat, Roshanfekran Volume II* (translated means, Intellectuals as providers of Service and as Traitors) (Tehran: Kharazmi Publication), p.13.
[34] Ibid., p.28.
[35] There are a number of websites through which information on Shariati's view and transcripts of his speeches can be obtained. However, for a clearer picture of his ideas see his books Shariati, A. (1974), *Masuliateh Shia Budan* (translated as The Responsibilities of being a Shia) (Tehran: Ketabkhaneh Melli), and Shariati (n.d.) *Tashiiyeh Alavi va tashiiyeh Safavi* (translated as 'Alavi and Safavid forms of Shi'ism') (Tehran: Hoseinieyeh Ershad Publications).
[36] Shariati, A. (n.d.) *Tashiiyeh Alavi va tashiiyeh Safavi* (Tehran: Hoseinieyeh Ershad Publications), p.47.
[37] Ibid., pp.162-63.
[38] Moin, B. (1999), *Khomeini, Life of the Ayatollah* (London: I.B. Tauris), p.177.
[39] Shariati, A. (n.d.) *Tashiiyeh Alavi va tashiiyeh Safavi* (Tehran: Hoseinieyeh Ershad Publications), p.300.
[40] He had studied such mystic writers as Mollah Sadra (who died in 1641) and the Sufi writer Jalal al-Din Rumi (who died in 1273). The study of mysticism is not seen as a normal activity in Shi'ite clergy tradition, as the view of many mystics are seen as heretical in Shia society. The influence of mysticism in Khomeini's thinking can be seen the concept of *velayat-e faqih*. For more on Khomeini's study of mysticism see further Moin, B. (1999), *Khomeini, Life of the Ayatollah* (London: I.B. Tauris), pp.39-52.
[41] For the background of Ayatollah Mottahari and other prominent figures in Iran's history see further the glossary.
[42] In many ways this idea of the inherent inequality of man, with each having their role to play in society was very Platonic in its ethos.
[43] Quranic verse 32, chapter on Wealth and Allurement.
[44] For an overview of Mottahari's view of society read his book Mottahari, A. (n.d.), *Jahan Biniyeh Tohidi volume I and II* (translates as The Unified WorldView) (Qom: Sadre Publications).
[45] Khomeini, R. (1981), *Hokumateh Eslami* (Islamic Government) (Tehran: Bozorg Bookshop), p.78.
[46] Khomeini, R. (1981), *Islam and Revolution*, translated by Algar (Berkeley: Mizan Press), p.79.
[47] Ibid., p.64.
[48] Khomeini, R. (1981), *Hokumateh Eslami* (Islamic Government) (Tehran: Bozorg Bookshop), p.49. Translation quoted in this text is taken from Abrahamian, E. (1998), *Khomeinism* (London: I.B. Tauris), p.61.
[49] See further 'Velayat Faqih', *Kayhan International*, April 12 1981, a similar point is make by Abrahamian (1998), in his discussion of Islamic government.
[50] Abrahamian, E. (1998), p.43 estimates that in the 1970s in Iran, the top seven clergy could all be connected through genealogy. It was a common practice to have clerical families inter-marry. There was also little outside or democratic influence when in came to position or title within the clerical hierarchy.

Chapter 6
A Great Revolution of the 20th Century[1] – the Installation of an Islamic Theocracy

> He who establishes a dictatorship and does not kill Brutus, or he who founds a republic and does not kill the sons of Brutus, will only reign a short time
>
> Machiavelli, Discorsi

This chapter marks the beginning of the final section of this work and deals with the more contemporary political issues that have developed in Iran during the post-revolution, post-Khomeini era. Previous chapters have looked at the theory of revolution, together with the various ideological perspectives that helped define the pre-revolutionary period in Iran. That analysis's was necessary for understanding the current political situation in Iran. The previous chapter has shown that Khomeini and his ideology were anything but orthodox or traditional. In fact, he showed himself to be an innovative and pragmatic leader in both a spiritual and political sense. These two attributes are even more in evidence in the post-revolutionary period, when faced with severe opposition to his plans to create a theocratic state and against all international expectations, Khomeini and his followers succeeded in the creation of the Islamic Republic, with Khomeini elevated to the position of *velayat-e faqih* or Supreme Leader for life.

The price paid by those who had underestimated Khomeini and his political potential was severe. Just as most revolutions inevitably 'consume their children', Iran in the aftermath of the Shah's overthrow saw many former revolutionaries cast into the political wilderness and some even beyond. Those opposition activists who gave so much to the overthrow of the Shah but who did not 'follow the line of the Imam' in the aftermath of the revolution, would have to pay the price for the success and continuation of Khomeini's Islamic Republic. In the immediate aftermath of Khomeini's return the task of rebuilding Iran and creating its new structures of government led to the initial break-up of the opposition alliance. Their sole area of agreement was that the government was to be neither a monarchy nor a dictatorship. Through a series of unpredictable events, the eventual political structures created have been termed 'a dictatorship by another name, disguised with the garb of religious morality'.[2]

An investigation into the causes of the revolution and the ideological battle that occurred in the immediate aftermath will facilitate our understanding of the divisions that fragment Iranian society today. This investigation begins with the contemporary history of Iran as an oft-colonised country, leading to increased nationalistic sentiments amongst its peoples and political elite. These sentiments were utilised and channelled by Khomeini and his followers to facilitate the achievement of their goals. Khomeini's distancing himself from the Islamic intellectuals, who had assisted in his return to Iran, was also to prove significant. His betrayal of them, would lead Iran and Khomeini on a path, not towards his vision of *velayat-e faqih*, but toward the establishment of an autocratic theocracy, which took on a life of its own, separate and distinct from it's ideologue.

The Causes of the Revolution

With hindsight the eventuality of the Iranian revolution should have been obvious.[3] To the many commentators at the time however, it appeared that the Shah would once against ride out this period of social unrest and would continue to control Iran with an iron fist well into the next century. Following the success of the revolution and the Shah's flight into exile, many tried to trace the roots of the revolution and explain why they failed to notice the emergence of such a powerful mass movement. Was it the Shah's ambitious White Revolution, his attempts at forced modernisation of a traditional state that destabilised Iranian society or was it a mixture of his autocratic rule and the economic downturn in the latter half of the 1970s that disillusioned his people? One can traces the roots of the Iranian revolution to the CIA engineered overthrow of Mohammad Mossadeq's nationalist government in 1953 or to the bloody suppression of the Khomeini led anti-Shah uprising in 1963. Whether one traces the roots of the revolution to any one of the above or to the earlier developments in the Iranian society, the fact remains that at no time before the period of 1972-77 had the socio-political exclusion from the Shah's regime reached such explosive levels of populist expression. The sale by President Nixon of an array of conventional weapons alienated not only the Shah from his people, at a time when they were suffering the effects of an economic downturn, but also brought the negative aspects of US influence on the internal affairs of the Iranian government into the limelight. The oil price boom of 1973 was followed by a sudden economic depression in the latter part of the 1970s, which affected the confidence and financial independence of much of the working class of Iranian society. The rising expectations in Iranian society resulting from the oil price boom were followed by disillusionment with the Shah's economic policies following the above economic downturn. This is almost a textbook example of where the theory of rising expectations foresees the development of a revolutionary situation. Furthermore, the creation of the *Rastakhiz* Party in 1975 symbolised the height of the Shah's repressive policies and compounded his dislocation from the plight of his people. The result was a revolution born out of the ashes of discontent and resulting in the country being enveloped in chaos.

In truth it was a combination of all the above, which led to the downfall of the last monarchy in Iran. The 1979 revolution has a number of roots, which are spread over the decades preceding the revolution. The Shah's father Reza Khan was an ardent secularist who believed that the only way in which Iran could modernise was through the adoption of western practices. Basing his early development programmes on those of Kamal Ataturk, he steered the government towards an increasingly anti-Islamic stance. He made western dress mandatory, banned the Islamic veil and brought areas such as education, which were the traditional domain of the clergy, under governmental control. Many of these policies were continued and expanded under the reign of his son Muhammad Reza Shah; however, he did not possess the strength of character with which his father dominated the clergy. The Shah's White Revolution became a rallying call for opposition activism, with the clergy viewing the law that enfranchised women, as being a direct attack against the future of the Shia faith in Iran.[4] Secularists argued against the referendum that was to confirm the Shah's rule as being unconstitutional. While both the clergy and the secularists argued against the Shah's policies, their reasons for doing so differ significantly. That said, the underlying divisions were temporarily cloaked by their mutual agreement that the Shah's arbitrary rule was contrary to the needs of the country.

The Shah's response to any form of opposition was both repressive and heavy-handed. His suppression of the basic freedoms of speech and association, together with the curtailment of the independent press, united opposition groups at home and brought condemnation from human rights groups abroad. The Shah might have survived the turbulent period that surrounded his government in the late 1970s, had his response been both measured and consistent, however it was neither. Even if we look at Khomeini's early opposition, its purpose was to exact change and was not necessarily intended to overthrow the system of monarchy. The Shah's failure to deal effectively with the legitimate demands of the opposition, mixed with his autocratic rule, resulted in a situation where the opposition was unable and unwilling to compromise. The Shah's over-dependence on US support and advice did little to add consistency to his rule. President

Nixon sold the Shah whatever advanced weaponry he needed, to fulfil the American administration's desire that Iran be its surrogate 'policeman of the Gulf'. Such action contrasted distinctly with the Democratic administration of President Carter, whose human rights policy suggested that any country guilty of human rights violations would be deprived of both American aid and military support. Such words encouraged the opposition movement in Iran, while it worried the Shah sufficiently for him to waiver in his response to the opposition. The Shah's indecisiveness can be see in his frequent change of Prime Minister during the 1970s, as he fluctuated between attempts at compromise and a severe crackdown on opposition activity.

His toleration of the opposition movement from 1977 onwards can be understood in another light, when we consider the Shah's failing health. The Shah's weakness during this period can be attributed to his ongoing treatment for cancer; the medication must inevitably have had an effect on both his demeanour and his judgement. In addition, he was overcome with the need to prepare for the possibility of his premature death and the desire to ensure the continuation of the Pahlavi dynasty. Upon the Shah's death the throne would pass automatically to his son, however being a minor, the regency of the throne would go to Queen Farah. While from mid-1977 the Shah's public appearances were noticeably few, Queen Farah was often depicted in the midst of some socially worthwhile activity, with a look of regal determination.[5] Such propaganda was an attempt to prepare the public for the possibility of the regency of Queen Farah.

The Shah's illness had other adverse effects for his administration; he rarely appeared in public and when he did he looked weak and sickly, thus giving the public the impression that the Shah's position was weakening. A further incident that gave the opposition movement heart and damaged the Shah's image domestically occurred during his visit to Washington in 1977. Hostile opposition demonstrations from exiled Iranians awaited the Shah during his visit, the video footage of which was shown live on Iranian television and showed the support that the opposition movement had abroad. Furthermore, during a reception on the White House lawn, the demonstrators became so vocal that police tried to disperse them with tear gas. Unfortunately, the wind shifted direction and sent the tear gas across the White House lawn towards the reception; scenes of the Shah fleeing with tears in his eyes gave a welcome boost to the opposition movement watching the broadcast at home.

President Carter's stance in defence of human rights gave many the perception that America was wavering in its support for the Shah. This encouraged the opposition to believe that without US support for the

Shah, his regime was fragile and its hold on power tenuous. The US however, fearful of the loss of an ally in the Gulf and uncertain about the outcome of the Islamic movement in Iran, shifted their position from one of neutrality in early 1977 to one of outright support for the Shah by the end of that year.[6] The change in the US stance towards Iran and its human rights record, can be attributed to a combination of fear towards the possibility of instability in the Gulf region, together with the Shah's support for a freeze on oil prices as proposed by Saudi Arabia

The end of 1977 saw another change in Prime Minister and marked the beginning of the final stages of the revolutionary movement that would remove the last Shah of Iran. While the change of Prime Minister was officially due to economic problems, in reality it was a feeble attempt by the Shah to show that he was willing to enact change in the face of opposition demands. The removal of Prime Minister Hoveyda and the appointment of Amuzegar, did not lead to any significant changes in government policy. The latter was the head of the *Rastakhiz* party, which further highlighted to the opposition the Shah's unwillingness to make any real meaningful change to government policy. The new Prime Minister also had to deal with a dire economic situation, with inflation steadily increasingly; the Iranian economy was severely overheating. While attempts were made to counter both of these economic phenomena, the administrations unwillingness to reduce the amount spent by the government on US military equipment, showed the severity of its dislocation from public sentiment and economic suffering. The return of US support also meant a return to the regime's tough stance towards opposition activity. The end of 1977 marked the return to arbitrary arrest and harassment by SAVAK, the regime's strong arm and (not so) secret police. However, the tide of protest and the momentum that the opposition movement had built up was proving to be impossible to reverse.

One of the greatest threats to the regime during this period was the student movement. Their support could not be coerced by economic blackmail, which made them a more formidable opposition than their counterparts in factories and state run industries. Furthermore, the Shah's policy of increasing accessibility to education meant that university attendance was now widely available to Iranians across the class spectrum. This brought a diversity of social and political opinions in the sphere of third level education, thereby increasing the diversity of the political discourse amongst the student community. Many students during this period were also given the financial assistance necessary to study abroad. Abroad they were introduced to ideas and concepts, which they found increasingly difficult to reconcile with the policies and practices of the regime in Iran. The increase in the student population strained the resources of the exchequer, while increasing the expectations of the student community; these expectations could not be satisfied during the period of high unemployment in the latter part of the 1970s. The result of all of the above was a series of student protests throughout the 1970s. Until 1977, however, these protests were mainly confined to student campuses and student issues such as housing and academic standards. When national demonstrations against the administration erupted in early 1978, the student's were equipped with the idealism and organisational skills gained through their previous years of protest. Many Marxists, as well as religious groups within the student community were increasingly active throughout this period. Iranian student's abroad played no small part in the revolutionary process, offering ideas and financial assistance, bringing the plight of their compatriots at home to the wider international audience, through the Confederation of Iranian Students Abroad.

While the student movement effectively utilised the western media abroad, other groups had alternative ideas of how the opposition movement should overthrow the regime. The *Mujahedin* and the *Feda'iyan-e Khalq*, who both had links to Bazargan's Freedom Movement, advocated the use of guerrilla tactics espoused by Marxists throughout the developing world. These groups began a campaign of intimidation and armed struggle that brought the opposition movement into direct military confrontation with the regime. While their guerrilla tactics of bombings and assassination did not provoke the mass upheaval that was expected, their experience was to play a vital role in the final push to depose the Shah and his regime.

In the latter half of the 1970s the Shah through his policies unknowingly managed to alienate vast sections of Iranian society. The *bazaaris*, a traditional source of both political and economic power, were alienated through the Shah's economic policies and the monopolisation of all large trade agreements by his extended family.[7] Moreover, his plans at modernisation that included the importation of western goods and the establishment of western-styled supermarkets encroached on the traditional areas of production and distribution formerly controlled by the bazaar. Being traditionally aligned to the religious classes, the *bazaar* became a major source of financial support for religious organisations that opposed the Shah and his modernisation plans, such as Khomeini's Coalition of Islamic Societies. Financial assistance was given in the hope that a change of government would lead to a return of their previous position of economic influence, not to mention their economic affluence. This gave the clergy financial independence thus enabling the ulema to withstand the organised assault on their resources by the Shah's administration.[8] It did not however protect them against the political backlash after 1977.

The Course of the Revolution

While the regime continued to imprison and exile various leading clergy, they severely underestimated the religious threat that faced the government. In January 1978, an article was published in a semi-official newspaper *Ettela'at*, which directly attacked the character of Ayatollah Khomeini. The article entitled 'Iran and Red and Black Colonisation', attacked the clergy as black reactionaries and their leader Khomeini as being in the employment of a foreign government. The article went further and attacked Khomeini's character. It's publication sparked serious demonstrations in Qom. The publication of this article identified Khomeini as a major opposition figure and vastly underestimated public support for the clergy; it was both an untimely move and a misevaluation on the part of the government. Khomeini in the aftermath of the article's publication was elevated out of his exiled obscurity. For a number of years the government's activities against secular opposition left the movement without a charismatic leader behind whom they could unite. The Shah had inadvertently placed the persona of Khomeini into a position behind which all shades of opposition could unite. The consequences of this action was to be felt in the post revolutionary period, but for now neither the Shah nor his government could have foreseen the far reaching consequence of their ill-advised actions.

In response to the defamatory article against one of the leading clergy, the Iranian ulema organised demonstrations, strikes and sit-ins in protest. The government's response was swift and merciless, with a number of deaths reported. The ulema sensing the beginning of an unstoppable momentum utilised the forty-day memorial services for those killed, to organise further demonstrations and protests. The government was caught in an impossible situation, they could not declare the memorial services unlawful gatherings, nor could they prevent them from being turned into political protests. Invariably government troops would intervene to quell disturbances and more deaths would result and thus began the forty-day cycle of deaths and mourning and demonstrations over the next months, which was to finally lead to the collapse of the regime.

These demonstrations were augmented by a series of strikes, which began in May 1978. Here the alliance between the workers, the *bazaaris*, the students and the ulema came to the fore. The ulema mobilised the masses through the mourning ceremonies and Friday prayers, while the *bazaaris* were instrumental in financially supporting the strikers and the families of the victims killed by the state security apparatus. The diverse group of opposition activists with varied ideological interests meant that the riots that ensued attacked not only government installations but also the symbols of foreign political and economic interests in Iran. As the intensity and the extent of the protests increased, it began to engulf both urban and rural centres, while transcending class divisions and increasing the geographic reach of the revolution. While many of the Shah's attempts at modernisation, such as the emancipation of women, were seen as being for the benefit of the middle and upper class Iranians, these classes objected to the regime largely on the grounds of a difference in political ideology.[9] In addition, the working and religious classes had both economic and cultural reasons to object to the shah's rule. Whatever their grievances or their economic background, all shades of opposition and class were united for a time in their joint goal of toppling the Shah and his government.

Women too played a major part in the success of the revolution; they were active across the opposition spectrum, from the leftist guerrilla movements, to the traditionally religious classes, to the *petite bourgeoisie*. This wide range of interests encompassed in the women's opposition movement can be seen from the variety of slogans used during women's protest marches throughout 1978. The slogans ranged from a desire to have free and open elections, to increased democratic institutions, to the return to the chador[10] and segregation for women. Opposition sentiment reached such heights by mid-1978 that opposition to the regime was characterised as anything that was contrary to the current government's policy. Any announcement by the incumbent administration of possible reforms was taken as false, as were the many propaganda announcements made to alienate the growing opposition movement. This can be evidenced by the government's attempts to blame the fire in a theatre in Abadan in August 1978, which killed over a hundred people, on opposition activists. The vast majority of people did not even consider that the fire could have been accidental. If the government tried to blame it on the opposition, then it was inevitable that the SAVAK were responsible.[11] Although possible, it is unlikely that the Shah would have ordered the burning down of the theatre; however in the end it was public perception of what occurred that turned the Abadan incident into a catalyst for even greater protests and demonstrations.

The Shah's response to this increasingly unstable environment was a mixture of concession and repression. He changed his Prime Minister once again in 1978, replacing Amuzegar with Sharif-Emami, who tried to appease the opposition with policies that encouraged greater political freedom. These policies had little chance of acceptance by the opposition movement as they coincided with a continuing SAVAK crackdown on any dissident behaviour. This dual policy did little to legitimise the Shah's leadership or to quell growing opposition demands. Some changes did occur under Sharif-Emami, a ministry was established to protect religious affairs, casinos that offended religious sentiment were closed down and the new imperial calendar[12] was abolished resulting in a return to the Muslim calendar.[13] While the opposition movement continued to be harassed, there was substantial movement towards greater political freedoms during Emami's two-month premiership, however many considered it a matter of too little too late. Events in any case were soon to surpass the changes that were occurring within the political environment of Iran. In early September a series of peaceful demonstrations were held throughout Tehran. Some attracted mass crowds, estimated at over a million people. One such demonstration on September 8th held in Jaleh Square in central Tehran, erupted in violence as government troops fired upon unarmed demonstrators, the result was the death of between 500 and 900 people.[14] The Jaleh square massacre, its attempted cover-up and the ensuing installation of martial law was a turning point for much of the opposition movement, where the door was shut on any possibility of compromise with the regime. The Shah was uncertain in his response and oscillated between compromise and crackdown. His decision to replace Emami with General Gholam Reza Azhari was seen by many as a sign of what was to come.

In the mass sense of hysteria and revolutionary fervour, the uncompromising attitude of Ayatollah Khomeini became increasingly popular amongst the Muslim masses. While Khomeini began to stress that the current problems facing Iran could only be solved by a return to Islamic values and Muslim ways, few people were familiar with his proposed ideas for Islamic government. While many younger people had heard of Khomeini, few were aware of his role as an opposition figure, equating him solely with the disturbances of 1963. This was about to change, with a number of events bringing Khomeini back into the limelight. The *Ettela'at* article and ensuing demonstrations brought him to the forefront of the opposition movement in Iran and out of his previous obscurity. With the imprisonment of all of the other major clerical figures, such a Taleqani and Shariatmadari, Khomeini's brand of Islamic radicalism was increasingly becoming the only source of Islamic inspiration for the revolutionary movement. In October 1978, under pressure from the Shah, Khomeini was forced to leave Iraq. Having been refused entry into Kuwait, he proceeded to Paris. In hindsight, forcing Khomeini to leave Iraq had to have been the most serious miscalculation on the part of the Shah. Travel between Iraq and Iran was limited and could be controlled. Therefore, Khomeini's ability to influence the opposition movement in Iran was seriously curtailed while he remained in Iraq. In France by comparison, Khomeini faced no governmental control of his activity and had open and unlimited access to the international press. Travel between France and Iran was frequent and many of his declarations and sermons were easily smuggled into the country. Khomeini increasingly became the only visible opposition leader in the eyes of the international community. His numerous interviews concerning the Shah's human rights record put the beleaguered regime under increasing international pressure. At home, a strike in the oil industry began to cripple the already faltering Iranian economy. Leftist guerrilla movements, the *Feda'iyan* and the *Mujahedin*, began a bombing campaign targeting government installations and personnel. This tactic of open conflict with the regime won them new adherents and led to the belief that the regime could be defeated, causing many ordinary Iranians to rethink their support for the government.

Khomeini for his part was continually updated on developments within the opposition movement. Realising that he needed pan-opposition support for his post-revolutionary ideas, Khomeini began to gather support amongst other fringes of the opposition movement. While in principle he was unwilling to compromise, Khomeini did try to augment his religious credentials with secularist supporters, to this end he issued a statement with the National Front leadership declaring that Islam and democracy were the principle ideals of the revolution. While the notion of western liberal democracy was never in Khomeini's plan, this joint statement had the desired effect on both the international and the Iranian audience. Internationally, his association with a constitutional democratic movement such as the National Front gave his movement increased legitimacy. This was especially important when the United States was considering alternatives to the Shah's regime. Their willingness to talk, albeit unofficially, to Khomeini supporters about the post-revolutionary make up of Iran, showed the ignorance many had of Khomeini's true beliefs. In Iran, the declaration meant the cementing of the Islamic-secular alliance. In the absence of any charismatic leadership to represent the secular movement, it also meant that Khomeini became the unconditional leader of Iran's revolutionary movement.

When the end came for the regime, it was relatively swift. *Ashura* 1978, which fell on the 11th of December, saw mass commemoration ceremonies turn into political demonstrations all across Iran. In Tehran, Khomeini's unchallenged leadership of the opposition movement was confirmed when the demonstrators passed a 'resolution' calling on Khomeini to lead the country. The Shah's attempts to pacify or quell the opposition through force had all but failed. His aspiration that his son should follow him as Shah of Iran was becoming increasingly improbable. His refusal to abdicate, however, meant that a peaceful transition of power was becoming unlikely. At the end of December 1978 the Shah was convinced to hand over power to Shahpour Bakhtiar, a National Front politician who believed in parliamentary democracy. His former National Front colleagues immediately denounced Bakhtiar and his attempts at reining in the opposition movement with mass concessions on political prisoners and drastic changes in economic and foreign policy were to no avail. His position was tenuous from the beginning. On the 16th of January 1979, Mohammad Reza Shah, the last Shah of Iran, left his country and went into exile. Behind, he left a country in turmoil and a provisional government weakened by his weeks of indecision.

The Revolution in Retrospect

While the events of 1979 have been surpassed in the western imagination by the fall of Communism, the Iranian revolution remains one of the most significant events of the twentieth century. It is comparable in significant to both the French and Russian revolutions, as it saw the establishment of a new form of government, never seen before in the modern era It is all the more important because of its setting in the developing world. There have been many governments and autocratic rulers overthrown throughout this region *coup d'etat's* and change of government personnel through revolt is a common occurrence. In Iran in 1979, however, it was not only the Shah's rule that was called into question; it was the whole system of government and the nature of the state that he represented. It was an upheaval against foreign domination, against the politics of bi-polarity, against oppression and modernisation at all costs. Anthony Parsons, the British ambassador at the time of the revolution, spoke with the Shah just before his exile and concludes that 'the basic reason (for the fall of the regime) was that he (the Shah) tried to turn the people of Iran into something which they were not, and they had at last rebelled under the leadership of their traditional authorities, the religious classes'.[15] He goes on to compare the Shah's predicament in January 1979 to that of Nasr Din Shah during the Tobacco Crisis of 1892 and of Muzaffer Din Shah during the constitutional crisis of 1906. In each case, the people of Iran overwhelmingly rejected 'development' at the expense of cultural, political and economic independence. Through each of the three revolts in Iran, it was an alliance between the clergy, the intelligentsia and the *bazaaris*, which forced change. History, it appears, had a tendency to repeat itself. It was for this reason, among others, that the clergy were reluctant to return to their mosques and seminaries as they had done in the early part of the 20th century.

In chapter three we defined a revolution as having a number of distinctive characteristics. It possesses some form of violence, leads to societal value change more in tune with the socio-political environment and it creates an institutional and political framework together with a political elite that is significantly different from the previous regime. While Iran in 1979 fits all of the above criteria, it differs from previous revolutionary movements, as it simultaneously attempted to create a new institutional structure while endeavouring to return to a traditional value system. The new structure of government was clearly distinct from the Shah's administration; in fact it was a unique creation. Whether it is possible to simultaneously move forward in a political sense and return a society successfully to a previous, and some would say restrictive, value system is questionable. It is possibly a case of trying to return the contents to Pandora's box after they had taken flight. This is the dilemma facing the Islamic Republic today and will be dealt with in subsequent chapters.

What is not in doubt is that the Pahlavi rulers drastically changed the political and social landscape of Iran in the fifty years of their rule. They undermined the traditional position and strength of the clergy and the age-old bazaar based economy, in favour of secularisation and a modern industrial and financial sector. Reza Shah utterly destroyed the ethnic power structure within Iran, together with the tribal and feudal system that had been in place since the Arab invasion. In its place he established a highly centralised administration, based loosely along the lines of the Western European (French) system of government. Mohammad Shah in his turn created an urban society, extending educational and health services, together with an economy based on industrial output rather than agriculture. There are many aspects of the Pahlavi's rule that were, in part, commendable, however they achieved this development at the expense of the traditional balance of power. The clergy, the bazaar merchants and the very concepts of liberty and freedom, suffered as a result. Here we have the true misunderstanding of the revolution. Khomeini and his financial backers in the bazaar, wanted to re-established the socio-political balance which the Pahlavi's had deemed fit to cast aside in the name of progress. The intelligentsia, while also disagreeing with the social and the political system the Shah had created, did so for very different reasons, mainly the lack of transparency and accountability in a system that was increasingly autocratic. If 'development' can be termed a revolution, as it has been with the industrial revolution in Western Europe in the 19th century, then it can be said that what the Pahlavi's attempted in Iran, was in some sense revolutionary in nature. If this is so, than the opposition to the Shah can be categorised in two ways. The clergy and the *bazaaris* were counterrevolutionaries, as they desired to undo the changes that had occurred in Iranian society over the previous sixty years. The intelligentsia, the Islamic intellectuals and the secular constitutionalists, on the other hand were the actual revolutionaries of 1979. They did not desire a return to the socio-political culture of the late 19th century, but viewed the interplay of Islam and politics together with Iran's cultural and historic heritage in an original light. Their slogans of the revolution were not wholly against modernisation but were against the restraints on personal freedoms, which the political structure used to push through its excessive reform programmes.

Viewed in this light, the opposition alliance created in the process of overthrowing the Shah, had different goals and aspirations and was inevitably going to falter. In the aftermath of the Shah's departure, the immediate goal of the Bakhtiar government was to prevent the return of Khomeini. However, the level of protest and the uncompromising attitude of Khomeini and his followers meant that Bakhtiar could not hold out for long. On the morning of the 1st of February 1979, on board an Air France jet, Khomeini returned to his native Iran to a tumultuous welcome.[16]

The Installation of a Theocracy

During his brief stay in Paris Khomeini was surrounded by western educated intellectuals such as Abol Hassan Bani-Sadr, Saqeq Qotbzadeh and Ebrahim Yazdi,[17] however on his return his insular network of former students and associates from the Coalition of Islamic Societies took over. Once back in Iran, Khomeini appointed the most senior of these, including Ayatollah's Beheshti, Musavi-Ardabili and Mahdavi-Kani as well as Hojatoleslam Bahonar and Rafsanjani, as his revoluticnary council that was to rule the country until a new form of government could be established. The council also contained some secular politicians, the most notable of which was Mehdi Bazargan, as well as two sympathetic generals. As for Khomeini, he declared his wish to withdraw from political life and return to the religious center of Qom. While Khomeini may physically have been in

Qom, due to the loyalty of his disciples, he was never far from the political scene.

After a number of meetings of the revolutionary council, Khomeini realised that the secular politicians were hampering progress towards the creation of an Islamic government. In a move to eliminate this obstacle, to buy the council more time and to assuage the fears of the intelligentsia, Khomeini requested that Mehdi Bazargan form a government with his secular colleagues. Bazargan was a widely respected politician and so his appointment by Khomeini gave many secularists the impression that the clergy would now return to their mosques and allow the intelligentsia to rule the new administration. Bazargan's cabinet incorporated the various shades of constitutional politics, being composed of members mainly from his Liberation Movement and the National Front. There was also one leftist representative and one cleric, however, the Islamic nature of the cabinet was not what was emphasised, it was more inclined towards ensuring the formation of a democratic rather than theocratic government. The Revolutionary Council, however, remained in force and was supplemented in the absence of Bazargan and his colleagues by Islamic intellectuals seen as sympathetic to Khomeini's ideas. Thus started the clerical tradition of shadow institutions, which has remained in force up until the present day. The revolutionary council, while officially having no legislative or executive role, continued to be the centre of political power in Iran without having to suffer the constraints of accountability. They continued to issue statements and to organise the new state, undermining Bazargan's cabinet at every turn.

Bazargan and his colleagues sought an orderly change in the immediate post-revolutionary period and while being Muslim they largely followed the belief in a separation between religion and the state. Some leading clergy, most notably Ayatollah's Shariatmadrai and Taleqani supported them in this view. Some within the clerical fraternity believed the revolution to be Islamic in nature but believed that a separation between government and religion was necessary to prevent the corruption of one by the other. This appeared to be the minority view amongst the clergy, who likened their exclusion in the Bazargan government to that of Ayatollah Kashani's exclusion from the Mossadeq administration in the early 1950s. They wanted political representation and viewed the revolutionary council as the most effective method to obtain this. There was a problem, however, in that the clergy had little experience in the running of government affairs or the administration of a functioning bureaucracy. Ayatollah Beheshti, an ardent supporter of Khomeini and a firm believer in the establishment of a theocracy, believed that the secular bureaucracy could provide the necessary expertise, whilst the clergy could provide the necessary leadership and guidance. The council continued to undermine Bazargan's government and began to extend their control over society through the rapid development of local revolutionary *komitehs*. The *komitehs* find their origin in the early period of the revolution, when vigilante type groups began to be formed around each local mosque. These groups organised, mobilised and controlled the civilian population throughout the progress of the revolution. Following the revolution, the clergy used the *komitehs*, who were in every town and neighbourhoods throughout Iran, to confirm their control over the country. In the post-revolutionary period the *komitehs* independence meant that a return to centralised government was increasingly difficult. Bazargan's government had no control over these organisations and this, together with the work of the Revolutionary Council, severely hampered the government's attempts to regain control over society.

The appointment of Bazargan provided Khomeini with the time he needed to assess the post-revolutionary situation and to plan his strategy for the implementation of an Islamic State. Bazargan, whose intentions always appeared to be honourable and in the best interests of the Iranian people, had been manipulated into believing that it was Khomeini's intention to take an indirect role in governing the country. Instead, Khomeini and his followers set about establishing their own shadow administration, with which they intended to replace the official government institutions. While it could be argued that this was a sub-conscious act in their will to control society, primary research shows that this was a concerted and organised endeavour to undermine the democratic institutions of the state.

By August 1979, Khomeini and his organisation was sufficiently prepared to directly challenge the authority of the transition government. Khomeini's speeches became more critical of Bazargan's government; even Bazargan's Islamic credentials were called into question, as were his attempts to maintain relations with the United States.[18] Taking into consideration Iran's past turbulent relations with western powers, being labelled pro-American or pro-British was tantamount to a death sentence. In support of Khomeini's anti-imperialist and non-consensual language a group calling themselves 'Students following the line of the Imam' stormed the American embassy in November. The students continued to hold the embassy and its staff hostage for 444 days and quickly surpassed the *komitehs* as the transitional government's main problem. The student take-over occurred at a time when Bazargan was trying to create an atmosphere of rapprochement between his and the American Government.

While it appears that neither Khomeini nor his followers directly sanctioned the take-over,[19] they were the main beneficiaries from the events that followed. Bazargan, following the seizure, felt that his position as Prime Minister was untenable and resigned. The Embassy take-over and seizure of American personnel as hostages isolated Iran internationally. The leadership vacuum left by Bazargan and any possible influence that western powers could have wielded on the internal developments in Iran ended with the western condemnation of the student's actions and the international isolation that ensued. This vacuum was soon to be filled by Khomeini and much to the surprise of the 'students' Khomeini came out in support of the take-over, perceiving the resultant instability as being of use in his push for an Islamic constitution.

In the aftermath of the fall of the monarchy, much debate occurred as to what form of government should replace the former institutions. Khomeini, who viewed the revolution in terms of monarchy versus Islamic government, believed that the people had already spoken and therefore further consultation with them was not necessary. Western democratic models or such ideals had no place in Islam. Therefore for Khomeini the path forward was clear, the rule of God did not need ratification by the people and as the representative of God on earth, the clergy had a natural right to rule. The content or ideology of the government was not considered a matter for the people. As a result, when it came to a discussion on the type of government that Iran would install, Khomeini would not agree to anything less than an endorsement of an Islamic Republic. 'Republic' being the only concession that he was willing to make to those who favoured a western democratic form of government.

The referendum was held in late March 1978 and the wording of the referendum was a sign of things to come. It asked the Iranian electorate, 'Do you approve of an Islamic Republic', with the implication that the alternative was a return to monarchy. There was overwhelming support in favour of the referendum proposal, as it was held a mere fifty days after the return of Khomeini from Paris and with the revolutionary and religious fervour of the people still intense. Following the referendum, Khomeini ordered the provisional government to draft a proposal for a new constitution. The first draft was a mixture between the 1906 Iranian constitution and that of the French Fifth Republic. Completed by June, it made no mention of *velayat-e faqih*, nor did it envisage any of the provisions laid out by Khomeini's vision of Islamic government. Khomeini's only public statement was that he required that the constitution should be specific in ensuring that women could not be appointed to either the position of a judge or to the Presidency.

Instead of publicly voicing his overwhelming disagreement to the constitution Khomeini stated that a Constitutional Assembly should be appointed to revise the proposed document, to ensure its adherence to Islamic teachings. While he favoured a small select group of Islamic jurists, *foqaha*, there were others in the clergy who, realising his intentions, pushed for a larger group over which Khomeini's influence would be diminished. Other secular politicians and those believing in the formation of western democratic institutions argued that a purely clerical assembly would result in the establishment not of a democracy but a theocracy. It was agreed finally that an Assembly of seventy-three elected members would review the constitution. The debates on the constitution that followed were indeed comprehensive and signified the diverse opinions that were present in Iranian society.

Khomeini had based many of his assumptions for Islamic government on a passive society that was willing to adhere to the rule of the clergy as if it were the will of God. The debate on the constitution shattered whatever notion he held of a passive society willing to accept his version of Islamic government. The clergy were severely divided, other opposition groups all had different views on the format of the constitution, with many believing that Islam should not play a direct role in whatever form the government should take. During the initial stages of the debate, it became obvious to the followers of Khomeini that an Islamic constitution might not emerge naturally from these discussions. From this point on we can see a change in the public statements of Khomeini and his followers. Khomeini spoke out harshly against the draft constitution, criticising its lack of Islamic character. His supporters for their part brought the concept of *velayat-e faqih* into the public domain, calling for its implementation and inclusion in the new constitution. Further public debate was stifled in this manner and the conservative assembly produced a blueprint for an Islamic state in November, which declared Twlever Shi'ism as the state religion and created a government based around Khomeini's ideology, whom they named as *faqih* for life. He, as the *velayat-e faqih*, was given total supremacy over the political and social life of the country, while *Shar'ia* was to become the basis of the legal system.

The Defeat of Democracy

With the acceptance of the Islamic constitution and the establishment of the Islamic Republic, the theocracy craved by Khomeini and his followers was almost wholly established. Some, however, still believed that Khomeini and his supporters did not have the organisational experience to successfully administer the government. While they may have controlled the hearts and minds of the masses, it was Bazargan and his cabinet of professional politicians who had the experience necessary to run a modern bureaucracy. Bazargan's resignation and the take over of the American Embassy, however, dealt a severe blow against the possibility of establishing a pluralist society.

Within the clergy Ayatollah Shariatmadrai was the most vocal in his opposition to the new constitution and the absolute rule of the *faqih*. His supporters in Tabriz formed the Muslim People's Republican Party (MPRP)[20] and staged a revolt. In January 1980 Khomeini outlawed the party, put Shariatmadrai under house arrest and declared that he was no longer to be considered an Ayatollah. This was a turning point in the new regime, where Khomeini showed his intolerance of any sort of opposition, even from those within the Shia clergy. The declaration to disrobe Shariatmadrai of his position as an Ayatollah has no legal or religious precedent in Islam and was a sign of the anti-Islamic means that Khomeini was willing to use in order to enforce his rule. Here it could be effectively argued that Khomeini was utilising the same tactics of harassment and intimidation that the Shah had used to silence his opposition.

In an attempt to counter other opposition parties and to establish a base of political support for the new regime, an Islamic party (The Islamic Republican Party - IRP[21]) was established under the leadership of Ayatollah Beheshti. Its ideology was simple; it advocated a devotion to Islamic principles and the rule of the *faqih* over the country. More impressive than its ideology, was its militant wing the *Hezbollah* (or the Party of God), established to forward its goal of a 'true' Islamic society. The *hezbollah* were used to disrupt opposition meetings and were responsible for attacks on opposition headquarters and personnel. In the days and weeks following the revolution both the *komitehs* and *hezbollah* were effective tools in excluding all shades of opposition from taking part in the discussion on the future shape of Iranian society. The ideals of the *hezbollah* can be best understood through the words of one of their ideologues, the now famous Hojatoleslam Sadeq Khalkhali,[22] who was all too willing to confirm the rule of the new regime through the spilling of the blood of anyone unwilling to accept Islamic rule. Khalkhali once claimed to have sentenced to death 2,000 prisoners in one week and claimed that 'human rights mean that unsuitable individuals should be liquidated so that others can live free'[23] and that 'those who are against killing have no place in Islam. If the survival of the faith requires the shedding of blood, we are here to perform our duty'.[24] Trials were arbitrary and pleas of innocence were often dismissed on the grounds that if the accused were innocent then the judge was merely hastening their passage to paradise.

Throughout the early chaos that followed the revolutionary period, the IRP, the *hezbollah* and the *komeiths* managed to undermine, physically attack and force all legitimate opposition underground or abroad. In the words of Bazargan, 'the *komeiths* are everywhere and no one knows how many exist, (they create an atmosphere) of instability, terror and fear ... (They) turn our days into night'.[25] The *Mujahedin,* the *Tudeh* Party, the National Front, the *Fedayeen Khalq* and the Islamic People's Republican Party all suffered under the regime of terror that followed the installation of the Islamic Constitution. Open opposition was no longer tolerated and many believed that the only way to exact change was through a return to the tactics used previously to undermine the Shah's regime. While not all groups believed this, both the *Mujahedin* and the *Fedayeen* returned to the guerrilla tactics, of bombing and assassination in their attempts to loosen the clergy's grip on power.

As for the new Islamic regime, their recently acquired power was less applied to the creation of a new society and was more inclined towards the deconstruction of the old political and economic system. While the constitution laid out the basic structure that the government was to take, society in general was edging towards anarchy. The clergy was more concerned with destroying all the vestiges of the Shah's influence on Iranian society, giving little thought as to what should replace it. The IRP stressed the regime's opposition to capitalism, colonialism and economic oppression, without providing any viable alternatives through which Iranian society could function. The clergy advocated the nationalisation of the vast majority of Iranian industry, which was formerly run by the Shah or foreign interests, while having little managerial experience to effectively run such large undertakings. The striking workers, who had facilitated the Shah's departure, were reluctant to follow the clergy's call for a return to work. Many leftist parties, such as the *Tudeh* and the *Fedayeen*, had strong associations with the workers and were unwilling to be docile followers of the Islamic government. The workers established committees to fight for workers rights, while the government established Islamic alternatives to these worker organisations. These Islamic committees gradually gained authority over the workers and this together with the all-out ban on strikes, resulted in a slow movement towards the resumption of economic activity. That said, many of those with managerial experience had fled the country following the fall of the Shah and while advocating an anti-capitalist stance on economic issues, the IRP failed to provide a viable Islamic alternative.

Looking for an Islamic alternative to economic policy was difficult, while agreeing that any new policy should be anti-capitalist, few could agree on what this should represent. While the Quran provides some alternatives, it is far from a cohesive policy for a modern economy.[26] Being against usury, Islam prohibits the charging of interest on loans and in banking the sole purpose for an Islamic state to become involved in economic activity is for the purpose of redistribution of wealth within society and to provide for the needs of the poor. State intervention in the economy of Iran, did little to increase output, while Iran's international isolation following the take-over of the American Embassy, did even less to assist the economic recovery necessary to quell worker disquiet and to alleviate the economic hardship that was gripping the post revolutionary society of Iran.

The Power Struggle in Post-Revolutionary Iran

The decline in the economic sector was not the only result of the hostage crisis, pluralist politics was also a casualty in the immediate post-revolutionary period. Bazargan's resignation enabled Khomeini to appoint the Revolutionary Council as the caretaker government. With the Council now as the sole decision-making power in the State, together with the new Islamic Constitution and with the Presidential Elections in sight, it appeared as if Khomeini's vision of an Islamic state was becoming a reality. His instruction to the Revolutionary Council to purge all 'corrupt elements of the former regime'[27] was taken literally. Islamic organisations were established not only throughout the industrial sector but also within each government ministry. The purpose of these organisations was to provide the means by which to control and vet the ideological compatibility of workers with the new regime. Those who refused to join these Islamic worker organisations or who were accused of assisting the former regime or indeed of being a supporter of foreign interests were often removed from their position or in some cases detained and executed.[28]

Secular politicians and Islamic intellectuals alike saw the forthcoming Presidential Elections as their final attempt to limit the control of the forces of theocracy. The IRP for its part, due to its extensive and formidable grass roots network, was in a prime position to capitalise upon the revolutionary momentum and rhetoric. Khomeini, in a surprising move, decreed that no clergy should be allowed to stand in the Presidential Elections. It is difficult to comprehend such decision by Khomeini, as his close associate and former student Ayatollah Beheshti would have been the IRP's obvious candidate and a formidable contender for the Presidency.

Omid is of the view that Khomeini's decision was based upon his unwillingness to decentralise clerical leadership and supremacy to any other office bar his own.[29] While this is a possibility it is more likely that Khomeini viewed the revolutionary period as being incomplete, perhaps foreseeing the potential difficulties that lay ahead. Khomeini saw that a non-clerical President would be a useful scapegoat. By preventing a clerical candidate, Khomeini effectively handed the election to Bani-Sadr, an Islamic intellectual who was with Khomeini during his stay in Paris, but who did not fully share his views on Islamic government. While receiving 75% of the popular vote in the presidential election, this did not automatically transform itself into political power for Bani-Sadr.

Even though the Constitution places the President second only to the Supreme Leader in the Executive Branch of Government, the clergy with control of the Assembly of Experts, the Guardian Council[30] and their effective manipulation of the masses, managed to undermine any possible power that Bani-Sadr might have wielded. Following the Presidential Elections the clergy showed little sign of handing over power to the incoming Presidential administration. Both the Revolutionary Council and its appointees in the various ministries were unwilling to cede power to those nominated by the President. Some even refused to recognise the President himself, arguing that only the *majlis* (which the IRP was expected to dominate) could confirm his position, arguably opposing the very idea of a directly elected president. The result was a multiplicity of decision-making centres throughout the government administration. There was the official 'elected' government and the unofficial 'clerical' government, each with opposing views on the direction that policy should take. The unofficial government, however, was well entrenched within the administration and was able to utilise both the media and the student population to rally against Bani-Sadr and his colleagues. In addition, the 'students following the line of the Imam' had not only managed to isolate Iran internationally but the global attention generated by their continued presence in the US embassy compound, made them a formidable obstacle for any new administration. Bani-Sadr's attempts to find a peaceful end to the hostage crisis led to criticism from both the students and the IRP, who painted him and other democrats as tools of foreign powers. The IRP's own police force, the revolutionary guards, joined the students in the embassy compound and acted as the strong arm of the IRP on the streets of Tehran, arresting those who did not adhere to the IRP's and the Revolutionary Council's decrees. This included Bani-Sadr's nominated foreign minister, and former Khomeini ally, Sadeq Qotbzadeh, who dared to denounce the level of media censorship imposed by the IRP and the Revolutionary Council.

The IRP's victory in the initial parliamentary elections did little to clarify the division of power within the state. The decentralised nature of political power continued, the judiciary did little to uphold the rule of law as outlined by the Constitution and the bureaucracy had been purged to such an extent that it barely had the ability or expertise needed to function. The country was on a self-destructive course; with the excesses of the new regime being countered by open demonstrations against what many were beginning to believe was 'political despotism under the guise of religion'.[31] Even the clergy were divided over the direction of the new regime. It is difficult to surmise the extent to which Khomeini agreed with those who used violent means to implement their version of Islamic justice. It is obvious, however, that he was as wary of conservatives within the clergy's ranks as he was of those who espoused democratic values, often setting them against each other in an attempt to maintain his own position.[32]

A new phase of the revolution began on the 22nd of September 1980 when Iraqi forces invaded Khorramshah[33] and proceeded further eastward into Iranian soil. Iran and Iraq had always had an uneasy relationship, even under the Shah. It partly stemmed from the old Ottoman-Persian (Sunni-Shia) conflict from the time of the Safavid Empire, and partly due to the desire of both countries to play a more significant role in the Gulf region. The revolution in Iran and the regime's new rhetoric calling on the entire Shia faithful around the world to join the path of revolution threatened to destabilise many of the countries bordering the Persian Gulf. Many of these states were based on monarchical systems similar to that of the former Iranian regime. Most has significant Shia minorities and as a result viewed the intentions of Iran's new regime with distrust. For Iraq, it viewed Iran's call to arms of the Shia faithful as a significant enough threat to contemplate a direct assault on Iranian territory.[34] Saddam Hussein, the Iraqi leader, perceiving Iran to be politically and militarily in disarray and foresaw a swift victory. With Iran internationally isolated, Saddam Hussein correctly assumed that the international community would not condemn his actions. In fact, he was financially and morally supported by other Arab states who perceived Iran as a direct threat and by western powers who saw Khomeini's Islamic movement as a destabilising factor in the region.

More importantly, however, was the effect that the Iraqi invasion had on the power struggle that was developing within the Iranian political structure. With Bani-Sadr as President, those who believed in the division between the state and religion had hoped that they could change the structure from within. With the outbreak of the war and the call to defend Iran's territorial integrity, all official opposition was put on hold. All shades of political persuasion supported the political regime and fought to defend the Islamic Republic, as almost all perceived the threat to Iranian territory as greater than the internal threat of clerical autocracy. In many ways this meant that a political discourse on the direction of the revolution was put on hold until the end of the war, which lasted eight years and exacted a heavy price, in economic and social terms, from the Iranian people. Not all the opposition groups adhered to the unofficial truce declared at the outbreak of the war. The *Mujahedin* used the disarray caused by the onset of the war as a platform through which they could destabilise the theocratic state. To many the *Mujahedin's* action was perceived as treason, putting one's personal agenda ahead of the national good. This resulted in their becoming a spent political force in the internal politics of Iran. For the hard-line clergy, the war provided them with an opportunity to consolidate their power in the political vacuum that followed the onset of hostilities. While Bani-Sadr believed that his landslide election victory was a mandate to re-direct the revolution back onto its true path of liberty and pluralism, he was seriously misguided in the ability of his office to achieve such a task. Furthermore, with the IRP winning a majority in the *majlis* elections, a political stalemate developed where the conservative *majlis* blocked all of Bani-Sadr's attempts to name his cabinet and to implement change. Increasingly frustrated at his inability to exact change, Bani-Sadr began to concentrate more on the war effort, leaving Tehran for the War Front he left behind the IRP who began to consolidate their position and to monopolise political power.

Bani-Sadr had hoped that his role in the war effort would allow him to build up a base of popular support amongst the soldiers at the front and their families at home. The units at the front were a disorganised mix of official army units, revolutionary guards and the unofficial *basijj*. The official army had been seriously discredited for its support of the Shah prior to the revolution and as such was mistrusted by the clergy. The clergy established their own army units through the revolutionary guards, while the *basijj* were militias, whose training was organised through the numerous mosques and seminaries throughout the country. The *basijj* were largely untrained and under-equipped, often composed of under aged units, who believed that they were fighting a religious war to safeguard the Islamic State. Therefore, Bani-Sadr's impact at the front was confined to the regular army, who were blamed for being disloyal when offensives failed. As a result Sadr's idea of establishing a political base at the front was misguided and his continued absence from the political scene in Tehran facilitated those who wanted to see an end to any discourse related to democracy or representative politics.

There was a significant movement in support of Bani-Sadr and against what many saw as the 'Stalinist methods' of political control used by the IRP. The IRP controlled all the institutions of power and the state broadcast media and through these methods they were able to counteract any opposition moves with state sponsored propaganda. Friday prayers became more than religious ceremonies, becoming places of political activism, where the boundaries of the state and religion were torn away. With such a grass roots network provided by the Friday prayer meetings, together with their control of the state media machine, there was little that the opposition could do to get their message out. When the opposition held rallies, the *hezbollahis*, the *basijj* or the revolutionary guards disrupted them with violence, something that the opposition was unwilling or unable to counteract.

Throughout this period, Khomeini appeared to continue his support for Bani-Sadr as President. Khomeini even tried at times to mediate between the office of the President and the IRP, urging that a spirit of consensus rather than conflict was in the best interest of Iran. Bani-Sadr, during the early days of the revolution was often referred to as a 'devoted son' of Khomeini. He was also close to Khomeini's son Ahmed and therefore was believed to have the ear of the Supreme Leader. However, when Bani-Sadr went as far as to criticise the very institutions that Khomeini had helped establish, Khomeini's support of Bani-Sadr was found to be finite. Therefore, with opposition groups uniting behind Bani-Sadr's call for greater openness and democracy, and with his attacks on the very institutions of the Islamic Republic, Bani-Sadr's days in power were numbered. With the withdrawal of support by Khomeini, the *majlis* drew up the papers of impeachment against Iran's first democratically elected President. The *majlis* debated the motion on the 20th and 21st of June 1980, however, the outcome was pre-ordained, without Khomeini's support Bani-Sadr fate was decided.[35]

In many ways Bani-Sadr was the only person able to give Khomeini an alternative view on the future of the revolution. He was the only voice amongst the many advising the Supreme Leader who advocated the partial or whole separation of religion and politics. With his voice quashed from the inner circle of Khomeini's advisers, Khomeini came under the influence of hard-liners within the clerical ranks, who were intent on little more than absolute political and economic control. Whether due to his age, his fear of secular politicians or a desire to safeguard his position and political legacy, Khomeini facilitated the betrayal of the revolution and its ideals, turning the 'just' battle for increase freedom into an authoritarian regime.

Ayatollah Montazeri, the once chosen successor to Khomeini, has recently published his memoirs on the internet from his Qom residence where he remains under house arrest. These memoirs document the post revolutionary period from the perspective of a high-ranking official within Khomeini's administration. They shed much light on the inner workings of the murky world of Iranian politics and seriously question the Islamic nature of Iran's new Republic.[36] A review of the Iranian Constitution and structure of government highlights the difficulty with decision making within the Iranian structure. With a multitude of decision making centers, further complicated by the 'behind closed doors' attitude of many of the institutions, it is difficult if not impossible to clearly outline and understand the decision making process of Iranian politics. It's lack of centralisation together with its parochial attitude to decision-making, means that political and economic power in Iran has often been divided into individual fiefdoms. Furthermore, with such ambiguity surrounding who has decision making ability, 'unofficial' interest groups have far more influence in the decision making process than elsewhere. One group's belief that they are doing 'God's work' is sufficient for the circumvention of the constitution or the disregard for internationally accepted principles. It is for this reason that the international community has difficulty in assessing the true intentions of Iran's stance towards the outside world. Furthermore, its population is subject to arbitrary interpretation of the law, with little support available from constitutional institutions. It was with the awareness of such a political environment that the Iranian electorate went to the polls in May 1997 to elect a new president. While the world waited, the Iranian people cast their votes, which would decide their political future.

Notes

[1] An argument could be made that Iran was the 'Last Great Revolution of the 20th Century', as put forward by Wright, R. (2000), *The Last Great Revolution: turmoil and transformation in Iran* (New York: Random House). While I would agree with this many theorists might disagree, especially with the fall of communist throughout Central and Eastern Europe in 1989. The reason for naming Iran as a 'Great Revolution' is dealt with in Chapter 5.

[2] Interview with an opposition activist, Tehran, September 1999.

[3] Two interesting first hand accounts of the build up to the revolution were written by the British and American Ambassadors to Iran at the time. See further Parsons, A. (1984), *The Pride and Fall: Iran 1974-79* (London: Jonathan Cape), and Sullivan, W. (1981), *Mission to Iran* (London: Norton).

[4] It is interesting to note the transition of Khomeini's views concerning women in politics. His initial views were against giving women the vote in 1963, changed to being a champion of women's rights in post revolutionary Iran. He never rescinded women's voting right (which had been given under the Shah) and in fact lowered the voting age to fifteen, to

match the age that men can vote. For a further insight in the transition of Khomeini into the role of defender of women's rights see further Wright, R. (2000), *The Last Great Revolution* (New York: Random House), pp.133-160.

[5] Keddie, N. (1981), *Roots of the Revolution* (New Haven: Yale University Press), p.232.

[6] President Carter on a Christmas visit to Iran in 1977 praised the Shah for his leadership, noting that his people evidently wholeheartedly supported him.

[7] While the bazaar may be viewed a basically a market for goods, in many Middle Eastern countries, it provides an economic function far beyond that of retailing. While being independent of government, it is estimated the traditional bazaar accounted for over two-thirds of economic activity in Iran in 1976, their control of the lucrative carpet industry accounted for much of the influx of foreign currency into the economy. However, the Shah's family had begun to encroach on the bazaar's traditional role, when through state owned enterprises they began to monopolise all large state capital projects. There were also serious claims of corruption against his immediate family that were largely overlooked by the Shah's administration. See further Graham, R. (1979), *Iran: The Illusion of Power* (London: Croom Helm) and Keddie, N. (1981), *Roots of the Revolution* (New Haven: Yale University Press).

[8] For example, in 1977 the Amuzegar government dramatically cut the state subsidies to the *ulema* and the Shah's policy of state control of education also reduced the *ulema's* resources and influence in society.

[9] These new middle classes wanted a form of western liberal democracy, while the Shah wished to preserve his regime.

[10] Chador is widely recognised as an Islamic mode of dress for women, covering the hair, hands and which extends to cover the feet. The chador is actually the black cloak-like cloth, traditionally held in place by ones teeth and that are used to cover the women's clothing, from head to toe.

[11] Indeed theories abound that those responsible were somehow linked to a religious or clerical group. The weight of the anti-government sentiments that resulted appears to suggest that the opposition had most to gain from implicating the government. However, no conclusive proof has ever been put forward to substantiate either argument.

[12] The imperial calendar commences at the time of Cyrus the Great and was an attempt to emphasise the monarchical, pre-Islamic history of Iran.

[13] The Muslim calendar begins with Mohammad's *hijra* as year zero.

[14] Exact accounts were difficult to ascertain, due to the imposition of martial law and the government's attempt to prevent knowledge of this event seeping into the public domain. There were accounts given of mass graves on the outskirts of Tehran, where government forces dumped bodies to distort exact numbers of victims been accounted for, such ideas were expressed to me during primary research interviews.

[15] Parsons, A. (1981), p. 126.

[16] For an eye witness account of the lead up to Khomeini's return together with his triumphant return to Iran, see further Simpson, J. (1988), *Behind Iranian Lines* (London: Robson Books Ltd).

[17] These three men are a good representation of the fate of Islamic intellectuals in the post-revolutionary theocratic state. Having assisted Khomeini in his bid to return to Iran, Bani Sadr became the first elected President of the Islamic Republic but was later impeached and forced into exile. Ibrahim Yahdi was Iran's foreign minister but was disgraced and forced to remain on the fringes of Iranian politics. Sadeq Qotbzadeh also became foreign minister in the early years of post-revolutionary Iran but was subsequently executed for treason.

[18] Bazargan's attempts to maintain relations with the US were with good reason. Under the Shah the US had become a major trading partner for the Iranian economy. Following the

revolution and the economic devastation, restoring the economy was one of the priorities of the new administration. Also the Iranian military was largely equipped with US made weaponry, good relations with the US was therefore necessary to maintain the military and the ensure the supply of the necessary spares.

[19] In fact, during a previous take over a month earlier Khomeini ordered that the students leave the Embassy premises. In an interview with one of the student leaders (September 1999) involved in the embassy take-over, any direct involvement or sanctioning of the action by Khomeini was denied.

[20] The Muslim people's Republican Party (MRPR) is an Azeri based organisation in Tabriz, situated in the heart of Iranian Azerbaijan. Their main goal was greater autonomy for Azerbaijan. They called for a boycott of the referendum in December 1979 that was intended to confirm the new constitution. The organisation was seriously hampered in its activities following a crackdown by the government, who executed many of its leadership and placed its spiritual leader Ayatollah Shariatmadrai under house arrest.

[21] IRP – Islamic Republican Party, was an attempt in the post-revolutionary period to unite all Islamic forces under the one banner and to facilitate the establishment of a one party state. Established by Ayatollah Beheshti, it was constantly troubled by internal division, which lead to it being disbanded in 1986 on Khomeini's orders.

[22] Hojatoleslam Sadeq Khalkhali is better known as 'the hanging judge' or the 'Butcher of Tehran' for his role as a religious prosecutor in the days following the revolution.

[23] Simpson, J. (1988), p.97.

[24] Ibid., p.215.

[25] Bakhash, S. (1990), *Reign of the Ayatollahs – Iran and the Islamic Revolution* (New York: Basic Books), p.57.

[26] For an insightful look at the concept of Islamic economy with specific reference to Iran see further Keddie, N. (Ed.) (1983), *Religion and Politics in Iran: Shi'ism from quietism to revolution* (Yale: Yale University Press), pp.145-166.

[27] *The Observer*, November 11th 1979.

[28] Details of these worker organisations were obtained through a number of interviews with employees from government departments and others. Interviews took place between February/March 1999.

[29] Omid, H. (1994), *Islam and the Post Revolutionary State in Iran* (London: Macmillan Press), p.92.

[30] For a more in-depth look at the powers of these institutions see further Appendix II.

[31] A termed used by Bani-Sadr in an article in the newspaper *Enqelabeh Eslami*, May 14th 1980, as quoted in Omid, H. (1994), p.94.

[32] This can be seen most evidently in his decision to forbid clerical participation in the first presidential elections of the Islamic republic.

[33] Khorramshah, is in the western province of Khuzestan, it sits on the Iranian side of the mouth of the Shattel-al Arab.

[34] There was also the additional issue of the Shattal al Arab waterway, which both Iran and Iraq laid claim to but which Iran possessed. It was seen by Iraq as the gateway to the Persian Gulf, access to which was seen as vital for Iraqi trade.

[35] For a more in depth discussion on Bani-Sadr's fall from grace and the many issues surrounding his impeachment see further Bakhash, S. (1990), *Reign of the Ayatollahs - Iran and the Islamic Revolution* (New York: Basic Books), Chapter 6. Or for Bani, Sadr's personal view of this period, see his book Sadr, B. (1991), *My Turn to Speak; Iran, the Revolution and Secret Deals with the US* (Washington: Brassey's Inc).

[36] The website was subsequently closed by the Iranian government.

Chapter 7
The Election of Khatami – Iran from Revolution to Realpolitik[1]

May 1997 marked a further stage in the development of the Iranian revolution. If we are to view revolution without the constraints of time, it could be argued that the election of President Khatami commenced the final stage of the implementation of the revolution, which began in the 1970s. President Khatami and his philosophy is representative of the Islamic reformation that is sweeping through not only the Iranian clergy but also Shia thinking in general. It is the continuation of the religious transformation which began with Shariati in the 1960s and which is continued with Soroush today within Iranian society.

President Khatami's election has been dubbed the 'second revolution', which marked the beginning of the 'Third Republic'.[2] The Third Republic makes the distinction between the two previous periods of post-revolutionary Iran. The First Republic occurred just after the 1979 revolution, the distinguishing factor of this period was Khomeini's use of social mobilisation to unite the masses and guarantee the continuation of the state during the heady days of the Iran-Iraq conflict. The Second Republic begun with the realisation that mass mobilisation would not suffice to guarantee the continuity of the revolution. This period occurred following the end of the eight-year war with Iraq. Iran's economy was in ruins and it was internationally isolated. The Second Republic is possibly best understood in the context of the then President Hashimi Rafsanjani, a political pragmatist whose administration concentrated on rebuilding the economy. The Third Republic by contrast, is the first period since the revolution where Iranian society is not in some political or economic abyss. Therefore, the population and the political elite concentrate more on creating an ideal society rather than the one necessary for survival. Khatami's call for a society based on respect for, and sovereignty of, the rule of law is profoundly reshaping the social fabric of Iranian society. His administration called for the creation of a civil society, based upon an open political system. It has unleashed a plurality of voices that would never have been accepted under the previous two republics.

The 1997 Presidential Election – Defining the Opposition Movement

Khatami's election provided, for the first time, a serious ideological alternative to the direction that the Iranian State and government might take. Previously the opposition movement was defined by its desire to disband the Islamic state and as such alienated many within Iran who, while believing in an Islamic state did not necessarily believe in the government's interpretation. Today talk of civil society, pluralism and inclusive politics has entered the language of the Iranian government and this has all occurred within the context of the Islamic administration. Khatami has attempted to create an Islamic State not based upon the previous method of theological authoritarianism but has tried to utilise a new brand of Islamic government based upon the Islamic enlightenment, to mobilise the masses and to ensure the continuation of a system that he personally agrees with. While his attempts to change the system while maintaining it has the potential of increasing societal conflict in the future, it has succeeded in mobilising a diverse electorate throughout Iran under the umbrella of political development. Not everybody in Iranian society welcomed Khatami's election victory. Many are sceptical, indeed worried that attempts to institutionalise democratic values and practices would result in the eventual overturning of the theocratic system. Many believe that an open discussion of issues such as equality and equal rights is counter-productive to the ideals and the very existence of the revolution.[2] However, Khatami's election while wholly unexpected was a sign that Iranian society is ready for change.

There has been much debate in Iran and elsewhere as to how Khatami could have achieved election victory in 1997 out of relative obscurity. Initially leading up to the elections it was assumed that the conservative figure Nadegh Nouri, who had the support of the Supreme Leader, was assured of victory. Khatami became a candidate for an umbrella coalition of a variety of reformist factions. The Roohaniyun[4] religiously supported Khatami, while the Agents of Construction Party[5] financed him and the Bureau for Solidarity[6] provided the support of Iranian youth. While more than 200 people ran for the election, the Guardian Council of Elections approved only four candidates.[7] Khatami was the only real reformist amongst the candidates, the others – Nadagh Nouri,[8] Reshari[9] and Zavarei[10] were perceived, and correctly so, as being from the conservative faction of Iranian politics. Coming out of relative obscurity, the Guardian Council did not believe that Khatami's candidature posed a serious threat to the conservatives on the ballot. Khatami's background is very religious,[11] while his political credentials are decidedly reformist.[12] This can be seen as the main reason for his broad based popular support, since he was the only candidate who appealed across class, religious and political spectrums.[13] While initially the conservative factions did not take his candidature as a serious threat, his growing popularity meant that the alliance of reformist movements had the potential of wrestling part of the government from conservative control.

The election process was also interesting in that it defined, for the first time, the divisions present in the ruling establishment. The election represented the beginning of the movement away from conservativism, while it highlighted the lengths to which the conservatives were willing to go to maintain their grasp on power. During the election campaign, the power of the 'unofficial rulers' of Iran became worryingly evident; their leadership was unknown while their ability to undermine the democratic process became evident. Much was done to destroy Khatami's reputation and attacks on gatherings of his supporters became almost commonplace. The most notable supporter who suffered personal attacks included Hashemi Rafsanjani's daughter, Faiza, owner of a female newspaper and a *majlis* member. In fact, even the Supreme Leader's brother, a supporter of Khatami and his policies, was not spared from physical attack. In the state media, controlled exclusively by the conservatives, Nouri was seen as being loyal to the leader, while Khatami was depicted as Iran's second Bani Sadr, associating with politically bankrupt people.[14]

The most astonishing debacle, now known as the '*Ashura* incident', showed the depths that the conservatives would go to discredit the Khatami campaign in the eyes of the electorate. Occurring during the mourning month of *Muharram*, *Ashura* remembers the martyrdom of Imam Husayn. It is a particularly sensitive time holding much significance for the Shia faith. During the election campaign, an unidentified group opposed to the election of Khatami produced a twenty-minute video in which young people, whose appearance was of an affluent background, were chanting slogans in support of Khatami on the eve of *Ashura*. In the video a young women (who was wearing make-up) was asked who she would vote for, she replied Khatami, asserting that he will give the youth freedom (taking off her head scarf). The videotape was sent to every mosque throughout Iran, with the request that it should be played during Friday Prayers. While the tape was later proven to be false, its contents were sufficiently contrary to the values and norms in Iranian society to lead many to believe the opposition claims that Khatami's election was detrimental to the continuation of the Islamic State. This was not the sole ruse used by the incumbent administration to prevent a reformist take-over of the presidential office. The election also shows how far out of touch with public sentiment the conservatives were. Many believed the revolutionary fervour demonstrated during the early years of the revolution was a expression of religious conservatism; this was a serious miscalculation. At one stage the conservative factions contesting the elections rumoured that if Khatami were elected satellite dishes would be allowed into the country. In the aftermath of the election it is estimated that this declaration by the conservatives actually assisted the Khatami campaign, as most people either already had a satellite dish or wanted to get one. Furthermore, when the list of candidates was published it was not in alphabetical order which was the norm and which would have put Nouri at the bottom of the list and Khatami near the top. Instead Nouri was put on top, so that the electorate would implicitly understand that he had the support of the leader. This did not change the outcome, the electorate related to Khatami's demeanour and his promises of a more open society. Few people considered that as President he would have minimal influence in a system that was still overwhelmingly controlled by the conservatives, however, they were willing to believe his promises and wait to see how the conservatives would react. However the fact that Khatami came from relative obscurity to be President of Iran is food for thought. A lecturer in political science from the University of Tehran put forward the question of how the head of the national library could possibly become President, especially in a country where the circulation of books was so small and where bookshop owners cannot sell their wares. Furthermore, Khatami supported civil society and civil politics – concepts that even political scientists have difficulty explaining. To the question of why did the electorate support these ideas, the answer inevitably lies in the psyche of post-revolution Iran. Out of a sense of apathy, a large segment of the population had not voted since the revolution. However following the campaign against Khatami by the establishment, people believed that if the establishment was against Khatami, therefore he must be good.[15] Khatami was elected less for his political ideology, than for the fact that he was not part of the ruling establishment.

Since his election President Khatami has attempted to steer the country away from its previous international isolation and by doing so hoped to have Iran accepted as a legitimate international actor. The path of reform in Iran is a difficult one to follow; the many factions within Iranian politics and society make it a very precarious journey. A journey to be taken only if assured of the people's support and even then it should be traveled with care. President Khatami was a total outsider in the 1997 presidential elections. For most of the campaign he was trailing in fourth place, unheard of outside of his brief period as Minister for Culture and Islamic Guidance in 1994. His main asset during the campaign was, paradoxically enough, the high level of anti-Khatami propaganda spread by the hard-line factions within the Iranian political establishment. They misread the political atmosphere; Khatami was depicted as a liberal, which endeared him to the youth of Iran. Iran is a country with a young population, over 60% of whom are under twenty-five years of age. Therefore a large segment of the voting population were not old enough to remember the rigours of the revolutionary period and remained unaffected by the politics of the Iran-Iraq war. Their support could not be won by revolutionary or nationalist rhetoric and it was their support that was of vital importance to the outcome of the election.

Since his election President Khatami has shown himself to be an astute political character. He is aware of the power of the hard-line factions, their power is not to be discounted and their control of the vital arms of the government, such as the judiciary, should not be underestimated. For that reason it was important that Khatami choose his political battles well. The reinstatement of the local councils, a decree of Ayatollah Khomeini that was suspended during the Iran/Iraq War, was a good place for Khatami to start, as it was a policy sure to be accepted. On the other hand any attempt to undermine the traditional power base of the hard-liners would be toughly contested.

The local elections in March 1999 were a further watershed in post-revolution Iran. For the first time since 1979, and possibly ever, power and democracy were being pushed as close to the people as possible. However while the election was an overwhelming success for Khatami's supporters, the future role of the local councils has yet to be clearly defined. As an elected member of the Tehran council pointed out 'the original role was that people should rule through these councils, not the government ... The fact is that conservatives are trying to imply that councils should only run the cities (e.g. traffic, electricity and other techno-functional needs). This is very low politics for groups that have a high political agenda. More participation in politics increases peoples interest in politics, we (Khatami's supporters in the local councils) want to instill a culture of political participation'.[16] While over two years have passed since the inauguration of the councils, the exact role they will play is still not clear. That said, they have succeeded in facilitating a more open political debate and their goal of increased political participation has been fulfilled. Having wrestled a segment of additional power from the hard-line clergy during the local elections, the battle lines were drawn in the contest for a further bastion of the hard-line authority, the very *majlis* that impeached Khatami years before.

Post 1997 – a Revolution in Reverse?

Khatami's presidential victory, while being hailed around the world as an unequivocal movement towards openness and 'democracy', was less a victory than an astonishing achievement. The conservatives still controlled the Parliament, the Judiciary, the armed forces, and most importantly the ultimate socio-political center of power, the Supreme Leadership. The President was in essence a lone bastion of liberalism, with limited influence upon a system, overwhelmingly supportive of the conservatives.

Khatami while having many opposition factions to thank for his success in the election was not going to alienate his administration within the political system by trying to fulfil all the promises made prior to the elections. The President, as we have seen from the previous chapter, can be easily removed by the Leader or by the Parliament. Such a fate befell Bani-Sadr, who believed his views of liberal democracy where those predominately held by the system. It was a costly mistake and following his swift impeachment and his imminent arrest, he escaped to France where he continues to live in exile. It is not the intention here to compare Khatami to Iran's first President, as their views on government and society differ in a number of areas. It is fair to say, however, that Khatami has learned the lessons of his predecessor and realising the precariousness of his position he has not openly challenged the Islamic system. Instead, Khatami has concentrated on building up his power base within the system, appealing to the people directly when he felt public pressure could assist the achievement of his aims. In other words, he has chosen the battles that he can win to change the system from within. He has cleverly avoided all direct conflict with the Leader. At times, he has even done this to the detriment of those who have supported him, as can be seen from the student demonstrations in July/August 1999.[17]

At that time the students were demonstrating against the slow pace of political reforms and the imprisonment of opposition figures. When the security forces, together with the *basijj* violently broke up the demonstrations on what could only have been the Leader's orders, Khatami's absence or even verbal support for the students was a shrewd yet somewhat Machiavellian move by the President. It damaged Khatami's presidency to a certain extent, with the people realising that Khatami could not deliver the reforms necessary to assuage their appetite for greater political and social freedom. This realisation brought Iran closer to social unrest, than at any time since the revolution. With the realisation that change was not going to occur, or at least was not going to occur at the pace of their liking, many believed that the only other option for change was through greater open defiance.

The student disturbances were a worrying sign for Khatami and his moderate allies. It showed a growing unease amongst the youth of Iranian society. President Khatami was elected because he was seen as a reformist; the hopes and aspirations of many Iranians were invested in his election victory. The people's expectations are a heavy burden for Khatami's government to bear, especially as the path to reform is strewn with a variety of dangerous pitfalls. Many Iranians dislike any comparison to be made between Khatami's reforms in Iran and Gorbechev's policies of *Perestrokia* and *Glastnost*. *Glasnost* was the policy of more open and consultative government, while *Perestrokia* was the practice of restructuring the economic and political system. In essence, Gorbechev was attempting to reform the Soviet system, while at the same time maintaining communism as the dominant ideology. With the benefit of hindsight, one might argue that it was the attempt to open up Soviet society while increasing the availability of information, which eventually led to the break up of the Soviet Union. The comparison made between Khatami and Gorbechev, is furiously contested within Iran, however, the idea that both leaders believed in their respective system of government yet tried to bring it into the modern era, stands firm.

The tension on the streets of Tehran is still tangible. Ever since the bloody demonstrations in July 1999, the population has been holding their breath awaiting the next conflict to arise. Instead of an open conflict, the hard-liners have changed tactics and have attempted to undermine Khatami's government and the electoral prospects of the moderate wing of Iran politics. The first blow came with the imprisonment of the former mayor of Tehran and electoral adviser to the president, Golam Hussein Karbaschi. He is highly respected by the people of Tehran, for his success in giving Tehran the structural face-lift it deserved and was instrumental in the formation of the liberal political grouping the 'Party for the Agents of Reconstruction', which successfully contested the 1995 *majlis* elections. Being a cleric, though not one who wears clerical dress, Karbaschi was tried on charges of fraud by the Clerical Court and imprisoned for 5 years.

Politics came onto the streets of Tehran again during the last Friday of the holy month of *Ramadan* in January 2000, a day when the people of Iran commemorate the 'Universal day of Jerusalem'. The late leader of the revolution, Ayatollah Khomeini, inaugurated this event to raise anti-Israeli sentiment amongst Muslims; however, this year it became the stage on which a further act of internal strife between the various political factions was played out. While the President took part in the commemoration, his message was one of restrained accommodation, 'on the eve of a new century, mankind needs peace, freedom, justice and security more than any time before ... we hope we will witness the promotion of peace for all men, through peaceful co-existence, mutual respect and peaceful negotiations'.[18] His sentiments were not altogether echoed throughout the crowd. Posters bearing the signature of the *Hezbollah* (Party of God), alleged to have been responsible for the bloodshed during the previous July's student protests, attacked the character of not only of Israel but also of reformists such as the imprisoned Iranian cleric Abdullah Nouri.

Such polarised views between the political actors and the audience in Iran, was further evidenced during the celebrations marking the 21st anniversary of the revolution in February 2001. While the President struck a conciliatory tone in his speech, preferring to speak of his government's successful economic policies rather than the usual anniversary rhetoric decrying western imperialism, the crowds were divided in their response. The crowd's cries of 'death of America, death of Israel, death of liberalism', drowned out by the President.[19] The Supreme Leaders absence from the official rally was also noted; as was the fact that he gave his own speech full of the usual rhetoric, later in the day at Tehran University. The crowd were predominately supporters of the hard-liners, with many reformers preferring to remain away for the annual demonstrations for fear of an outbreak of violence. The President's unusual speech therefore did not meet with overwhelming support amongst the crowd, which was seriously diminished in scale from previous years.[20] While the fear of violence can explain the decrease in the numbers participating in this annual pilgrimage in remembrance of the revolution, a more probable reason is the populations' disillusionment with the regime's empty revolutionary rhetoric. Rhetoric that they believe no longer adequately defines their goals, their society or their political objectives.

With the loss of the Presidency to a reformist and with local councils eating away at their traditional power base, the conservatives in Iranian society were not going to sit idly by and watch their economic and political control of Iran wither away. The parliamentary elections in March 2000 were to be the next step in the contest between the conservatives and those who wanted reforms. The conservatives had, and still have, a two-pronged strategy to regain total control of Iranian politics. The first prong was to make the lines of demarcation between the two main factions disappear. Iran does not have an official party system; therefore it is often difficult to know to which faction each politician belongs. This meant that it was relatively easy for many conservatives to reinvent themselves as reformists, while not forsaking their true ideological intentions.[21] The second prong of the strategy of the hard-liners was to directly attack the key areas of reformist strengths; this meant the reformist media and their main political activists. Since the election of Khatami, many newspapers began to appear printing a wide spectrum of political views. This has resulted in a political discourse into the future of Iranian politics, which hard-liners found increasingly threatening. In the last two years, the hard-liners have physically and 'legally' attacked many of these papers on the basis of their alleged 'opposition to Islam and the Islamic Republic' and these actions have resulted in the closure of over thirty publications in the last six months alone. The attacks on opposition activists have had a more devastating impact on Iranian politics. In 1998 a number of assassinations of opposition activists was later proven to be the work of renegade members of the Ministry of Information, a hotbed of hard-line sentiment under the direct control of the Supreme Leader. Others activists and close associates of President Khatami were arrested and imprisoned. Some of those included clerics, who had impeccable revolutionary credentials and whose loyalty to the republic could not be doubted. One such cleric was Abdullah Nouri[22] whose sentencing by the unconstitutional Clerical Court is an example of the extent to which the incumbent regime will go to rid themselves of the opposition from within.

Abdullah Nouri first came to political prominence over two decades ago, when he was appointed as the late Ayatollah Khomeini's personal representative to the Organisation of Construction – Jihad.[23] He was also a member of the *majlis*, from 1983 to 1987, representing the district of Esfahan, where he was head of the budget and planning committee. Through this committee he developed a working relationship with, the then *majlis* Speaker, Ali Akbar Rafsanjani.[24] This long-standing relationship between these influential figures may hold the key to the success or failure of the moderates following their gains in the March 2000 parliamentary elections. Nouri received a further promotion in March 1989, this time as Khomeini's personal representative to the Islamic Revolution Guards Corps (IRGC). In his appointment of Nouri to this highly trusted military organisation, responsible for countering 'anti-revolutionaries', Khomeini asked the 'learned, faithful, combatant, religious and politically quite wise' Nouri to 'supervise all cultural, political, ideological, religious, propaganda publications, security and legal activities of the IRGC as well as having the final say to any promotion and dismissal of IRGC Commanders'.[25] A striking recommendation from the spiritual leader of the day. Days before Ayatollah Khomeini's demise, he appointed the influential Nouri, together with 23 other top political figures[26] to the special Council for Constitutional Amendments. Two months later, the constitutional amendments were passed in a constitutional referendum and

Hashemi Rafsanjani was elected Iran's new President. Abduallah Nouri, was appointed Interior Minister, and was accompanied at cabinet table by Mohammad Khatami as the Minister for Culture and Islamic Guidance.

In the aftermath of Abdullah Nouri's trial and conviction widespread protests in his defence swept throughout Iran. Tehran University was awash with posters protesting against Nouri's conviction. The motto of the student gathering was 'rejecting injustice, supporting oppressed students and clerics', students gathered outside the university's mosque to the chant of 'we think like Nouri, arrest us too!', 'shut down the unconstitutional court of clerics', 'the conviction of Nouri is a perfect example of the inquisition' and 'Nouri, Nouri, God bless you, you are our Majlis Speaker'.[27]

Nobody epitomises the development in political ideals over the period of the revolution better than Adbullah Nouri. He is representative of many Iranians who had believed wholly in the revolution but who also believe that the political system present in Iran today is not what the revolution was fought for. 'Persevere, as your son has been imprisoned for his faith and religion' were the words of Ayatollah Montazeri during a phone call to Nouri's father following his son's imprisonment. It is hard to believe that this conversation occurred in the Islamic Republic and that Nouri was being persecuted for his Islamic beliefs, it is more likely that this would have occurred during the Shah's regime, instead it took place in late 1999. Indeed, Montazeri once destined to succeed Khomeini as Leader of the Islamic Republic, is now under house arrest, placed there by what he describes as 'club-wielding' clerics, part of a regime which he and Nouri both helped to install.

It appears that the revolution has almost come full circle. Under the Shah, clerics were imprisoned for their religious belief; under the current regime those same clerics find themselves again imprisoned. It is not only the clerics who are finding themselves ostracised from the regime that they helped create, both the student movement and the ordinary people who helped the revolution succeed are now finding themselves forced unwillingly into opposition. Many ordinary Iranian who were initially in favour of the Islamic Republic and who vehemently opposed the regime of the Shah, now find themselves persecuted again because they are labelled liberals for their views in favour of greater political participation. As one student leader who was involved in the US Embassy take-over and who now is a reformist member of the Tehran City Council[28] – summed up the paradox of the current situation, 'sometimes there are those (like Nadegh Nouri) who call student groups liberals. If that means the erosion of religion then we are not liberals. If you define it as meaning (the) fight for people's rights then we are liberals. Conservatives are reactionary; they do not want people to take part in politics. Dr. Soroush, and Mr Kadivar were arrested because of their thoughts. We can't work under these conditions, this type of regime. People should be allowed to express their voice, not just in the higher levels of the political processes'.[29] The revolution appears to have come full circle with the suppression of political freedom being the definitive common point between both of the regimes that have straddled the revolutionary period.

Perhaps the reasons for the former revolutionaries becoming disillusioned with the system of government that the revolution created can be found in the nature of that system. Following the revolution one of the only areas where the diverse coalition of opposition forces agreed upon was that the post-revolutionary government should take on the form of some sort of republican government. For republicanism was the only form of government that was totally contrary to the personal, hereditary, lifelong and arbitrary rule which had defined Iranian history for the previous 2,000 years. During the negotiations following the Shah's departure it was overwhelmingly agreed that the provisional government should be neither monarchical nor dictatorial. In Iranian history monarchical and dictatorial rule are in effect one and the same, in many cases constitutional monarchs such as Muhammad Ali Shah, showed themselves to be more dictatorial then their predecessors. Following the revolution, republicanism was an attempt to de-couple dictatorship and monarchy from the Iranian political system. However, both the Iranian and Shia culture is steeped in a tradition of strong leadership, embodied in a single father-like figure. Therefore, the post-revolutionary form of republicanism found it difficult to move far from these deeply embedded traditions. What has become known as Islamic republicanism is a distinctly Iranian invention, while the hereditary, monarchical domination was rejected; it was replaced by a system based on hierarchical clerical rule. As Islamic republicanism developed it became evident that was still dictatorial in nature, in as far as political power remained within a exclusive group of revolutionary elite. Furthermore, this group attempted to regulate their society based on their personal beliefs. The result for the Iranian population was less political openness and a return to arbitrary rule. The arrest of Abdul Nouri, his trial and his outstanding defence brought home to many the cyclical direction that the Iranian administration had taken. During his defence Nouri highlighted the true republican ideals that were an expression of the revolution, as delineated by the Constitution. He argued that the revolution had come full circle and that the tyranny, for which the Shah was overthrown, was now present again in the Iranian political system.[30] While Nouri was found guilty and imprisoned, his demands for a return to a true republican government, to a State based on the rule of law and against the concepts of monarchy or dictatorship, were taken up during the campaign for the elections to parliament in March 2000.[31]

This renewed call for the re-instatement of republican ideals is of great interest because it is being made by the religious classes who are perceived to be the backbone of the Islamic government. This new form of republicanism tries to combine political liberalism with religious conservatism. It is an attempt to meet the needs of a modern society while not denying the religious fabric that defines their society. The very people who manned the barricades during the revolution that now are pushing forward this agenda for a return to republican ideals. They are predominantly religious, educated within the Islamic system, veterans of the eight-year war and of the revolution itself. Many are in prominent positions within the current administration and almost all believe that the revolutionary process was hijacked or took a detour some years after the overthrow of the Shah. These people are not traitors to the revolution or to Islam; they are in fact its guardians, battling against tyranny and dictatorship even if it comes from within their own religious hierarchy.

A Revolution Unresolved?

By looking at the binary opposition between the state and the people before and after the revolution,[32] we can see that the changes instilled by the Khatami government, while being somewhat significant, were not sufficient enough to bring Iranian society into a zone of relative equilibrium. The power to define their political future still remains outside the grasp of ordinary Iranians. The main reason for this was that all candidates for election are firstly screened by the Guardian Council for their 'Islamic' values and adherence to the principle of *valeyet-e faqih* (Supreme Leadership), only then could they be put before the electorate. However, both the *majlis* and the office of the Presidency, the two elected arms of government, still only possess a limited potential for implementing change, with most power vested in the position of the Supreme Leader who is not directly elected by the Iranian people. The Supreme Leader has the final say on any social, religious or political policy that is enacted by any institution of the Republic. The guardian council's role is to ensure that all laws are in line with the teachings of Islam. The main problem from a religious and a political perspective is that the basic ideology (religious and political) governing the Republic is a creation of the 'religious elite'. As we have seen in the previous chapters, Khomeini's interpretation of Islam and

Islamic government is unique and therefore the Iranian government's brand of 'Islam' is not necessarily representative of the people. Therefore, from a religious and political sense it is possible to say that the level of binary opposition between the people and the authorities (religious and political), has remained relatively the same and in a religious sense has even expanded from the pre-revolutionary state. Therefore, an analysis of the Iranian revolution can conclude that the original objectives of the revolution have remained unachieved in the Islamic State.

The second point to be raised by our above discussion relates to the time span of a revolution. In chapter four we concluded that to define revolution by a specific date in time is to misrepresent a struggle, which may have occurred over many years. For example, to identify 1949 with the Chinese communist revolution, is to leave unacknowledged over twenty years of guerrilla warfare and struggle. It is so with the Iranian revolution; the republican ideals mixed with a belief in Shi'ism that suitably represented the majority of the opposition to the Shah, remains unfulfilled over two decades after the Shah's departure. Post-revolutionary Iran is still in a state of revolutionary flux. In many ways the Iraqi invasion and the need for national unity to expel the aggressor put the revolutionary process on hold. As one veteran of the revolution aptly put it, 'we had the revolution not to replace the Shah with the clergy. The revolution did not occur because of poverty but because of freedom. The revolution was about spreading freedom. But the war put all of these ideals on hold. When our independence was threatened, we had to all pull behind the government and stop asking for more democracy but now the war is over ...'. It was only after the end of the war and following the period of economic and social reconstruction that the Iranian people could repeat the calls made in 1979 for increased political and religious freedoms. Many pinpoint early 1981 as the time when the revolution was betrayed. Many in the Iranian administration view the presidency of Bani Sadr as the betrayal of the revolution because of his belief in the separation of religion and politics. It was Khomeini's retraction of his support for the democratic process and its elected president that was the true betrayal. As one insider explained, 'the Imam was convinced by the conservative factions within the post-revolutionary establishment that Bani Sadr's intentions were to betray the clergy just as Mossadeq had over thirty years previously during the installation of his nationalist government'.[33] Mossadeq's unwillingness to acknowledge the decisive role the clergy played in the departure of the Shah in 1950 and his reluctance to recognise the role that the clergy could play in Iranian politics was to affect the course of the revolution that even he could not have foreseen.[34] Khomeini feared that Sadr, a non-clergy and believer in parliamentary democracy while being an unreserved member of the Islamic movement, would sell out the clergy and prevent them from their goal of officially fusing religion and politics.

The devastating protracted eight-year war with Iraq left no family untouched and no community unscathed. The need for national unity meant that much of the early opposition to Islamic government was put on hold until the war was over. However, this time was crucial in providing the conservative clergy with the opportunity to consolidate their power within the Iranian system. From the onset of the revolution the clergy either controlled the political institutions or else established shadow institutions through which to exert their influence and control. This development will be analysed in more detail later, suffice to say at this stage that these shadow institution effectively undermined attempts at creating a stable and democratic government in the post-revolution period. With most of the secular opposition living in exile, which seriously discredited their leadership in the eyes of the Iranian people, the main opposition force left in Iran of any substance were the *Mujahedin*. However, the *Mujahedin's* decision to side with Iraq following the onset of the war did little to endear them to the larger Iranian population. In addition, the *Mujahedin's* terrorist campaign, while resulting in many high level IRP[35] casualties,[36] provided the government with the excuse necessary to eradicate whatever opposition remaining within Iranian borders. Therefore with the opposition from within the state constrained by the war with Iraq, the misappropriation of the revolution was all the easier.

The election of President Khatami and the subsequent trial of Abdullah Nouri made some things very clear, the divisions within the Iranian political elite became obvious. On one hand the supporters of a dictatorial Islamic state, while being caught off guard by the election of Khatami, had every intention of participating in Iran's political future and were unwilling to hand over the reins of power without a serious contest. On the other hand, the Islamic reformists were now in a position to battle for the hearts and minds of the Iranian electorate on an equal footing with the conservative right. The reformists, while being committed to the democratic participation of religion within the Iranian political system nevertheless have brought the true ideals of republicanism back into the political debate. It remains to be seen, however, whether the debate that began with the election of Khatami will result in the amount of change necessary to quell the calls for greater political freedom from the Iranian electorate. In many ways, Khatami provides the reform movement with a serious dilemma. While being the saviour of the reformist movement in 1997, he now poses one of the greatest threats to the success of that movement. As Khatami wants to maintain the system of clerical rule, there will come a time in the near future where the reformist movement may have to oppose Khatami's support for the continuation of the current form of government, in order that their goal of a truly democratic government can be achieved.

The Politics of Parallel Institutions

As previously discussed, the shift in Iranian politics towards a more pluralistic political scene, based upon the true principle of republicanism, is a trend that will be difficult for the traditionalists to stop. In many ways this shift back towards the ideas that fuelled the revolution was made possible due to the success of the new regime in consolidating their power over the state apparatus as well as over society. While the consolidation of the conservative control of the state can be open to criticism, their goal of building state institutions enabled Iran to survive during the early turbulent period following the Shah's departure.

That said, building state institutions should not be confused with a co-ordinated system of institutionalisation. In fact, in the post revolutionary period, the attempts to create state institutions often resulted in a number of similar institutions being established, while control over them remained politically diverse. In other words, the initial period of state formation led in many ways to institutional pluralism. The political consolidation in the post-revolution period, as discussed earlier, was swift and in many cases merciless. The institutions of the *ancién regime* were taken over; while social institutions went about their business of Islamising society. In many cases where control of an institution was not guaranteed to the religious authorities, shadow or parallel institutions were created. This occurred more prominently in the military, where the new rulers of Iran did not trust the armed forces. The revolutionary guards, who could be trusted to defend the Islamic State, were therefore established. Most of this consolidation was carried out through the IRP, and while it was later disbanded because of continuous internal disagreements, its swift handling of the transition period enabled the Iranian State to survive.

With no serious counter-revolution coming from the royal forces, nor from the secular opposition, there was little need for total ideological conformity within the ruling establishment to counter an outside force. With the onset of the Iraqi war much of the political opposition to Islamic republicanism was muted. However, within the confines of the IRP and the clergy there was much debate on the fundamental differences in the ideological direction of the Islamic leadership. Indeed, with little need for ideological conformity, the social division within the coalition of Islamic leadership began to show. The *bazaaris* who had financed the revolution out of necessity because of the Shah's family's almost total control of the economy, wanted to received the spoils of their victory. Other sections of the Islamic alliance also wanted some returns from the revolution. The clergy wanted to further Islamise society, while the poorer sections of Iranian society wanted some tangible economic returns for their years of struggle. In essence, all three members of this successful coalition were competing for the same economic resources to fulfil their goals. For a time the war with Iraq and the powerful presence of Ayatollah Khomeini managed to subdue these differences for the common goal, however, the overwhelming differences existing beneath the surface continued to grow. This led ultimately in 1986 to the abandoning of the idea of a one party state under the IRP banner.

In many ways the purpose of the position of *velayet-e faqih*, as initially held by Khomeini, was to provide the central ideological leadership necessary to keep society from fracturing too much. Khomeini managed to play this role well, remaining above the fray on many occasions and only becoming involved when he deemed it of vital importance. Nevertheless, as the war with Iraq raged on, Khomeini could not even quell serious internal divisions concerning the operation of the state. It was only Khomeini's deathbed decision to take the blame for the mismanagement of the war that prevented the Iranian State from dissolving into bitter dispute. What has become evident since the death of Khomeini was that the position of *velayat-e faqih* was very much a position suited to the unique personage of Khomeini. Khomeini was inimitable, the mixture of personal charisma, religious seniority and revolutionary credentials made it possible for a wide variety of people from across the social and political spectrum to unite behind him. His successor, the former President Ali Khameni, had neither the charisma nor the religious credentials necessary to be a unifying force in Iranian politics and so the many divisions within the ruling elite, which had been held in check by Khomeini, re-erupted into the political void upon his death.

The Islamic revolutionaries were more than capable of building the Islamic State post 1979; nevertheless it did not lead to the total centralisation of economic and political power. With the death of Khomeini this became all the more apparent, when the previous united factions attempted to gain control of various state political and economic apparatus. The Iranian state controls the most important economic resources in the country, this was increased following the revolution with the nationalisation of the oil industries and take over by the state of the many production facilities controlled by supporters of the former regime. The various factions that made up the successful alliance against the Shah were able, in the post-revolutionary period, to gain control of segments of the economy, turning industry into a number of economic fiefdoms. With economic control came political influence and the increased establishment of parallel institutions from which pressure could be brought to bear on the political apparatus.

On a political level each faction, at different historical junctures, was able to establish their own political institution, or at least re-define the power of a political institution following their association with it. There is no greater example of this than the oddly named Council for the Determination of Exigencies, established in 1987 by Khomeini in an attempt to end the legislative deadlock by the Guardian Council who continued to veto reformist legislation passed by the *majlis*. He assigned this institution the task of arbitrating between the *majlis* and the Guardian Council, however it was an ineffectual institution from the onset. That was until Hashemi Rafsanjani, the former President and the leader of the modern right faction, became its chairman. The modern right faction in Iranian politics has much economic power within the Iranian State and this transformed itself into significant political influence following Rafsanjani's appointment to the Council. This previous lacklustre institution was transformed overnight into one of the most influential institutions in the state, with a role far exceeding what was originally envisaged. Another example of such an institution unforeseen in the original constitution, but which has none the less wrestled a significant amount of influence from the formal structure, is the Special Clerical Court. This court has been responsible for the conviction of many liberal clergy or clerical supporters of Khatami's administration over the past number of years, including Nouri and Kadivar. Acting outside of the constitution and established as a result of the far right's interpretation of a decree from Khomeini, there is little possibility of state or political control over this renegade institution.

By the mid-1990s, the political system in Iran did not merely embody those institutions envisaged by the constitution but was a patchwork of official and unofficial institutions, which have become a permanent feature of the Iranian political system. It is fair to say that few political systems in the world have such a complicated decision making process, with a plethora of interconnected and parallel institutions having varying degrees of influence. There is neither transparency nor any organisational chart through which to map out the hierarchy of one institution in relation to another. In such a fluid and competing political system, it is a wonder that the post-Khomeini period has not been characterised by open conflict. Indeed, the state has survived mainly through moving away from its ideal of an Islamic form of democratic centralism. It has made few attempts to rein in the various centers of decision-making and instead has become the medium through which competing claims could be articulated rather than resolved.

Attempts at Economic and Political Centralisation

There have been attempts throughout the 1990s to bring all these extra institutions under 'state' control and to re-centralise the decision making process. This initially took the form of economic centralisation following the end of the war and the election of Rafsanjani as President (1989-1997). During the war there was a need for a highly centralised economic structure to fulfil the production and distribution needs of the war effort Following the war it was assumed that this formal structure would fracture into a multitude of parts. It was assumed that the traditional bazaar would take over much of the previous work carried out by the state. While this did occur, it was organised by the traditional right under the guidance of their political representative-Rafsanjani. In many ways this alliance, at a political level, of the traditional bazaar with the conservative right, brought some form of economic centralisation. It was further augmented during the 1992 elections when the ultra conservative Guardian Council expelled many candidates from the traditional left from the electoral process.

Rafsanjani's eight-year presidency is characterised by attempts to develop an economic plan that would centralise control of the economy under the state apparatus. This occurred simultaneously as he tried to appease those, mainly the *bazaaris*, who had assisted his bid for power but who also wanted a more decentralised economic plan. At the heart of this debate on centralisation was the control of the very wealth 'Foundations', which were technically non-governmental/religious organisations that aided the oppressed, the orphans and the widows of the martyrs of the revolution and the eight-year war. These foundations control a large segment of the Iranian economy and have the potential to change economic results, thereby giving them a direct influence at the political level.[37] Rafsanjani's attempts at centralisation put his administration on a collision course with the traditional right, who wanted to consolidate their position of economic control and to augment it with political authority.

The traditional right decided that the election campaign to the fifth Islamic parliament would be the platform on which they would build their bid for political control. The coalition of the right that had shared the control of the economic and political life of Iran over the previous fifteen years began to crumble. The traditional right, believing that they had the potential to take full control of the state apparatus decided to discard their former allies. Previously the coalition of the right had offered the electorate a list of candidates, which adequately reflected the full spectrum of politically right views in Iranian society.[38] This time, however, the traditional right rejected the moderate right candidates, together with the any suggestions made by Rafsanjani for changes to their list. The split between the traditional right and what became know as the modern right, allowed the previously defeated and demoralised Islamic left to remerge as a vital political force. While the traditional right is best described as conservative, the modern right are a fluid group made up of modern state builders, who believe in economic and political centralisation while at the same time favouring the rule of the Islamic elite. The Agents of Construction Party were initially supportive of the modern right, until they found their natural place in the centre left of the political spectrum during the 1997 presidential election campaign.

Indeed, the 1997 election was indicative of the very real divisions that had erupted across the political spectrum. The traditional right came into the campaign full of confidence, with their candidate having received the unofficial backing of the Supreme Leader; they believed that the election was theirs for the taking. However, the 1997 political scene was very different from the elections contested previously throughout the late 1980s and early 1990s. Public sentiment and the knowledgeable Iranian electorate were not easily won over with empty slogans of security, prosperity and justice. The traditional right, therefore, had seriously misread the political landscape. The united forces of the political left had a simple slogan advocating their views against *'enhessar'*, against monopolies. The electorate did not need an explanation as to who controlled the political and economic monopolies; the slogans coupled with an appealing presidential candidate assured the resurgence of the previously lacklustre left.

The result of the presidential election was tantamount to a political coup; the office of the president was the bridgehead with which the forces of the political left would attempt to regain control of the institutions of the state. The traditional right had seriously underestimated the public's readiness for a more pluralistic and transparent political system. The public had put up with years of abuse, intrusions into their private lives, economic scarcity and elitism. Now the public were energised and united in their calls for the government to retreat from the private lives of its citizens. By electing a relatively unknown presidential candidate the electorate were no longer the aggrieved partner of state policy but had now become a serious player in an increasingly more complicated game for control of the State's institutions.

The traditional right, however, were unwilling to quietly become a part of Iranian history following their defeat at the 1997 presidential elections, as they still controlled the *majlis*, the judiciary, the Guardian Council and the vital position of *velayat-e faqih*. Through utilising these institutions they hit back at the political left who had orchestrated the election victory and the electorate who were their partners. The 1997 election re-energised the left and under the pragmatic leadership of Khatami, they focused on winning a few crucial battles, while avoiding all out war with the ruling system. As for the electorate, for the first time since the revolution, they believed that their vote counted and that the civil society that was promised by Khatami was within their grasp. As previously mentioned President Khatami was in a precarious position, the electorate wanted drastic change while the traditional right became even more conservative in their political outlook. The stage was set for intensive negotiations between Khatami and the fifth *majlis* regarding his cabinet appointments.

While willing to compromise in the areas of traditional importance to the political right (such as commerce), Khatami steadfastly sought control of two vital ministries that were needed to fulfil his reform package. The Ministry for Islamic Culture and Guidance and the Interior Ministry were vital to Khatami's future plans. The Ministry for Islamic Culture and Guidance is responsible for providing licenses to the publishing media while the Interior Ministry is in charge of Iran's internal security, including the appointment of provincial governors, which would give Khatami's reformist movement political control at a local level. Under his direction the Ministry for Islamic Culture and Guidance continued to provide licenses to reformist and pro-democracy newspapers, as quickly as the Judiciary were closing them down. Through this policy, papers that were closed reopened almost immediately with the same staff and editorial policy but under a different name.[39] It also provided the public with a variety of opinions and opened up a political discussion that would not have been possible only a few years previous. Furthermore, the interior ministry had been a bastion of traditional right support since its formation in 1983 and had been one of the leading tools used against any opposition to their rule.[40] Following the election of Khatami, the Interior Ministry was implicated in a series of opposition murders, which had been blamed on foreign agents. Khatami's choice of these two ministries for the base of the reformist resurgence was vital. Over a three-year period leading up to the 2000 parliamentary elections, these ministries eroded the previous autonomy that the traditional right had held, which enabled them to set the political agenda. This provided a more open, just and honest debate concerning the future of the Iranian nation.

Both the presidential election in 1997 and the parliamentary elections in 2000 marked a further stage in the political maturity of the Iranian electorate. Both elections were relatively free from manipulation, without the assistance of the Interior Ministry, the Guardian Councils ability to disqualify candidates was greatly reduced. For that reason, as well as the public discourse initiated by the reformist press, Iranian politics was able to move above the previous practice of street politics and towards the ideal of a democratic Islam. The victory in the presidential, parliamentary and local election by the reformists over the past four years does not necessarily signal the end of factional politics in Iran. The power struggles between the traditional right and the reformists for control of state institutions continues unabated; the issues have remained the same however the playing field has now moved. The traditional right still maintains control over vital areas of the state, areas where both the electorate and the reformists have minimal influence. Both the Guardian Council and the Judiciary are under the firm control of the Supreme Leader, who also controls the army and revolutionary guards. No faction on the Iranian political scene can ignore the political, as well as the economic, influence that these institutions yield.

Furthermore, just as the right wing of the Iranian political spectrum has split between the traditional and modern right, the reformist camp also holds equally diverse opinions within its ranks. The reformist coalition is made up of groups that include similar views to the modern right and the traditional left, together with all the diversity of opinion in between. The traditional left is also divided about the future structure that the Islamic State should take. There are those, including Khatami, who believe that the Islamic government including the institution of the *velayat-e faqih*, is the only way to ensure the survival of the Islamic state. While others would hold a more liberal democratic perspective, which would entail a seriously decreased political role for the *velayat-e faqih*, some would even see the elimination of this all-powerful position as being the only way to truly ensure democratic reform. Even if the traditional right has been dealt a severe blow by the electorate over the past number of years, there is nothing like electoral defeat to assist as a unifying force in Iranian politics. There are already signs that the previous rift between the traditional and the modern right is being healed, with the traditional right placing the unofficial leader of the modern right, Rafsanjani, on the top of their electoral list for the 2000 parliamentary elections. Furthermore, there is the sign that the traditional right is even more aware of the necessity of winning the confidence of the electoral and, therefore, there appears to be moves within the traditional right to try and re-invent themselves as an ideologically centre right political movement. This face lift of the traditional right has meant that they have taken on many of the policies of the modern right, providing a façade of reformist credentials in an attempt to woo voters back into their ranks.

Perhaps it is too little too late, however with the unpredictable nature of Iranian politics a resurgence of the traditional right in the future, in some shape or form, is not to be discounted. What is certain however is that regardless of the political actors in the future, the electorate has developed to a great extent over the past number of years. Their expectations of the political leaders are much higher than previously, their knowledge of individual rights and their awareness of democratic values have all increased substantially.[41]

Notes

[1] Idea of the chapter title was taken from Waxman, D. (1998), *The Islamic Republic of Iran: between revolution and realpolitik* (London: Research Institute for the Study of Conflict and Terrorism).

[2] The term 'Third Republic' has been increasingly associated with Khatami's administration following been popularised in the editorial of the monthly *Kian* (June-July 1997). According to the editorial (the editor at the time being Mashallah Shamsolvaezin) 'we are on the verge of entering the era of the "Third Republic"'. The division of the history of Iran since 1979 using the notion of republics was previously used by Ehteshami, A. (1995), *After Khomeini: The Iranian Second Republic* (London: I.B. Tauris).

[3] Indeed, during the last Friday prayer meeting held before the 1998 No Ruz (new year) celebrations, at the Imam Khomeini memorial, I heard Ayatollah Mesbah Yazdi, head of the judiciary and long time conservative say that a 'Belief in equal rights for all is worse than cow worship.'

[4] The two main religious groupings within Iranian politics can be divided as follows: *Roohaniat* is seen as the continuation of the Islamic Republic Party (as established by Ayatollah Beheshti after the revolution but which was disbanded in 1986 on the instruction of Khomeini), it is perceived as being conservative in nature. Viewing those who are associated with its membership can substantiate this assertion; they include Rafsanjani, formerly Khameini (former president and current *velayat-e faqih*), Yazdi head of the Judiciary) and Nadeg Nouri. The other political grouping was *Roohaniyun*. While also being clerical this groups is seen to be more reform minded and believing in political transparency. Members of this grouping include Karubi (former Iran's representative to the Hajj in the same year of the bloody Friday massacre in Mecca, he is also the head of the Organisation of Martyrs, called the father of all fatherless children, he became the Iranian *Majlis* Speaker during the Iraq/Kuwait war), Mussavi Khoeiniha (publisher of the *Salam* Newspaper and formerly Iran's top prosecutor, head of the Hajja and pilgrimage organisation) and a somewhat odd inclusion is Khalkhali (know after the revolution as the *Butcher of Tehran*, for his role as a religious prosecutor)

[5] This party was formed by Golam Hussein Karbaschi, Tehran's former mayor, he is a cleric (although he never wears clerical dress) and was imprisoned following his dubious conviction by a clerical court on charges of fraud. The party was formed in 1995, during the

Majlis elections and the party's name is an indirect reference to Rafsanjani, who as President at the time was given the name of 'Master/Lord of Iranian Construction'. The Party of Construction cannot be understood without the character of Rafsanjani, who has no official position but is a back seat driver. It is a unofficial party and was financed privately (nobody knows by whom). The main loud speaker of Mr. Karabachi and his party was the *Harshari* (Fellow Citizen) newspaper, which has subsequently been closed down. Other founders of the party (who were all high bureaucrats) include Mr. Adali (Central bank Governor and formally Iran's Ambassador to Canada; he has been criticised for the current wave of inflation, is committed to a floating exchange rate and free market economics, and he is said to be an agent of the IMF, who implements their policies in Iran), Dr. Nourbash (the current Governor of the Central Bank; he was also the governor during the brief presidency of Bani-Sadr. As the finance minister during the 2nd term of office of Rafsanjani, he was impeached due to his inability to run the financial affairs of the country. The night he was impeached he was appointed by Rafsanjani as his personal financial advisor and was then put into the position of Governor of the Central Bank) and also Mohammad Hashemi (brother of former president Rafsanjani).

[6] Bureau for Solidarity is an umbrella student organisation.

[7] The Guardian Council had twelve members, six clerical and six jurists. The six jurists are proposed by the judiciary and accepted by the Majlis. The six clerical members were approved directly by the leader.

[8] Nadagh Nouri is not to be confused with the reformist namesake Abdul Nouri. Nadegh is an archconservative and former Speaker of the House. Was seen as the choice of the Supreme Leader during the 1997 presidential election and was expected to achieved the post with a landslide victory.

[9] Mr. Reshari is a clergyman and former Minister for Intelligence. Notorious for toppling Ayatollah Montazeri, the named as successor to Ayatollah Khomeini (but who was deemed too liberal by many). In fact Reshari wrote a book, called *Political Memories*, in which he basically says that he was instrumental in Montazeri's fall from grace and furthermore states that he was right. He was in the Rafsanjani cabinet but was removed. Then he became the Leaders representative to the Hajj organisation.

[10] Mr. Zavarei was a non-clergy and worked in the Judiciary.

[11] Khatimi's father was a respected Ayatollah who had great influence in Yadz province and was the Friday prayer leader there. Furthermore he was the Imam's representative in Yadz province. *Personal note* – during the author's time in Yadz (Khatami's home province) it became evident to the author that while the population are very religious, this does not necessarily mean they follow the line of the conservative religious leadership in Iran. In fact, while pictures of the Supreme Leader proliferate throughout other towns and cities, it is the visage of Khatami and his father that adorn the shops and homes of Yadz.

[12] Khatami was formerly the Minister for Cultural and Islamic Guidance but because of his liberal practices he was impeached by the conservative Majlis in 1990/91 and subsequently sent into exile at Iran's National Library, where he stayed until the 1997 elections. During his tenure as Minister for Culture he did much to liberate the press and the arts from the constraints placed on them in the post revolutionary period.

[13] Speaking to a member of the leadership committee of the student movement, the Bureau for Solidarity, who were the first to propose Khatami's name as a possible candidate, I was told that his reformist credentials and his religious background were the deciding factors in their support for his candidature.

[14] In one interview, an unknown conservative likened Khatami to those who were responsible for the death of Imam Hossein. In Iran where religious mythology is very powerful such an assertion was seen as an act of desperation on the part of the conservatives.

The 'politically bankrupt people' being referred to here are the Freedom Movement of Iran, an outlawed opposition movement

[15] I saw an example of this phenomenon myself following the arrest and imprisonment of a relatively unknown cleric Muhammad Kadivar because of his liberal writings that were seen as destabilising to the state. In an editorial in the daily Salaam, the editor thanked the authorities for choosing the people's next leader. While Mr. Kadivar remains in prison his wife has been elected to the parliament in the 1999 elections.

[16] This interview took place on the 9th of March 1999.

[17] These protests took place to voice disapproval of the closure of the reformist newspaper *Salaam*.

[18] As quoted in the Daily Newspaper *Emrooz*, Sunday January 2, 2000.

[19] This is not usually the practice. Throughout all Friday prayer ceremonies and official speeches, the speaker traditionally stops to allow the crowd to vent their anger against imperialism or foreign governments (such as the US, Israel and England), in fact there is usually a person who incites and directs the crowd's chanting before and during speeches. The person responsible for this action in Tehran, Mr. Mortezai, is fondly known as the unofficial 'Minister for Slogans'.

[20] In fact, the official figure given by government sources was that one million demonstrators participated in this annual event. However, in reality from my personal observation, I believe the figure to be much less. Indeed, the serious decline in numbers from previous years could explain the reason why members of the Ministry for Information confiscated my camera during the demonstration (I was taking pictures of the crowds at the time).

[21] This was the case with Hojatoleslam Sadeq Khalkhali, the 'hanging judge', while nobody can doubt his hard-line ideology, he presented himself at the last elections as a reformist candidate.

[22] See further Nouri, A. (1378/1999), *A Hemlock for the 'Advocate of Reform'* (Tehran). This was the name given to the book published giving the account of Abdul Nouri's defence, it reads as a defence of republicanism and the ideals of political pluralism.

[23] A revolutionary centre established to facilitate the reconstruction of the 'ruins' inherited from the Pahlavi dynasty and to provide rural areas with more facilities.

[24] In a recent interview Hashemi Rafsanjani, recalled those *'Golden Days'* with Nouri in Parliament. See further *Hamshahri*, Monday the 10th of January 2000.

[25] Taken from (1990) *The Book of light, a collection of Imam Khomeini's Guidelines* (Tehran: The Organisation for Cultural Documents of the Islamic Revolution), pp. 104-105.

[26] Including Mr. Ali Khameini (the then President and now current Spiritual Leader), Hashemi Rafsanjani (the then Speaker of the Parliament) and Mir Hossein Mousavi (the Prime Minister).

[27] See further *Azad*, Tuesday December 14th 1999.

[28] This student leader subsequently found himself on the run following his part in the student riots, with calls by conservatives in the parliament for his execution for crimes against Islam.

[29] Interview carried out March 1999.

[30] Nouri, as he was a cleric was tried by the Special Clerical Court, which acts outside the constitution. His main argument in his defence was that the court was unconstitutional, as its creation had never been envisaged. Furthermore the court was charging Nouri with press violations, which he argued was outside the remit of the court as there was already a Press Court in the Iranian judicial system. Throughout his defence Nouri relied solely upon the Islamic Republic Constitution as passed following the revolution and which was amended in 1989.

[31] An interesting book by Abdi, A. (1378/2000), *Enqelab Aleyheh Tahir (Revolution against Humiliation)* (Tehran: 13 Bahman publications), makes a comparison between the pre-revolutionary state run by the Shah and the post-revolutionary administration of Hashemi Rafsanjani. The comparison is based upon the political and economic rule of the hierarchy.

[32] See chapter 4, where the binary opposition in the pre- and post-revolutionary system of government is measured. While there is a significant reduction, the level of binary system within the current system would lead us to believe that the potential for social unrest has not left Iranian society.

[33] Interview carried out March 1999.

[34] If one is to review correctly the history of Mossadeq's nationalist government, it becomes evident that the return of the Shah and the re-installation of the monarchy were assured when the clergy withdrew their support for Mossadeq. This was the true betrayal, not only of Mossadeq but also of the political freedom desired by every Iranian. Following the return of the Shah in 1953, the religious establishment were ostracised to a large extent from Iranian society. Yet their insistence to theocratic autocracy following the 1979 revolution has lead again to their current alienation in Iranian society.

[35] IRP – Islamic Republican Party, was an attempt in the post-revolutionary period to unite all Islamic forces under a similar banner and to facilitate the establishment of a one party state. Established by Ayatollah Beheshti, it was constantly troubled by internal division, which lead to it being disbanded in 1986 on Khomeini's orders.

[36] Most notably the second President of Iran Musavi-Ardabili and the founder of the IRP, a close disciple of Khomeini and the head of the Judiciary Ayatollah Beheshti.

[37] All figures related to the 'foundation' business are unofficial, however some estimates place their output at 3-4% of GDP, while others suggest that they account for up to 60% of annual economic activity. The largest Foundation *Bonyad Janbazan*, it is estimated to control between 20 and 30% of the Iranian economy, making it the largest non-governmental influence on the state's economic policy. Exact figures are impossible to obtain, as these foundations work outside the state structure and as 'religious' organisations do not have to pay government tax. The above estimates were obtained from an Iranian government source.

[38] Perhaps a brief note should be made that a spectrum of political views denoting left and right in Iranian politics, is very different in meaning when compared with what we would associate left and right in Western Europe. While the liberal/conservative (left/right) analogy is correct, in Iran it also denotes those who wish to reform the Islamic regime and those who wish to maintain it in its current form. There are also fractures along the left-right access. The left is also divided between left and right, with the left wanted to abolish the current form of government, while the right desire liberal reforms while wanting to maintain Islamic government. Furthermore the right can also be similarly divided between the modern right and the conservative right.

[39] Such as the newspaper *Jamea*, which after being closed down by the judiciary reopened under the name of *Neshat*, with the same personnel and layout. *Neshat* was also closed down, however the editors reopened, this time under the name of *Toose*. Over the past year and a half approximately 50 newspapers and journals have been closed and a variety of charges, from insulting Islam to undermining the State.

[40] This ministry was established in 1983 in an attempt to centralise the previously scattered job of intelligence gathering. Having been established through the amalgamation of a number of other bodies, it was highly factionalised, which is possibly one of the reasons for the revelations implicating the ministry in opposition murders in late 1988. The ministry was instrumental in providing information that would be used to disqualify potential reformists candidates for the *majlis* elections, to the Guardian Council. Following Khatami's election however and his gradual control over the ministry they issued a public statement stating that the ministry would no longer carry out this function.

[41] This conclusion is made from the interviews carried out with the electorate at a number of polling stations during the local elections in 1999 and the 2000 parliamentary elections.

Conclusion
Iran Today, Edging towards Unrest

Iran is at a crossroads, its revolution remains incomplete, its Islamic movement is in disarray and its system of governance is under attack, from within the system and from the general population. How Iran chooses to respond to its current situation is vital, not only for the people of Iran but also for the region and the international community. Stability in Iran is key to the region. When Iran is viewed in its geo-political environment, surrounded by countries with varying degrees of instability from Iraq to Afghanistan and the numerous former Republics of the Soviet Union, it becomes apparent that Iran's political and social development and its role as a stabilising factor in the region is of paramount importance to all who have concerns in this region.

In effect this work has involved the analysis of the Iranian political situation from three perspectives; Iran as an Islamic movement, a revolutionary movement and with reference to the complexities and intricacies of its unique political system. Through this research much can be concluded about the Islamic movement in general and Iran's attempts to Islamise society from above in particular. Iran is one of the few 'great' revolutions of the twentieth century and much can be learned about the process of revolution through viewing the development of Iranian society in this context. Finally, Iran's political system is a unique by-product of the social movement that overthrew the Shah. In fact, the current political structure is a fusion of the ideas of the revolution and the Islamic movement; it has been a defining factor in Iran's political development in the two decades since the fall of the Shah's regime.

Iranian Foreign Policy Development

Iran's maturation as an international actor can been seen through the development of its foreign policy over the past decade. The development of Iran's foreign policy from one based upon the exportation of the revolution to one espousing a 'dialogue amongst civilisations', is reflective of the changes that are occurring within Iranian society, as well as the dichotomy that is inherent in its political structure and ideology. Iran's relations with the outside world since the 1979 revolution have been difficult to say the least. It was largely isolated following the overthrow of the Shah and the takeover of the American Embassy in Tehran. It experienced a serious injustice during the Iran-Iraq war, when the fear of the Islamic movement and the desire to sustain their interests in the Gulf lead Western powers to financially and physically support the Iraqi regime against their neighbours. It was this policy that would come to haunt the West some years later with Iraq's invasion of Kuwait. While there is a need for reflection on the role of the West in the region, that was not the intention of this work. Suffice to say that Iran's political and foreign policy development did not occur in isolation and many developments in these policy areas can be traced to outside events. Khomeini's ideology, his view of society and the role of Islam, was given complete expression in his foreign policy statement of 'Neither East nor West but Islam'.

Khomeini initially viewed the revolution not in terms of boundaries but in terms of ideals. He viewed the Iranian revolution as being the culmination of the Islamic movement worldwide, as an example for other Muslim people to follow. He anticipated that the Iranian revolution would initiate an avalanche of Islamic sentiment and partnership that would see the perpetuation of Islamic theocracy abroad. Khomeini and his followers initiated a policy of 'exporting the revolution', where assistance was given to ideologically similar endeavours worldwide. The policy of exporting the revolution represents Khomeini's rejection of both communism and capitalism, and can find its roots in the Shia belief in fighting against oppression and tyranny. To fully understand this policy it has to be seen in the larger context of revolutionary theory. Promotion of a regime's ideology and revolutionary manifesto's abroad has always been a phenomenon of revolutions throughout history. The example of the American, French and Russian revolutions all bear witness to this. All states during this period tried to export their ideology, be it capitalism, communism or Islamic governance, viewed in this context Iran's exportation of the revolution was a means to achieve the same level of influence as other international actors. By intervention, America wants to make the world safe for democracy, witness the cases of Iran, Guatemala, El Salvador, Nicaragua and Afghanistan. By invasion, the Soviet Union wanted to make the world safe for socialism, witness the cases of Czechoslovakia and Afghanistan. By the exportation of its revolution, the Islamic Republic of Iran wanted to make the world safe for Islam, witness the cases of the Persian Gulf, Lebanon and Soviet Azerbaijan and Turkmenistan.[1] However, Khomeini's call for the oppressed of the world to unite remained unanswered. Many movements gladly accepted Iran's financial assistance, while shunning their advice and counsel. The advent of the Iran-Iraq war brought the utopian ideal of Muslim brotherhood to an end and with it the realisation that Khomeini's dream of a pan-Islamic movement, with him as leader, was impossible.

It is important to understand that such policies, as the exportation of the revolution, were a product of the chaos associated with a revolutionary situation and the irrational by-product of a new player in the international arena. Having replaced the previous regime the Islamic Republic in the initial years, found that it did not possess the experience or knowledge needed to formulate a cohesive foreign policy, based upon Iran's own identity and its place in the world. This in many ways led to Iran's international isolation and a high level of inconsistency in its policy dealings with the outside world throughout the early part of the 1980s. Iran entered into a new stage of policy development, as we have seen, following the end of the war with Iraq and the need for economic reconstruction. While during this period history continued to play a role in policy development,[2] its influence was decidedly decreased. Revolutionary idealism soon gave way to economic realism and a more pragmatic approach to foreign policy. Internally, the political atmosphere was more open. An open discourse on government policy began and newspapers were more critical in their discussions of current affairs. Externally, Iran was re-integrating into the world community after a decade of isolation. It was not as sensitive as during the war towards those who had taken Iraq's side. It was an Iran more aware of the political realities present in international relations. With the end of the war came the task of reconstruction. While Iran had succeeded in becoming almost self sufficient in the area of food production, due to the decline in the oil price during the 1980s outside investment was desperately needed to expand existing oil fields and to exploit new ones. Furthermore with the break-up of the Soviet Union and the dawning of the 'New World Order', a new international partner was needed. The European Union presented an interesting alternative for Iran. It could provide the economic support necessary for reconstruction, while enabling Iran to maintain its revolutionary ideals to some extent. In addition, the EU was viewed as a possible counter weight to the perceived US hegemony in the unipolar world created by the fall of communism. Furthermore; if monetary union was to become a reality the *euro* had the potential to rival the power of the US dollar on the international currency markets. That said, the Iranian system was still largely in the grasp of revolutionary zeal and so relations with Europe was justified to a large extent by the basis that they were based upon economics and had no real political content. Such a policy, while being economically expedient, did not show Iran to be a mature international actor, still viewing it policy formulation in terms of its history and revolutionary character.

The final stage of the revolution and Iran's foreign policy development occurred with the election of President Khatami in 1997. A new direction in foreign policy was taken and this is quite evident in the different slogans issued from the foreign ministry. Under President Rafsanjani the main foreign policy slogan was 'construction' therefore, all foreign relations were solely put into the context of economics. Under President Khatami the main slogan is one of 'development'. While this includes the ideas of construction espoused by Rafsanjani, it goes further and is not based solely on domestic needs. Iran began to view foreign policy in terms of culture and politics as well as economics. The ideas of the new administration are best espoused by Khatami's 'Dialogue Amongst Civilisations'. Dialogue Amongst Civilisations marks a new level of maturity in Iranian policy making and in Iranian State conduct. No longer is policy based on historical or purely economic considerations. Iran now appears, at least internationally, to possess the maturity to take its place as an international actor and potential guide to the Islamic community. Throughout the halls of power in Iran today, Khomeini's ideology, 'to perpetuate the revolution both at home and abroad',[3] is all but forgotten. In many ways we can see the development of Iran's foreign policy in tandem with the evolution of Iran's revolutionary process.

Khatami's call for 'dialogue amongst civilisations' provides the platform for the resolution of many of the questions that have remained concerning Iran's Islamic movement, revolutionary history and the instability inherent in the current political structure. A simple concept of dialogue amongst equals, of an open non-partisan discourse, has the potential to solve many of the problems that have faced Iran and the Islamic movement over the past two decades. The ethos of President Khatami's ideas can be implemented on a local, regional and international level. It has the potential to facilitate an open discourse within the Iranian political system, amongst Iran's fellow Muslim nations and between Iran, Islam and the world. For dialogue to commence in any setting, some basic fundamental ideals must be primarily accepted. Equality, acceptance of a diversity of opinion together with the recognition of those views that may not reflect your own, form the hallmark of both dialogue and democracy. Acceptance of dialogue internally in Iran can facilitate the peaceful transition from a revolutionary process towards a more stable system of politics that is both reflective of and responsive to the values of Iranian society. Furthermore, the recent attempts at *détente* between Iran and its neighbours, instigated again through the ideals of dialogue, has managed to turn the threat perception that previously existed in the region into potentially fruitful relations between Iran and its co-Persian Gulf countries. Possibly more profound than this, is the thawing of relations that has occurred between Iran and the international community. Beginning with President Khatami's speech at the United Nations in 1998, his subsequent interview with CNN's Christian Amanpour and his recent tour of European capitals, Iran since the election of Khatami was beginning to woo western leaders again. Indeed, in the aftermath of the US led coalition that toppled the Taleban, Iran was being perceived as a moderate Islamic nation and a potential ally in the region.

Iran and the Outside World

Iran's perception as a moderate Islamic nation appears to have changed somewhat in the aftermath of Bush's State of the Union Address in January 2002, when he declared Iran to be a member of the 'axis of evil' – a term coined by the US Administration to describe States that sponsor and export terrorism. Bush mentioned specifically Iraq, North Korean and Iran commenting that Iran 'aggressively pursues these weapons and exports terror, while an unelected few repress the Iranian peoples hope for freedom'.[4] Hailed as one of the most significant foreign policy speeches by his Administration, the 'axis of evil' comments have drawn criticism from across the Iranian political spectrum and have resulted in an evident hardening of positions, even from those within the reformist factions of government.[5] Scepticism as to the accuracy and the aim of these remarks by Bush was pronounced not only from within his own Republican party but also from the corridors of the NATO alliance. Iran's Supreme Leader accused Bush of speaking 'like a man thirsty for human blood'. President Khatami, who had earlier courted the possible opening of dialogue, criticised the remarks as being 'bellicose and insulting', while Kharrazi, the Foreign Minister, condemned Bush's 'arrogant remarks'. Secretary of State Powell later attempted to clarify the statement made by President Bush and to reiterate that the US was still willing to enter into dialogue with these States. However, it would appear that the damage had already been done and the possible thaw in relations that the operation in Afghanistan provided, has been missed. The consequence of this action by the US remains unknown. However, the alienation of reformist elements in the Iranian administration caused by the comments of the Bush administration does little to help the process of democratisation within Iran and the stability of the region as a whole. That said, while condemning the US comments the reformists were also quick to blame hard-line elements within Iran's political elite for facilitating these allegations of support for terrorism.

The categorisation of Iran as 'evil' came just as dialogue between Iran and the US appeared to be a distinct possibility, with overtures being made by Iran in recent years. During the CNN interview given by Khatami following his 1997 election, he spelled out his hopes concerning Iran's policy of dialogue, noting that America had 'an honourable' civilisation. Such statements are in stark contrast to Iran's Supreme Leader Khamenei's belief that anti-Americanism is 'the basic motto of the Iranian people' and must be 'preserved like a flag'.[6] Such contradictory statements are reflective of the Janus-faced policy that continues to emerge from the Iranian Administration and is due in no small part to the factionalised nature of Iranian politics. This has often resulted in Iran giving the international community conflicting versions of its true intentions. That said, Iran's handling of various regional disputes over the past decade has been commendable. It remained neutral during the Gulf War, while it had begun a dialogue with the United Arab Emirates over the Abu Musa island dispute. On the foreign policy front, since the election of President Khatami, Iranian officials had a number of successful meetings with their Saudi counterparts, have exchanged prisoners of war and begun the process of rapprochement with the other regional powers. Iran's response in the aftermath of the September 11th attacks was both sympathetic and measured. While condemning the attacks, the leadership also advocated a measured response. Their unwillingness to sign up to any form of US retaliation showed an independence of thought that few other countries were able to muster.

That said, Iran has rarely offered a unified image to the international community concerning its internal politics and its external intentions. The contradictory perspectives on politics and the fact that they can influence outside perceptions of Iran are a by-product of Iran's revolutionary process and the structure of its political system. Iranian society through the previous four elections[7] has overwhelmingly spoken in favour of reform. Although, through the analysis of Iran's revolution conducted in the writing of this book, it might better be termed a sign of support for the institutionalisation of the ideals of the revolution expressed prior to the 1979 overthrow of the Shah and his regime. These ideals have been described as a desire for republicanism (or rather a desire not to have power institutionalised within the confines of one political elite) and political, social and religious freedom. The Iranian movement was as much a social as a religious movement. It was a movement against the Shah's limitations of the political freedoms of his people, against his unwillingness to acknowledge the Islamic nature of Iranian society and against his family's monopolisation and abuse of the Iranian economy. These ideals are broadly representative of the opposition movement of 1979. In many ways, it was a movement in favour of greater pluralism – political, economic and religious. The question which part of this study posed was whether these ideals have been fulfilled through the creation of the Islamic Republic and the installation of a theocratic political system based on the ideals of Khomeini and his concept of *veleyat-e faqih*. This study has found that these ideals have not been fulfilled and that Iranian revolution remains wholly incomplete. Even though the Iranian political system espoused Islam as its guiding principle, many within the community believe that the system has lost touch with Islam and the feelings of the electorate. By ideologising Islam, the post 1979 administration brought a sense of rigidity to Islam that has seriously damaged its reputation amongst the faithful in Iran. One of the main tenets of Shia Islam is its support for, and guidance of, the oppressed in society. Ever since the time of Imam Husayn, the Shia ulema have acted as the moral conscience of the temporal leadership. The ulema's quietist approach to political leadership has often been criticised as being unofficially supportive of the status quo and various autocratic regimes. While the previous statement is true, the ulema's unwillingness to corrupt its values through direct political participation has enabled it to maintain its moral stance and to survive as a guiding force in Iranian society throughout the many changes in temporal leadership that have occurred.

Iran is the only product of the Islamic movement of the 1970s that turned its quest for a more Islamic society into direct political control. However, with over two decades of Islamic government in Iran, the question should now be asked whether the move to directly involve the clergy in the functioning of government has assisted or impeded the proliferation of Islam in Iranian society. While official figures are not available, the primary research of this work has found that attendance at religious services have consistently declined in Iran over the past decade. The Islamic movement in Iran is in perilous danger of becoming dislocated from the Iranian people, who view the values of their political system as being inconsistent with their own views on government and society. By indelibly linking Islam with the conduct of the Iranian State, the clergy have posed the most serious threat to traditional Islam in Iran, more so than any autocratic regime could ever have mustered through their oppression of the faith. Contrary to the image of Iran in the aftermath of 1979, when prayer meetings and religious gatherings became the method through which the government could mobilise the masses, Islam in Iran today is fast re-becoming a personal endeavour. The clergy and through them Islam has been tainted by political mismanagement and suppression.

Through the analysis of revolution and post-1979 Iran, it was suggested that Iran's revolution is a process that is still continuing. This claim was substantiated by the fact that the initial goals of the revolutionaries of pre-1979 Iran have remained unfulfilled. Furthermore, it is these same people that are leading the calls for reform within the current regime. Through the fieldwork carried out in Iran, these true principles of the revolution can be seen to be a desire for republicanism, political pluralism and an acceptance of Iran's Islamic culture and heritage. By focusing solely on the last of these ideals the clergy, the most organised political elite in the aftermath of the overthrow of the Shah, were able to misappropriate the revolution. While, in the aftermath of Khomeini's return from exile, the majority of the opposition activists from across the political spectrum were able to agree that republicanism should be the basis of the future government, they were unable to agree on what structure this future administration should take. Most views were conflicting and undeveloped, while Khomeini and his followers had a well-developed template for Islamic government. The true ideals of this template remained largely unknown, until after the referendum on the establishment of an Islamic government in late 1979. Khomeini's calls for the continuation of the revolution until all the vestiges of the former regime were gone, provided an atmosphere of chaos within which his plans for Islamic government could be developed uninterrupted. That said, the evidence points to the belief that Khomeini's initial intentions were to form a government where the Supreme Leadership was to have the role of moral guardian of society and not the undemocratic role, which we currently associate with the position. Much of Khomeini's early declarations and actions upon his return from exile point to this conclusion. The change in direction of the revolution, of the political system and the ideology of Khomeini came in early 1980, when the influence of conservative clergy came to the fore within his inner circle.

Those who supported Khomeini's movement – the traditional *bazaari* who provided the financial support and the clergy who mobilised the faithful – wanted their efforts to bear tangible fruit. The traditional bazaar financed the revolution largely because of their exclusion from the fruits of the Iranian economy, due to the monopolisation by the Shah's family of government contracts and the larger importation contracts. In the aftermath of 1979 it was the traditional bazaar who monopolised economic activity preventing the economic pluralism that was one of the cornerstones of the revolution. In turn, they continued their financial support for the conservative factions within the Iranian clergy who could ensure the continuation of their economic position. It was an alliance that had mutual benefits, as the conservative clergy used this financial support to monopolise political power and to ensure the continuation of their Islamic regime, in contrast to other pluralistic forms of government that could undermine this bazaar-clergy alliance. Whether Khomeini felt threatened by the strength of the conservative factions within the clergy, or whether he began to believe their rhetoric, (that democratic government would lead to the alienation of Islam within Iranian society) the fact remains that Khomeini effectively withdrew his support for political pluralism when he supported the impeachment of Iran's first democratically elected president Bani Sadr, by the conservative led *majlis*.

Iran – A Revolution Unresolved?

The analysis of the current available literature on the theory of revolution, found that the situation in Iran substantiated most of the theory available to explain this phenomenon. That said, the theories were found lacking when attempting to find an explanation for the developments that have occurred in Iran over the past two decades. If Iran's revolution was completed with the overthrow of the Shah and the establishment of an Islamic Republic, why is there continued socio-political unrest over two decades later? While many might argue that this unrest is not related to the previous events which overthrew the Shah, this study firmly repudiates such as assertion. Furthermore, the current available literatures' dependence on ambiguous ideas, such as the change in social values, together with the intangibility and difficulty in measuring such ideas, meant that a more representative definition of revolution was needed in light of the events that have occurred in Iran. Figure one was developed to assist the categorisation of socio-political upheavals and while this clarifies our understanding of the current literature, there was a need for greater tangibility in measuring when and where socio-political conflicts are likely to occur. To achieve this the concept of binary opposition was incorporated into the analysis on revolution, to assess the tangible changes in society that results from revolutionary activity. A definition of revolution was developed, that attempted to incorporate the ideas of socio-political change as outlined by previous theories and in addition it linked the notion of revolution with the idea of political evolution and electorate empowerment. At the core of this definition is the belief that, like Marxism, revolution is a result of an evolutionary process caused by alienation. However, this change is not provoked by economic considerations, but by the desire for greater political participation by the masses. The core of this new perspective on revolution is the idea that socio-political change is viewed in terms of the re-allocation of power within the state. It is argued that all forms of socio-political change from value alternation to elite change can be viewed in this context.

Understanding revolution in terms of the re-allocation of power, together with the belief that revolution is provoked by the desire for a greater political say by the masses (which is being prevented through either autocratic or dictatorial means), enables us to overcome the previous problems of intangibility presented by the other theories on revolution. Utilising binary opposition in the measurement of the allocation of power facilitates a quantification of revolutionary change. Binary opposition, in this respect, was defined as the difference between the state and the population, measured through the characteristics of the particular political system in force that reflects this relationship. The practical manifestation of these ideas was possible by analysing the pre- and post-1979 political systems in Iran and the results substantiated the idea that the Iranian revolution is a process continuing even today. Within the model developed, using binary opposition, the area after which socio-political unrest is decreased to the extend of being highly unlikely, is termed the zone of relative equilibrium and denotes a society that may not be fully content with its political system, but is content to the extent that they are unwilling to take to the streets to have it changed. The results of the analysis from the Iranian political system are interesting. The results show that significant progress has been made towards electorate empowerment in the years following the establishment of the Islamic Republic. However, it also highlights that Iranian society is still in a position of revolutionary flux. This is substantiated through a review of the contemporary politics of Iran, where the reformist and student movements have taken to the streets on a number of occasions in the previous year in their attempt to convince the government of the need for substantial changes to the Iranian political system. A further by-product of the binary opposition analysis is that the facets of the political system under review that cause the socio-political unrest can be highlighted. In Iran, it was evident from the primary research carried out for this work that the curtailment of voter choice through the pre-selection of candidates has lead to voter discontent. Furthermore, as the social protests over the last number of years have shown, the electorate do not believe in the ability of the Iranian political system to change or mirror the wishes of society. One of the main messages of Khatami's electoral campaign was the stamping out of 'monopolies', both political and economic. That said, the student protests of 1999 have shown the growing frustration and dissatisfaction with the ability of the Khatami administration to deliver these reforms.

The examination of the contemporary political environment in Iran corroborated most of the above conclusions. Religious participation is on the decrease, while disillusionment with the current political structure is increasing. The ability of the Khatami administration to bring about real change remains unproven. There are even signs within the administration itself of increased frustration at the conservatives ability to undermine liberal reforms, acting outside of the constitution on many occasions. In many ways the election of President Khatami in 1997 is representative of the changes that have occurred in the values of Iranian society. A majority of Iran's population is under the age of twenty-five, they do not remember life under the Shah, nor are they swayed easily by revolutionary rhetoric. Like the generation before them, they too crave the trappings of materialism, except now this is not expressed in support for Islamic associations but in opposition to the political structure that prevents them from achieving their goal. This section of society is aided and assisted in its task by the mass of revolutionaries who have witnessed the manipulation of their revolution. There is a wave of strong reformist sentiment in Iran today. If the conservatives do not accept the views of the overwhelming majority, there is a very real chance of further disruption to the precarious calm that resides over Iranian society. President Khatami is a product of the system; he is a cleric whilst being a reformist. He does not want to overthrow the political system of the Islamic Republic, but is attempting to implement changes to the system that can create a society based on economic and political pluralism. A task that is easier said than done. With the conservative and the traditional bazaar entrenched in control of the economic and political life of the country, it is difficult to envisage change without a serious overhaul of the current political structures. June 2001 saw the re-election of President Khatami with an overwhelming and majority. While his victory was assured following his announcement to seek re-election, the size of his majority was indicative of his support within the electorate. While his victory in 1997 could have been termed a vote against the establishment, the 2001 election was without doubt a vote in favour of reform. That said, Iran remains in a precarious socio-political position, with the Iranian population overwhelmingly in favour of change and an administration unable and in some cases unwilling to provide this change. The reformist movement in Iran now control the office of the president, the parliament and the local councils. Khatami's control of the key ministries of the Interior and, Islamic Culture and Guidance has done much to provide the Iranian people with a diversity of views and an open political debate. It also eroded some of the potential that the conservatives had to undermine the reformist movement. That said, through our previous analysis of the

Iranian political structure, it is evident that true political power rests outside of these institutions, in institutions that are neither responsible to nor dependant upon the support of the Iranian people. The main test of Khatami's second term will be his ability to reform the balance of power within the institutional structure of the State, for without such change other methods of instituting change will occur. If the people believe that they cannot encourage change through constitutional means, they will inevitable turn towards other means. Therefore, while Khatami was hailed as a hero of the reformist movement with his election in 1997, he may soon become its main stumbling block towards serious change. In many ways Khatami's election provided the reformist movement with the illusion of change, leading it to believe that reform was possible from within the system. While there has been a considerable movement over the last number of years in Iranian foreign relations with the West, including an increase in the freedom of the press, life for the majority of Iranians remains relatively the same. The battle that Khatami and his reformist allies are fighting is a limited one and perhaps a time will come, in the not to distant future, when the larger reformist movement will have to choose whether their goals can be achieve through working with Khatami and his allies.

The reformists are not assisted in their goals by the political structure that has developed since 1979. Through various stages of development a level of institutional pluralism has crept into the Iranian political structure. As such, no distinct or clear division of political power has occurred. Shrouded in ambiguity, Iran's political structure is tipped in favour of those institutions that act outside the system. From the clerical courts to the revolutionary guards and the Islamic foundations, all of these institutions act outside the constitution, are controlled from outside the political system and have immense influence on a system that is powerless to control or limit their power. The conservative clergy have a shadow political structure; they are not limited by the need for electoral support or the constraints imposed by constitutional law. This shadow political structure is utilised to impose their views and their interpretation of Islam and to maintain their monopolistic and autocratic control over the Iranian nation. How can those who believe in democracy defeat an enemy unrestrained by such principles? While the answer to this question must be, through democratic means, such restraint and patience is difficult for a population that suffers from the absence of a just political system. As it is, tensions within Iranian society have been on the increase since the conservatives lost control of the parliament to factions favourable to Khatami's reformist program. While the conservatives still have de facto veto through the Guardian Council over all reformist legislation that might be passed by the parliament, they have initiated a vigorous campaign to undermine and discredit reformist activists throughout the country. The Iranian institutional make-up since the re-election of Khatami has maintained its division between conservative and reformist. That said, the reformist movement encouraged by the re-election of President Khatami, has set about attempting to instigate his reform aspirations. The conservatives for their part have continued to undermine and directly attack the reformist power bases. Following a call from the Supreme Leader to stamp out corruption, the judiciary has begun to bring cases against a number of parliamentary deputies in early 2002 and have continued the closure of reformist newspapers and the imprisonment of journalists and editors. The judiciary is correctly seen as a bastion of right wing power. One of the main targets of their attack is Hossein Loghmanian, an elected member of the *majlis* for the western city of Hamedan. He was arrested in early January 2002 for remarks he made in the parliament concerning the judiciary. He was charged, found guilty and sentenced to ten month's imprisonment. This action on the part of the judiciary incensed already tense relations between the parliament and the judiciary, with over sixty members of parliament staging a walk out in support of their imprisoned colleague. By imprisoning Loghmanian the Judiciary, effectively violated the constitutional provision of parliamentary immunity. President Khatami's assertions that the rule of law and the supremacy of the constitution should be upheld was countered by the judiciary who contended that Loghmanian and other MPs had broken the law and that there should be no immunity for that. Calls for the Supreme Leader to intervene initially went unanswered, while the western press bemoaned the evident lack of freedom of speech within the Iranian establishment. It was only when the Speaker of the House Mr. Karrubi,[8] a reformist with close ties to the conservatives, threatened to paralyse parliament by leaving the Speakers chair empty, did the Supreme Leader intervene. The manner of the intervention however did little to quell the fears of the reformists nor did it clarify his view of the corruption investigation being carried out in his name by the conservative judiciary and revolutionary courts. Ayatollah Khamenei pardoned Loghmanian while not exonerating him of his charges. Many Iranians were left wondering about the Leader's view on the judiciary's handling of the anti-corruption campaign or whether he agreed with the reformist claims that the Judiciary was being used by conservatives to undermine the democratic institutions of the State. It left the political environment uncertain and the Iranian people to ponder what would happen when the next parliamentary deputy is jailed or when the 'anti-corruption' drive again threatens the immunity of parliament and the stability of political institutions. What the standoff between parliament and the Leader in January 2002 showed was that even the more conservative members of the Khatami's reformist movement (such as Mr. Karrubi) are becoming frustrated with the political in-fighting and pace of change. The move by Mr. Karrubi to force the Leader to take a position on the issue of Mr. Loghmanian's detention was a brave move and reminiscent of the Tobacco Boycott, which was one of the most important preludes to the 1907 Constitutional Revolution in Iran. Like the Tobacco Boycott, this stand-off proved that the conservatives were not invincible. It also stripped the Leader of his 'charismatic' position and reduced him to a mere political player. Furthermore, it clearly showed that the Leader was not all-powerful and highlighted that if the people (or their representatives) continue to insist on change, that the conservatives will inevitable have to grant that change or risk losing their privileged position.

September 11th has drastically changed the political environment within which Iran's leaders find themselves. The events of September 11th and the build up of the alliance against terrorism augmented the tensions within the Iranian establishment. There was varying views amongst ordinary Iranians. With such a large Iranian Diaspora and with close ties between many ordinary Iranians and relatives in the US, it was natural that there was a significant outpouring of sympathy for those who suffered from the attacks, with even a prayer vigil being held in Tehran for the victims. The Iranian government, echoing the sentiments of the world community, condemned the attacks. That said, Iranian society was still divided about the demands of support by the US administration. Relations between Iran and the US have always been tense, with US sanctions against Iran being perceived as unjust and the American presence in the Persian Gulf as being an example of its hegemonic design and imperialistic tendencies in the region. Ayatollah Khamenei whose speeches are usually splattered with anti-American sentiments, was unequivocal in his condemnation of the attacks, 'Mass killings of human beings are catastrophic acts which are condemned wherever they may happen and whoever the perpetrators and the victims may be.' He did however qualify his statement and Iran's position when he warned that Iran would also condemn any large-scale military operation against Afghanistan. The Iranian administration was by no means sympathetic to the Taleban regime, having almost gone to war with Afghanistan in 1998 following the killing of ten Iranian diplomats when the Taleban overran Mazar-i-Sherif. They were however even more sceptical of US interests in the region, viewing the placing of US troops in either Pakistan or another regional country, as a serious threat to Iranian interests and regional independence. President Khatami for his part, while condemning the attacks on the US, advised against a rash and emotional response by the international community and indicated that any response should be co-ordinated through the United Nations. All sides across the political spectrum in Iran are wary of the effect that a large scale US military intervention on its eastern border would have on the political stability in Iran. Not only because of the inevitable influx of refugees that Iran would have to deal with,[9] but also many were worried at how the conservative factions within the Iranian political elite would manipulate the situation. The conservative press in Iran while condemning the attacks were adamant as to the causes of the attacks. The *Tehran Times*, the English speaking newspaper in Tehran ran a headline in the aftermath of the attacks stating that the US was 'Paying the price for its blind support of a racist regime', alluding to the continued US support for Israel, adding that 'When a government is prepared to go against all internationally-accepted principles in support of a racist and criminal regime, it cannot expect to escape unscathed.'[10] Other right wing newspapers carried similar stories highlighting their views of America's misguided policies abroad being the cause of this attack on the American homeland, 'We are sorry for those Americans who have been ignorant of the implications of their governments' policies.' Many ordinary citizen across the Middle East and in Iran, equate what happened in the US as being directly related to failure by numerous administrations to find a solution to the Middle East crisis.

Throughout this period the United States has financially and militarily supported the Israeli State and therefore many throughout the Middles East equate Israel and America as being one and the same. As unseemly as it may appear, some in the Middle East believe that America was finally getting a taste of the destruction and suffering that its foreign policy has caused throughout the world. It was hoped by many that the carnage that was unjustly wrought on the United States would lead in some manner to a revision of American policies abroad, to the review of how and why the US is held in such negative light by many throughout the world. Instead, the US administration lashed out against more innocent civilians in a campaign that it termed as a battle of good against evil, democracy and freedom against fanatical terrorism. Far from solving the misunderstanding between the West and the developing world, it has widened the gulf of misapprehension and intensified the hatreds and grievances. The United States maintains its realist agenda in world affairs and appears willing to sideline the democratic values that it purports to be defending. Its 'with us or against us' policy has led the United States to work closely with the Pakistani administration of General Musharraf, the self-declared President of Pakistan, whose predecessors had financially and ideologically supported the Taleban regime.

As for Iran, the Taleban regime in Afghanistan has played an interesting role in the internal political development of Iran. Leaving aside the animosity between Iran and Afghanistan that goes back to the Afghan invasion in 1722, Iran always perceived the Taleban regime as a destabilizing force in the region. The Shia-Sunni divide did little to ease this disquiet, with the Iranian administration depicting the Taleban government as being fundamentalists and unrepresentative of the true message of Islam. This allowed many within Iranian society to question their own strict views on issues such as the freedom of women and the press. The government, in response, attempted to disassociate themselves from the Taleban version of Islam by allowing greater social freedoms. That said, the fall of the Taleban also brings to light some additional challenges to Iran as regards its regional policy and how its politicians will react to the developments on its eastern border. Regionally, both Iran and Pakistan have a strong role to play in ensuring, or rather in not preventing, that Afghanistan has a peaceful transition period and that its society does not slide back into political anarchy. Iran openly supported the Northern Alliance, who are largely Shi'ite and from non-Pustun tribes. The fall of the Taleban therefore was widely welcomed by Iran and it spent little time in exercising its influence throughout the western region of Afghanistan. That region that is now largely controlled by the Hezbi Wahdat and Jamiat-i-Islami, Shia factions within the Northern Alliance, who are sympathetic to Iranian interests in the region. They have also publicly supported the interim government of Mr. Karzai. There have, however, been reports that Iranian agents have been in and around the city of Heart, ensuring the local leadership there are sensitive to Iranian interests. Such reports together with the US continued insistence of alleging Iranian government involvement in international terrorism do not bode well for future relations between these two powers. While there is little doubt that Iran, in the early period of the revolution, gave financial and other support, to groups with ideological similar goals, there is also little doubt that if such support is continuing today it is most definitely not officially sanctioned. It is imperative for the international community and the Bush administration in particular, to have an understanding of the intricate and delicate balance within the Iranian administration: between the reformists and those who would prefer, and benefit, from a return to the isolationist and divisive relations of the 1980s.

In conclusion, Iran's Islamic movement has failed in its attempt to Islamise Iranian politics, instead it has politicised Islam and has damaged the reputation of the faith and the clergy, to the core. Iran's political system remains both complex and ambiguous, the balance of power between right and left, conservative and reformism, between government and non-government political influence remains blurred. The establishment of a party system could perhaps clear up much of this ambiguity, however the reformist movement will have to re-assess its goals and tactics in light of Khatami's re-election and the change in the geopolitical map following the September 11th attacks on the US. Iran's future is balanced precariously between Khatami's ability to implement the change and the system's apparent inability to accept it. He would do well to heed De Tocqueville's analysis of revolution,

> it is not always the going from bad to worse that causes a revolution. It happens more often that a people who have borne without complaint, and apparently without feeling, the most oppressive of laws, then throw them off violently so as their weight lightens. The system that a revolution destroys is almost always better than that which immediately succeeds it, and experience teaches that the most dangerous moment for a bad government is usually that in which it begins to reform.[11]

Notes

[1] Ramazani, R.K. (1983), 'Iran's Export of the Revolution: Politics, Ends and Means', in *Religion and Politics in Iran* (New Haven: Yale University Press), and Ramazani, R. (1986), *Revolutionary Iran - Challenges and Responses in the Middle East* (Baltimore, Johns Hopkins University Press).
[2] This time history being confined to who sided with Iran or Iraq during the eight-year war.
[3] Constitution of the Islamic Republic of Iran article 152 to 155.
[4] Taken form the transcripts of the State of the Union Address 2002
[5] In fact, following the speech and the absence of any attempt by the British government to distance themselves from Bush's comments. The Iranian government reject the appointment of Britain's new Ambassador to Tehran. Hopes of a thaw in British-Iranian relations therefore appear to have been put on hold.
[6] As quoted in Muravchik, J. and Gedmin, J., 'Why Iran Is (Still) a Menace', *Commentary*, July 1997.
[7] The presidential elections of 1997, the local elections of 1999, the parliamentary elections of 2000 and the Presidential elections in June 2001.
[8] Mr. Karrubi is one of the more conservative member of Khatami's reformist movement, he has a notorious record of radicalism (in a conservative sense) in 1980s, including heading the bloody demonstration in Saudi Arabia (during the Hajj pilgrimage) in 1987 which resulted in more than 400 deaths.
[9] Iran was already host to some two million Afghan refugees prior to the September attacks.
[10] Tehran Times 12th of September 2001.
[11] De Tocqueville, A., *La'Ancien Regime et La Revolution* (1856, Book II, Chapter 5).

Glossary I
People, Places and Organisations in Pre- and Post-1979 Iran

Ayatollah Ruhollah Khomeini – (1902-1989), an Islamic religious leader who was one of the main ideological leaders of the 1979 revolution and the main architect of the post-1979 political system. Named as *velayet-e faqih* for life under the 1980 constitution, he died in 1989 having left an indelible mark in the socio-political life of post-1979 Iran.

Ayatollah Seyed Ali Khamenei – is the current supreme and spiritual guide and the official successor of the late Ayatollah Seyed Ruhollah Khomeini. In keeping with the Shi'ia Islamic principles of governance, the Constitution of Islamic Republic provides for the establishment of leadership by a *faqih* (Jurisprudent) who, based on his qualifications, supervises and correlates government policies as *velayet-e faqih* (Leader) with divine decrees. As such, Ayatollah Khamenei is considered the leader of the Islamic Revolution, the Commander-In-Chief of the armed forces and the ultimate authority in Iran.

Hojatoleslam Mohammad Khatami – was elected as Iran's president in a surprising landslide victory in May 1997. He is generally considered to be a moderate cleric with liberal views on the role of women in the society. President Khatami's public resume since the revolution includes a seat in Iran's parliament (Majlis), the director of Iran's National Library, President's advisor in cultural affairs and his most controversial and significant job was as a cabinet minister for 10 years when he headed the Ministry of Culture and Islamic Guidance. It was this post from which he was forced to resign because he had become too liberal, allowing too much freedom in the media. In his post as the President of the Islamic Republic of Iran Khatami heads the cabinet and serves as chief of the executive branch and the government of Iran. Khatami's strong victory in both the 1997 and 2001 Presidential Elections was mainly contributed to the support of women and the youth of Iran who have placed high hopes in his promise of turning around the rising rate of inflation, moderating the social climate and creating new educational and economic opportunities for everyone.

Hojatoleslam Ali Akbar Hashemi Rafsanjani – ended his second 4-year term as the President of the Islamic Republic of Iran in July of 1997 when he transferred the powers of presidency to Mohammad Khatami. Rafsanjani is considered a charismatic cleric whose social and political views are somewhat more moderate than many hardline clergy but less liberal than the majority of the reformist movement. Rafsanjani's political activism dates back to the 1960s and 1970s when he fought against the U.S. backed regime of the late Shah of Iran. He quickly became a trusted and close aide of the late Ayatollah Khomeini. Rafsanjani's current position as the head of a powerful council of expediency (a consultative council whose members are chosen by the Leader) ensures his continued and powerful presence in Iran's political scene.

Ayatollah Hossein Ali Montazeri – The late Ayatollah Khomeini once hailed Hossein Ali Montazeri as 'the fruit of my life'. Montazeri was a leading religious figure in Iran, groomed as the future leader of the country. He was a long-standing companion of Khomeini, in the 1960s; he supported Khomeini, who had been exiled to Iraq. Subsequently, Montazeri was arrested and spent a couple of years in jail during the 1960s and 1970s. After the victory of the Islamic revolution in 1979, he was carefully groomed by Khomeini to become his successor and was officially ordained as the 'designated successor to the leader' by the all cleric body, 'the Assembly of Experts'. But relations between Khomeini and Montazeri began to sour after 1981 and the split became apparent after the leak in March 1989 of Montazeri's letters to Khomeini, in which he had sharply criticised a number of the ruler's decrees. Soon afterwards, Khomeini publicly disgraced Montazeri and removed him from his position. Today, the 79 year old Montazeri is a recluse, but not by choice. Two guards watch his house in the Iranian city of Qom, ensuring that he receives no visitors. His theological school has closed, his books have been banned, and his bank accounts have reportedly been frozen, leaving him with no source of income. He is a virtual exile in his own city.

Abdullah Nouri – is a cleric with impeccable revolutionary credentials, who was targeted by hardliners following the 1997 presidential elections for being too liberal. He was arrested and tried on dubious charges by the unconstitutional Clerical Court and was sentenced to 5 years imprisonment in 1999.

Abol Hassan Bani Sadr – is an Islamic intellectual and Iran's first post-1979 president. While originally viewed as a favoured 'son' of Khomeini, fear in his belief in liberal democracy led Khomeini to withdraw his support for Bani Sadr and this led directly to his impeachment and flight into exile. He currently lives in Paris.

Ayatollah Beheshti – was a close associate and former student of Khomeini's. He was the Head of the Judiciary following the 1979 revolution and was the leading force behind the formation of the Islamic Republican Party (IRP). He was killed in a MKO (Mujahedin-e Khalq) bomb attack in 1981.

Ayatollah Kashani – was the Islamic leader in the *majlis* in the early 1950s, his initial support for the Mossadegh's nationalist government enabled its survival. However, his feelings of 'betrayal' following his exclusion from Mossadegh's cabinet led to his withdrawal of support and hastened the return of the Shah in 1953.

Ayatollah Mohammad Hosayn Borujerdi – was the main ideological and religious influence on Khomeini following the death of Ayatollah Ha'eri. Borujerdi emerged in late 1946 as the highest-ranking Shia clergy in Iran (after the death of Ayatollah Hossein Qomi). Like Ha'eri he also believed that the clergy should remain out of politics, however the fact that he maintained an amiable relationship with the state led many to believe that he supported the *status quo* in Iranian politics. His death in March 1961 enabled Khomeini to leave behind his previous quietist approach to politics.

Ayatollah Mottahari – a former student of Khomeini's, he was Khomeini's main contact in the Coalition of Islamic Societies during his years in exile. He was also a prominent Islamic theorist of the time, whose views on society, religion and politics are in contrast to those held by Shariati. Rejecting any connection between Islam and Marxists, his views that man is created unequal can be seen as being Platonic in nature, with the clergy being the only ones in society with the depth of understanding of the Quran necessary to guide society effectively.

Ayatollah Shariatmadra – was a vocal opponent to Khomeini the absolute rule of the *faqih*. His supporters in Tabriz formed the Muslim People's Republican Party (MPRP) and staged a revolt, soon after the establishment of the Islamic Republic. In January 1980 Khomeini outlawed the party, put Shariatmadrai under house arrest and declared that he was no longer to be considered an Ayatollah. This was a turning point in the new regime, where Khomeini showed his intolerance of any sort of opposition, even from those within the Shi'a clergy.

Ayatollah Taleqani – was an Islamic intellectual and cleric of the Iranian opposition movement against the Shah. Taleqani viewed communism and Islam as being mutually compatible, citing the communal nature of Islam, its desire to combat class difference and materialism. While he became associated with the *Mujahedin*, he was closer to Islamic intellectuals such as Bazargan and his Freedom Movement, as he endorsed democratic ideals and the notion of a free pluralist society.

Coalition of Islamic Societies – was developed with the support of a number of *bazaari* merchants to support Khomeini's growing opposition movement. Khomeini placed his closest students and allies to supervise the Coalition's development. Many of the post-revolutionary leaders of Iran can trace their political roots to the Coalition and their role in disseminating Khomeini's word. The Coalition grew and its influence spread to other cities and other bazaars. In the years that followed, the Coalition became an indispensable tool for mobilizing the masses, for disseminating information and for the financial resources that were necessary to fund the course of Khomeini's revolutionary activities.

Confederation of Iranian Students Abroad – was an opposition movement against the Shah that was comprised of Iranian students studying abroad, mainly in the US and Europe. Through their offering of ideas and financial assistance, they brought the plight of their compatriots at home to the wider international audience.

Dr. Ali Shariati – was a political and religious philosopher. Dubbed the 'Luther of the Islamic world' his writings throughout the 1960s and 1970s reflect the changes that were occurring in the Islamic movement in Iran at the time. His views, while in many ways being similar to Khomeini's distrust of the clergy, ultimately put him in opposition to Khomeini's views of clerical rule. He died in 1978.

Dr. Soroush – a political and religious philosopher, in the tradition of Shariati. He currently resides in Tehran. His lectures and public speaking appointments are continually disrupted by more conservative elements of the political spectrum.

Ebrahim Yazdi – known as engineer Yazdi, he was a student in the lead up to the 1979 revolution. He joined Khomeini in Paris before his return and is an example of the fate of Islamic intellectuals in the post-1979 administration. He was initially appointed as foreign minister but impeached and forced to remain on the fringes of Iranian politics.

Feda'iyan-e Khalq – or the *Devotees of Islam* was established shortly after WWII and led by a young cleric Nawab Safawi. It was formed with the aim of representing the growing discontent with the reforms of modernisation of Reza Shah. Initially established as a forum for clerical opposition to the sidelining of Islamic law, it grew into an organisation representing the discontent amongst the bazaari's and the poorer segments of society that were left behind by Iran's modernisation programme. It became a radical organisation in the 1950s and 1960s and was allegedly responsibility for a number of assassinations of government officials, including the Prime Minister Hassan Ali Mansour in 1965.

Freedom Movement – was established by Medhi Bazargan and espoused Islamic and liberal democratic values. It influential in the transition government established by Khomeini upon his return from exile. However, continually side-lined by the Revolutionary Council, it was forced from the political scene following Bazargan's resignation as prime Minister in 1981. The organisation has remained in opposition to clerical rule ever since.

Haggani Seminary – was an influential (unofficial) political force in the post-1979 period. While prior to 1979, they advocated a quietist approach to clerical involvement in politics, however following the 1979 revolution, having tasted the trappings of power; this group of conservative clergy advocated the total control of the socio-political life of Iran by the clerical classes. They were instrumental in the overthrow of the Islamic intellectuals from power in early 1981 and remain a formidable political force in Iran today.

Ansare Hezbullah – play the role of foot soldiers for the Islamic conservatives. There is abundant evidence that the group receive organisational and financial support from the Office of the Leader, the Revolutionary Guards, the Intelligence Service, and those Islamic organisations such as the Organisation for Islamic Propagation and the Committee for [Public] Call to Prayers. However, Ansar categorically denies any connection with State–run institutes and claims to be a grassroots organisation with voluntary membership comprised of all sectors of Iranian society.

Hojatoleslam Khalkhali – was know after the revolution as the 'Butcher of Tehran', for his role as a religious prosecutor. He is an example of the re-invention of the far–right as reformists in the post-1997 period. While his hard-line credentials cannot be questioned, Khalkhali presented himself as a reformist candidate in the 2000 parliamentary elections.

Imam Ali – the first Imam and the fourth Caliph, he is equally revered by Shia's and Sunni's alike. The cousin and son in law of the Prophet Muhammad, he was seen to be the closest living relative by the Shia's and it was therefore argued that he should be the Prophet's natural successor.

Imam Husayn – the third Imam of the Shia faith, he is the second son of Ali, who defended the right of succession by the House of the Prophet. On the morning of the tenth day of the month of Muharram in 680 AD, Husayn and his small band of followers were met at Karbála (in modern day Iraq) by an overwhelming force loyal to the Caliph Yazid. Heavily outnumbered, Husayn and his followers perished but this date has become a watershed in Islamic and Shia history.

Imam Mahdi – the twelfth Imam (as believed by the Twelver sect of Shi'ism, which is the predominant sect in Iran), who went into occultation and who will return at the end of time to create a just and equal society. Also known as the Hidden Imam.

Islamic Republican Party (IRP) – was an attempt in the post-revolutionary period to unite all Islamic forces under the one banner and to facilitate the establishment of a one–party State. Established by Ayatollah Beheshti, it was constantly troubled by internal division, which led to it being disbanded in 1986 on Khomeini's orders.

Mehdi Bazargan – was the founder of the Freedom Movement. A firm believer in constitutional politics, he was a widely respected politician and so his appointment by Khomeini as the transitional prime minister in February 1979 gave many secularists the impression that the clergy would return to their mosques and allow the intelligentsia to run the new administration. However the storming of the US Embassy and Khomeini's support for the actions of the students, together with Bazargan's inability to control the growing power of the *komeiths*, led to his resignation in 1981.

Dr. Mohammad Mossadeq – leader of the nationalist government from 1950-53, he was the founder of the National Front, a party espousing parliamentary democracy and the nationalisation of Iran oil industry. While being the greatest hope for the establishment of a democracy in Iran this century, he was hounded from office by the West (who financially supported a counter coup to return the Shah to power) because of his desire for Iranian economic independence. On the return of the Shah he was placed under house arrest, leaving the secular opposition to the Shah without a visible leader, which inevitably left the door open for Khomeini to unite all shades of opposition to the regime.

Mohammad Hanifnejad – was the early ideological leader of the Mujahedin-e Khalq. He was an Islamic Marxist, greatly influenced by Shariati and Ayatollah Taleqani, viewing social exclusion and inequality in terms of Islam's battle against oppression.

Mohammad Reza Shah – was the second and last Shah of the Pahlavi dynasty. He ascended to the throne, when his father was forced to abdicate by Allied forces during WWII for his sympathetic Nazi views. An indecisive, arrogant and brutal leader, his dislocation from the values of Iranian society, eventually led to his downfall.

Mujahedin-e Khalq – or Holy Warriors of the People, represent the radical left wing Muslim organisation founded in the early 1970s. The group openly confronted pro-Khomeini forces in the late 1970s and early 1980s and has always alleged the arrest, torture and execution of is members under the Islamic Republic. In 1981 became a founding member of the National Council of Resistance (NCR), which is dedicated to the overthrow of the Islamic Republic.

Nadegh Nouri – was a former Speaker of the Majlis. He was seen as the choice of the Supreme Leader during the 1997 presidential election and was expected to win with a landslide victory. A candidate of the conservative right, he and his party misread the political landscape of 1997 Iran and suffered a serious defeat at the hands of the reformist candidate Mohamad Khatami.

National Front – is the political party founded by Mossadeq, advocating a philosophy of parliamentary democracy and economic nationalisation. It is current deemed an illegal organisation but continues to be active in the Islamic Republic. The party withheld their candidates from the local and parliamentary elections in 1999 and 2000, so as not to divide the reformist vote.

OIC (Organisation of the Islamic Conference) – 'is an international organisation grouping fifty six states which have decided to pool their resources together, combine their efforts and speak with one voice, to safeguard the interests and secure the progress and well being of their people and all of the Muslims in the world' – taken from organisations mission statement. See further www.oic-un.org. It was established in September 1969.

Pahlavi Dynasty – was founded in 1925 and lasted until the overthrow of Mohammad Reza Shah in 1978. This period is best defined as an attempt at modernisation, which failed to take into account the characteristics of Iranian culture, tradition and faith. Therefore the values of the regime did not reflect the values inherent in society, leading inevitably to socio-political unrest.

Prophet Muhammad – is the founder, ideologue and initial leader of the Islamic community. Born somewhere between AD 531 to 579, he died in 632 AD. His teachings (as depicted in the Quran) and traditions (*hadiths*) formed the basis of this vibrant faith.

Qajar dynasty – were the rulers of modern Iran from 1796 to1925, they governed over an increasingly decentralised country. Unlike the Safavids, the Qajars could not claim ascendancy from the Prophet and therefore did not exercise as much control over the Shia ulema. It was during the Qajar reign that the ulema re-asserted their control and influence over Iranian society.

Qom – is the ideological and religious centre of the Islamic Republic. This once dilapidated religious centre was re-vitalised by Ayatollah Ha'eri in the early part of the 20th century. Situated to the south of Tehran it became the religio-political centre of Iran in the aftermath of the establishment of the Islamic Republic.

Rastakhiz Party – was formed in 1975 when the Shah announced that all legal political parties would now be merged into a new single party entitled *the Rastakhiz* (resurgence) *Party*. The creation of this party symbolised the height of the Shah's repressive policies and compounded the psychological and financial dislocation of the regime from the economic difficulties of the people, leading to explosive levels of populist expression. Previous to 1975, in the early edition of the Shah's autobiography, *Mission for My Country*, he argued that one-party regimes were invariably either Fascist or Communist. After his creation of the *Rastakhiz Party* his stated views on one-party regimes was not re-printed in the later editions of his book.

Reza Khan (Reza Shah) – the founder of the Pahlavi dynasty, ruled as Shah from 1925 until his forced abdication in 1941. He believed that Iran needed strong leadership and based much of his political philosophy on Kemal Ataturk's modernisation plans in Turkey. His reform policies included social liberalisation together with attempts at undermining the traditional control that the religious ulema had over society. In many ways his policies went further than Ataturk's, such as the 1936 law passed which forced the unveiling of women.

Safavid Period – Shah Ismail Safavi (1487-1524) was the founder of the Safavid dynasty that ruled Persia from 1501 to 1736. Originally of Turkomen origin, they declared Shi'ism the State religion in 1501. Being able to claim ancestry from the House of the Prophet, gave the regime religious legitimacy and, therefore, during this period we see the decline in the influence of the Shia ulema on Iranian society.

SAVAK – was the internal security service created by Mohammad Reza Shah in the early 1950s. He used this new intelligence agency to undermine, attack and imprison those whom he saw as a threat to his rule. Under the wide banner of a 'threat', he saw the members of the former National Front, any leftist grouping and also the members of the religious classes who had opposed his right to rule. The treatment of these groups at the hands of the SAVAK over the next two decades can be described as both unjust and inhumane. The SAVAK were trained and assisted by both the American and Israeli security services, even though it became widely accepted by the early 1970s that the SAVAK were involved in the torture and forceful imprisonment of those advocating political opposition to the Shah's regime.

SAVAMH – are the internal security service of the Islamic Republic. It is generally agreed that this is the same organisation as the SAVAK but under a different acronym and with a different definition as to what is a 'threat' to the State.

Shahpour Bakhtiar – was a member of the National Front and a known parliamentary democrat. The sole politician willing to establish an interim government in late 1978 (his agreement was on the condition that the Shah leave the country). With the departure of the Shah and the imminent return of Khomeini, the fall of his government was inevitable.

Shaykh Abdul-Karim Ha'eri – was a Grand Ayatollah and one of the first teachers of Khomeini. His personal belief was that the clergy should not become involved in politics. Throughout his life, Ha'eri went to great lengths to remain above the political fray, even going as far as to move to Najaf (then a part of the Ottoman Empire) during the Constitutional revolution of 1906.

Tudeh Party – was an Islamic Marxist organisation that became increasingly popular during the 1950s among students throughout Iran. Their ideology finds similarities between the Marxist sense of social equality and justice, and similar ideals inherent in the Islamic faith.

Glossary II
Terms, Dates and Expressions

3rd of Khordad – marks the date of the election of Khatami to the Presidency of the Islamic Republic. Khordad is the third month of the Iranian calendar. Iranian months exactly correspond to the signs of the Zodiac or horoscope. So the beginning of the Iranian calendar is Aries (starts at March 21) and Khordad is Gemini (starts at May 21).
15th of Khordad – marks the date when in 1963, following Khomeini's anti-American and anti-Shah's speech, a nationwide riot broke out in the country, many people were killed and some public buildings were destroyed. Khomeini was subsequently arrested and exiled to Turkey. Each year in post-revolutionary Iran, this date is observed as the start of Khomeini's revolution. Khomeini himself passed away on Khordad 14, 1989.
Allah Akbar – translated means 'God is Greater than [any thing you can imagine]'; became the rallying cry of the Islamic movement.
Áshúrá – is the 10th day of the mourning month of Muharram and marks the date of the battle at Karbála, where Imam Husayn and his small band of supporters (which was said to be around 72 people) fell at the hands of the overwhelming army of the tyrannical Caliph Yazdi. Each year during this day Shia's repent for the death of Husayn.
Ayatollah – literally means 'the sign of God'. It is the title of high-ranking Shia clerics. In the Shia religious Hierarchy, the title of the most respected Ayatollah is Ayatollah Al-Uzma (or Grand Ayatollah). The clerics who are not Ayatollah (meaning that they are not considered to be knowledgeable enough to be called the Source of [spiritual] imitation) are called Hojatoleslam (the proof of Islam and the guide of Muslims). However, these concepts are very fluid and among clerics themselves have little technical significance.
Basijj – are the revolutionary militia force, which functions under the supervision of the Revolutionary Guard. Literally means 'Mobilised Forces' in Farsi.
Bazaar (bazaaris) – in Farsi means market (baz = again + aar = bring, therefore bazaar literally means that if you are not happy with your purchase, bring it back!). Bazzaris are consequently businessmen and merchants.
Caliph & Imam (and difference between the two) – **Caliph** is an Arabic word meaning the 'Representative'. But in political literature, this is the title of the Muslim ruler among Sunni Muslims. Sunnis believe after the death of the Prophet, there were four rightly guided Caliphs. By contrast, Shia's believe that only impeccable and sinless people could become the leader of Islamic society. So the leadership is confined to the Household of the Prophet, that includes Ali, as the Prophet's son-in-law as well as his cousin, and his eleven sons and grandsons. For Iranian Shia's, Ali is the first **Imam** (Imam is an Arabic word, meaning leader) and Mahdi (who is now in occultation for more than 12 centuries) is the Twelve Imam. Shia's think their Imams are able to execute miracles and see the Caliphs as unjust and tyrannical. While Shia's refer to their leaders (like Khomeini) as Imam, in fact they are not Imams, but the representatives of the Imam (in Khomeini's case, he was seen as the representative of Imam Mahdi), simply because, Shia's only recognise the household of the prophet as their Imams.
Chador – is widely recognised as an Islam mode of dress for women, covering the hair, hands and extending to cover the feet. The chador is actually a black cloak-like cloth, held in place by ones teeth and which is used to cover the women's clothing, from head to toe. As a matter of fact, Islam has no dress code in which it asks the believers to wear chador.

According to contemporary Islamic scholar, the late Ayatollah Morteza Mutahari (in his book titled the *Question of Veil*), wearing Chador is a pre-Islamic tradition in Iran that originated with the Zoroastrians, who believed other males should not see their female members. Wearing the veil is more a matter of taste and tradition and differs greatly from one country to the other. For instance, Iranian Chador is different from Arab or Afghan veils.

Ejazeh-ye ejtihad – represents the authorisation to issue religious decrees. Can be viewed as the religious equivalent of a Ph.D. When a clergyman reaches the level of canonical knowledge and spiritual purification, his professors (who are themselves Mujtahid or faqih) grant him *ejazeh-ye ejtihad*) acknowledge that he has become qualified as a Mujtahid (a source of spiritual imitation). As a result he can issue religious decrees for his followers and will be considered to be an Ayatollah.

Faqih or Mujtahid – is a religious scholar who knows Fiqh (Islamic Canon) and practices *ejtihad* (i.e. issuing religious decrees). This term is almost equal to Ayatollah, although Ayatollah is more of a popular title and has little religious significance, while *faqih* is a technical term.

Fatwa – is a religious decree. Only those of the level of Faqih or Mujtahid can issue such a decree and it is obligatory for all of his followers who have chosen him as their Source of Imitation.

Foqaha – is the plural of Faqih (religious scholars).

Hijrah – the withdrawal by Muhammad and his followers from Mecca to the northern city of Yatrib. It is often mistranslated as a 'flight', when in fact it was a well-organised and planned withdrawal from the city. It occurred in the year 622 AD and is an integral part of the Islamic consciousness even today. The event is the start of the Islamic lunar calendar (Hijri Qamari), according to which we are in the year 1422 AH (After Hijra).

Hojatoleslam – is the title of Shia clerics who are not yet Ayatollahs. The word itself is an Arabic term meaning 'the Guide of Muslims and the proof of Islam'.

Ijtihid or ejtihad – is an Arabic word meaning 'trying to gain access to knowledge through hard efforts'. Among Shia's, ijtihad is the learned opinion of a jurist (Mujtahid) on a religious subject. This opinion is obligatory and binding for the Mujtahid's followers (*Muqalids*).

Jihad – is an Arabic world meaning 'hard efforts or endeavor'. Also can be translated as campaign. According to the Quran, every Muslim is a campaigner who tries to help the good and fight the forces of evil. It can take place in any context and in any form: through helping each other, working hard for your ideas, even learning new sciences and finally if necessary, going to battle and fighting the enemy. The most difficult Jihad is the purification of your soul (which is called *Jihad Akbar* or the Great Campaign), while fighting the enemies of Islam is known as *Jihad Asqar* (the Small Campaign). Unfortunately, throughout history many military attacks and conquests were carried out under the name of Jihad and so for many people (both Muslims and non-Muslims), Jihad has become equivalent to violence and bloodshed in the name of God.

Komitehs – was the name, in the post-1979 period, of the religious police in charge of monitoring the every day life of the people and enforcing Islamic principles. In 1989, the komitehs were merged into the police department and now are an integrated part of the Iranian law enforcement structures.

Majlis – is an Arabic word meaning 'the place or the time where people sit down and discuss issues'. In Islamic political literature it means Consultative Council or Parliament.

Marja'taqlid – is a Source of Spiritual Imitation: The highest-ranking Shia cleric is the most senior Mujtahid. Only Shia's have Marja'taqlid.

Muharram – is a month of mourning in honour of Imam Husayn and the battle of Karbála. Muharram is the first month of the Islamic lunar calendar (Hijri qamari).

Mujtahid – somebody who can practice Ijtihad: a high ranking Shi'ite clergy man who can issue Fatwas, these are obligatoray for his followers (*Muqalids*).
Shar'ia – is Islamic law. It is also the penal code and civil law in some Muslim counties. Each Islamic denomination has its own interpretation of Shar'ia. So the Shari'ia of the Sunni regime in Saudi is quite different from that of Shia's of Iran.
Shia – literally means 'follower of Ali', denotes those who believe that Ali was the designated heir of the Prophet. While there are a number of divisions within Shi'ism, they all appear to be hierarchical in nature.
Sunni – is a word meaning those who follow Sunnah – traditions and practices– of prophet Muhammad. In contrast to the Shia's, Sunni's believe that the Prophet Mohammad died without designating an heir, leaving his followers to select his successor. This sect of Islam is generally based on the idea of consensus on religious affairs and constitutes some 90 percent of the population of the Muslim world.
Ulema – is the plural form of Alem (Religious Scholar) and has often been translated to mean 'clergy'. While this facilitates greater understanding, it is inaccurate. In Christianity the clergy are placed between Man and God, while the ulema in the Sunni tradition of Islam are not meant to intercede on man's behalf but are there to carry out other tasks, such as Islamic law and education. However, among Shia's due to the hierarchical nature of the faith, the ulema often play the same role as their counterparts in Christianity.
Velayat-e faqih – the rule of Faqih (or Islamic Jurist): a theory of governance first put forward by Ayatollah Khomeini in the late 1960s in his controversial book *Islamic Government*. In this book he argues that while the twelfth Imam of Shia's is in occultation, the responsibility of running the society will be with faqihs who are both pious and knowledgeable about religious affairs and are the sole rightful rulers who can act on behalf of the Imam. Based on this theory, Khomeini established his Islamic Republic in Iran after the 1979 revolution. However, many top clerics, including some prominent faqihs like Ayatollah Kh'uni and Shariatmadari, dismissed the idea and called it religious innovation.

Bibliography

Abd al-Qahir ibn Tahir (1935), *Moslem schisms and sects: the history of the various philosophic systems developed in Islam* (London Luzac).

Abdi, A. (1378/2000), *Enqelab Aleyheh Tahir (Revolution against Humiliation)* (Tehran: 13 Bahman).

Abrahamian, E. (1998), *Khomeinism* (London: I.B. Tauris).

Ahrari, M. (1984: Spring), 'Implications of the Iranian political change for the Arab world', *Middle East Review*; 16.

Al-Balagh Foundation (1990), *Imam Hussein and the Day of Ashura* (Tehran: Al-Balagh Foundation).

Al Ahmed, J. (1978), *Dar Khedmat va Khianat, Roshanfekran Volume I and II (Intellectuals as providers of Service and as Traitors)* (Tehran: Kharazmi Publication).

Al Ahmed, J. (1962), *Qarbzadegi* (Westoxification) (Tehran: n.p.).

Al-Tabari, A. (1988), *Muhammad at Mecca* (Albany: State University of New York Press).

Amann, P. (1962), 'Revolution: a redefinition', *Political Science Quarterly*, 77.

Ameer, A. (1949), *A Short History of the Saracens* (London: Macmillan and Co Ltd.).

Anderson, J. et al (Eds) (1995), *A Global World?* (Oxford University Press).

Amnesty International (1987), *Iran Violations of Human Rights: Documents Sent by Amnesty International to the Government of the Islamic Republic of Iran* (London: Amnesty International).

Amuzegar, J. (1998), 'Khatami's Iran, one year later', *Middle East Policy*.

Anders, J. and Jorgen, B. (Eds) (1997), *Islam in a changing world: Europe and the Middle East* (Richmond: Curzon).

Andrae, T. (1960), *Mohammad, the Man and his Faith* (New York: Harper and Row).

Anonymous, *The Imposed War - Defense Versus Aggression* (Tehran: The Islamic Republics of Iran War Information Headquarters).

Anonymous (1990), *Foreign Affairs Chronology 1978-1989* (Washington: Council of Foreign Relations Inc.).

Anonymous (1997), 'Meet Mr. Khatimi, The 5th President of the Islamic Republic', *Middle East Insight*.

Arendt, H. (1986), *The Origins of Totalitarianism* (London: Deutch).

Arjkomand, S.A. (1984), *The Shadow of God and the Hidden Imam: Religion, Political Order and Social Change in Shi'te Iran from the Beginning to 1980* (Chicago: University of Chicago).

Aristotle (1999), *Politics: books V and VI*, translated by David Keyt (Oxford: Clarendon).

Arnett, E. (1998), 'Reassurance versus deterrence: expanding Iranian participation in confidence-building measures', *Middle-East-Policy*; 6.

Aubin, J. (1970), 'La Politique religieuse des Safavides', *Le Shi'ismamite*.
'Ayatollah portrait: iron-willed fanatic', *US News and World Report*; 87 (1980).
Ayubi, N. (1991), *Religion and Politics in the Arab World* (London: Routledge).
Bakhash, S. (1990), *Reign of the Ayatollahs - Iran and the Islamic Revolution* (New York: Basic Books).
Baktiari, B. (1997), 'Iran's New President', *Middle East Insight*; 13.
Balfour, J.M. (1922), *Recent Happenings in Persia* (London: W. Blackwood & Sons).
Balyuzi, H.M. (1976), *Muhammad and the Course of Islam* (London: George Ronald).
Bani-Sadr, A.H. (1991), *My Turn to Speak, Iran, the Revolution and Secret Deals with the US* (Washington: Brassey's (US) Inc.).
Barzin, S. (1997, May 30), 'Khatimi's shock victory', *Middle East International*.
Bayat, A. (1997, 9-16 July), 'A Post Islamic Society', *Al Ahram Weekly*.
Beardsworth, R. (1996), *Derrida and the Political* (London: Routledge).
Bharier, J. (1971), *Economic Development in Iran 1900-1970* (London: Oxford University Press).
Bill, J.A. (1988), *The Eagle and the Lion: The Tragedy of American-Iranian Relations* (New Haven: Yale University Press).
Bill, J. (1982: January), 'The politics of extremism in Iran', *Current History*; 81.
Bishai, W. (1968), *Islamic history of the Middle East: backgrounds, development, and fall of the Arab Empire* (Boston: Allyn and Bacon).
Bistolfi, R. (1995), *Islam: a new element in the culture of Europe* (Birmingham: Centre for the Study of Islam and Christian-Muslim Relations).
Boland, B.J. (1982), *The struggle of Islam in modern Indonesia* (The Hague: Nijhoff).
Boyce, M. (1991), *A history of Zoroastrianism* (New York: Brill).
Brinton, C. (1965), *The Anatomy of Revolution* (Englewood Cliffs: Prentice Hall).
Bull, H. (1995), *Society and Anarchy in International Relations* (London: Macmillan).
Calvert, P. (1967), 'Revolution: the politics of violence', *Political Studies*; 15.
Carrere d'Encausse (1982), *Lenin Revolution and Power Vol. I* (London: Longman).
Centro Culturale Islamico Europeo (1989), *Revolution and Terrorism in Iran* (Roma: Centro Culturale Islamico Europeo).
Chehabi, H. (1990), *Iranian Politics and Religious Modernism: The Liberation Movement of Iran Under the Shah and Khomeini* (New York: Cornell University Press).
Clawson, P. (1993), *Iran's Challenge to the West, How, When and Why?* (Washington: The Washington Institute for Near East Policy).
Cohan, A.S. (1975), *Theories of Revolution – An Introduction* (London: Thomas Nelson and Sons).
Cohen, M. and Fermon, N. (Eds) (1996), *Princeton Readings in Political Thought* (Princeton: Princeton University Press).
Corbin, H. (1978), *En Islam Iranien* (Paris: Gallimard).

Cordesman, A. (1998), 'The changing military balance in the Gulf', *Middle-East-Policy*; 6.
Cottam, R. (1979), *Nationalism in Iran: updated through 1978* (Pittsburgh: University of Pitttsburg Press).
Cottam, R. (1982: Autumn), 'Nationalism and the Islamic revolution in Iran', *Canadian Review of Studies in Nationalism*.
Dahl, R. (1970), *After the Revolution* (New Haven: Yale University Press).
Davies, J. (1971), *When men revolt and why: a reader in political violence and revolution* (London: Collier-Macmillan).
Derrida, J. (1995), *Writing and Difference* (London: Routledge).
Dickey and Lau (1998, 19/1/98), 'US Officials are scrambling as a new, more moderate Iran proposed a dialogue, soccer diplomacy may be the first step', *Newsweek*.
Downes, M. (2000: Autumn), 'The Islamic resurgence: the case of Iran', *History Studies 2*.
Downes, M. and Keane, R. (2000: Spring), 'Dialogue Amongst Civilisation – the road to deconstructing unipolarity', *Iranian Journal of International Studies*.
Dunn, J. (1989), *Modern Revolutions, an introduction to the analysis of a political phenomenon* (Cambridge: Cambridge University Press).
Edwards, L. (1970), *The Natural History of Revolution* (Chicago: Chicago University Press).
Eichengreen, B. (1997), *Hegemonic Stability Theories of the International Monetary System* (CEPR Discussion Papers).
Elm, M. (1992), *Oil, power, and principle: Iran's oil nationalization and its aftermath* (Syracuse: Syracuse University Press).
Enayat, H. (1982), *Modern Islamic Political Thought* (London: Macmillan Press).
Esposito, J.L. (Ed.) (1990), *The Iranian Revolution: Its Global Impact* (Miami: Florida International University Press).
Etheshami, A. (1995), *After Khomeini: The Iranian Second Republic* (London: I.B. Tauris).
Etheshaimi, A. and Varasten, M. (Eds.) (1991), *Iran and the International Community* (London: Routledge).
Farazmand, A. (1989), *The State Bureaucracy and Revolution in Modern Iran: Agrarian Reforms and Regime Politics* (New York: Praeger).
Farhi, F. (1990), *States and Urban-Based Revolutions: Iran and Nicaragua* (Chicago: University of Illinois Press).
Fuller, G.E. (1991), *The Center of the Universe: The Geopolitics of Iran* (Boulder: Westview Press).
Fuller, G.E. (1991), *Islamic Fundamentalism in Northern Tier Countries: An Integrative View* (Santa Monica: Rand Publishing).
Fuller, G.E. and Lesser, I. (1995), *A Sense of Siege: The Geopolitics of Islam and the West* (Oxford: Westview Press).
Gabrieli, F. (1968), *Muhammad and the conquests of Islam* (London: Weidenfeld & Nicolson).
Gallagher, Laver and Mair (2001), *Representative Government in Modern Europe – institutions, parties and governments* 3rd edition (London: McGraw Hill).

Ghani, S. (1998), *Iran and the rise of Reza Shah: from Qajar collapse to Pahlavi rule* (London: I.B. Tauris).
Gowing, P. (1988), *Understanding Islam and Muslims in the Philippines* (Quezon City: New Day Publishers).
Graham, R. (1979), *Iran: The Illusion of Power* (London: Croom Helm).
Grey, C. (1873), *A Narrative of Italian Travels in Persia, in the Fifteenth and Sixteenth Centuries* (London: Hakluyt Society).
Gurr, R. (1970), *Why Men Rebel* (Princeton: Princeton University Press).
Habermas, J. (1987), *The philosophical discourse of modernity: twelve lectures*, translated by Lawerence, F. (Cambridge: Polity Press).
Hairi, N. (1358 (1979)), *Mosahebah Ba Tarikh Sazan-e Iran (Interviews with History Makers of Iran)* (Teheran: Revolutionary Documentation Center).
Hakeem, F.R. (1988), *La vie de Mohammad* (London: Islam International).
Halliday, F. (1979), *Dictatorship and Development* (Middlesex: Penguin Books).
Halliday, F. (1996), *Islam and the Myth of Confrontation: Religion and Politics in the Middle East* (London: I.B. Tauris).
Halm, H. (1997), *Shi'a Islam: from religion to revolution* (Princeton: Markus Wiener).
Hamidullah, D.M. (1945), *The Muslim Conduct of State* (Lahore: Muhammad Ashraf Publishing).
Haroon, S. (1984: August), 'Khomeini's crusade: an emerging global "third force"', *World Press Review*; 31.
Haykal, M. (1983), *The return of the Ayatollah: the Iranian revolution from Mossadeq to Khomeini* (London: Deutsch).
Herzog, C. (1988), *The Arab-Israeli wars: war and peace in the Middle East from the War of Independence to Lebanon 2nd Ed* (London: Arms and Armour).
Hicks, H. (1998: Nov 8), '"As fragile as a crystal glass": press freedom in Iran', *Human-Rights Watch*.
Hourania, A. (1980), *Europe and the Middle East* (California: California Press).
Hunter, S. (1990), *Iran and the World: Continuity in a Revolutionary Decade* (Indiana: Indiana University Press).
Hunter, S. (1992), 'Iran after Khomeini', *The Washington Papers*.
Huntington, S.P. (1993: Summer), 'The Clash of Civilizations', *Foreign Affairs*, vol. 72, no. 3.
Huntington, S.P. (1968), *Political Order in Changing Societies* (New Haven: Yale University Press).
Husain, S.A. (1974), *The Glorious Caliphate* (Lucknow: Academy of Islamic Research and Publication).
Hossein, M. (Ed.) (1992), *Iran: Past, Present and Future* (Ministry for Industry: Islamic Republic of Iran).
Hussain, A. (1983), *Islamic movements in Egypt, Pakistan and Iran* (London: Mansell).
Ibrahim, S. (1993: Spring), 'Crises, elites, and democratization in the Arab world'. *Middle East Journal 47*.
Iqbal, A. (1961), *Diplomacy in Islam* (Lahore: Institute of Islamic Culture).

Iqbal, S.M. (1977), *Islam as an Ethical and Political Ideal* (Lahore: Pakistan, Islamic Book Service).
Jafri, S. (1979), *Origins and early development of Shi'a Islam* (London: Longman).
Jiddo, G.B. (1997: September 3rd), 'Khatimi Yujaddid Intiqadhu as Taqlidiyyin', *Al Hayat*.
Joffe, G. (1999, April), 'At a turning point', *World Today*; 55.
Johnson, C. (1982), *Revolutionary Change* (London: Longman).
Jones, P. (1998: Autumn), 'Iran's threat perceptions and arms control policies', *Nonproliferation-Review*; 6.
Keane, R. (2000: February), *Dialogue amongst civilisation, creating an institutional framework* (Tehran: IPIS Conference Paper).
Keane, R. (2000), *Creating space in which to live; deconstructing binary opposition – The case of Bosnia and Herzegovina* (Limerick: University of Limerick).
Keddie, N. (1979), 'Oil, Economic Policy and Social Conflict', *Race and Class*, vol. 21, no. 3.
Keddie, N. (1981), *Roots of the Revolution - An Interpretative History of Modern Iran* (New Haven: Yale University Press).
Keddie, N. (Ed.) (1983), *Religion and Politics in Iran: Shi'ism from quietism to revolution* (New Haven: Yale University Press).
Keohane, R. (1989), *International Institutions and State Power – essays in International Relations Theory* (Colorado: Westview Press, Inc).
Kepel, G. (1995), *The Revenge of God* (Cambridge: Polity Press).
Kepel, G. (1995), *L'Ouest D'Allah* (Paris: Points Seuil).
Kepel, G. (2000), *Jihad Expansion et declin de L'Islamisme* (Paris: Gallimard).
Khomeini, I. (1406 (1985)), *The Practical Law of Islam* (Tehran: Islamic Propagation Organisation).
Khomeini, I. (1357 (1978)), *Zendego -Nameh-Ye Imam Khomeini (The Life of Imam Khomeini - 2 Volumes)* (Tehran: 12 Moharram Publications).
Khomeini, R. (1981), *Islam and the Revolution: Writings and Declarations of Imam Khomeini*, translated by Hamid Algar (Berkeley: Mizan Press).
Khomeini, R. (1981), *Hokumateh Eslami (Islamic Government)* (Tehran: Bozorg Bookshop).
Khomeini, R. (1984), *Nahzat-e Imam Khomein*, Vol 1 *(Imam Khomeini's Movement)* (Tehran: Imam's Way Press).
Kornhauser, W. (1960), *The Politics of Mass Society* (London: Routledge & Kegan Paul).
Kuhn, T. (1962), *The Structure of Scientific Revolutions* (Chicago: University of Chicago).
Lapidus, I. (1983), *Contemporary Islamic movements in historical perspective* (Berkeley: Institute of International Studies).
Leedy, P. (1989), *Practical Research 5th edition* (New York: Macmillan).
Lenin, V.I. (1947), *The Essentials of Lenin* (London: Lawrence & Wishart).
Lenin, V.I. (1970), *What is to be Done?* translated by Utechin P. (Oxford: Clarendon Press).
Lipset, S.M. (1976), *Political Man* (London: Heinemann).

Lloyd, J. (1982), *Explaining Foreign Policy* (London: Prentice Hall Inc.).
Long and Reich (1995), *The Government and Politics of the Middle East and North Africa*, 3rd Edition (Oxford: Westview Press).
Lombard, M. (1975), *The Golden Age of Islam* (Oxford: North-Holland Publishing Co).
Lotfian, S. (1994: Spring/Summer), 'Human Rights and the challenge of ethnic separatist movements in the Middle East', *Iranian Journal of International affairs*, vol. VI (nos. 1 & 2).
Mao Tse-Tung (1967), *Selected Works of Mao Tse-Tung, Vol. I* (Peking: Foreign Language Press).
Marlowe, L. (1997: December 17), 'Ideological battles of the Ayatollahs seems certain to resurface', *Irish Times*.
Marlowe, L. (1997: December), 'Islam seeks consensus amongst contentious issues', *Irish Times*.
Marlowe, L. (1997: December), 'Iran welcomes former Islamic foes to summit', *Irish Times*.
Marlowe, L. (1997: December), 'Leaders with opposing views of Islam battle for the soul of Iran', *Irish Times*.
Marlowe, L. (2000: April), 'God given right of Mullahs to rule queried by dissident', *Irish Times*.
Marx, K. (1983), *Karl Marx and Fredrick Engels, Selected Works, Vol. 1* (Moscow: Progress Publishers).
Masci, D. (1998), 'Reform in Iran: are moderates changing the Islamic Republic?' *CQ-Researcher*; 8.
Maududi, S.A.A. (1955), *The Islamic Law and Constitution* (Lahore: Pakistan, Islamic Publications Ltd).
Mawdudi, S.A.A. (1984), *The Islamic movement: dynamics of values, power and change* (London: Islamic Foundation).
Mazzaoui, M. (1972), *The Origins of the Safawids* (Wiesbaden: F. Steiner).
Melville, C. (Ed.) (1993), *Safavid Persia: the history and politics of an Islamic society* (London: I.B. Tauris).
Menashri, D. (1990), *Iran in a Decade of War and Revolution* (New York: Meiers and Holmes).
Mitrany, D. (1966), *A Working Peace System* (Chicago: Quadrangle Books).
Moore, B. (1991), *Social Origins of Dictatorship and Democracy: lord and peasant in the making of the modern* (London: Penguin).
Moore, W. (1963), *Social Change* (New Jersey: Englewood Cliffs).
Moaddel, M. (1993), *Class Politics and Ideology in the Iranian Revolution* (New York: Columbia University Press).
Moin, B. (1999), *Khomeini, Life of the Ayatollah* (London: I.B. Tauris).
Mojtahed, Z.P. (1994: Spring/Summer), 'A Geopolitical triangle on the Persian Gulf, Actions and Reaction amongst Iran, Bahrain and Saudi Arabia', *Iranian Journal of International affairs*, vol. VI (no. 1 & 2).
Monashri, D. (1990), *The Iranian Revolution and the Muslim World* (Boulder: Westview Press).

Morgenthau, H. [1958] (1993), *Politics Among Nations: The Struggle for Power and Peace* (New York: McGraw Hill College).
Mottahari, A. (undated), *Jahan Biniyeh Tohidi (The Unified World View) vol. I and II* (Qom: Sadre Publications).
Muir, W. (1912), *The life of Mohammad: from original sources* (Edinburgh: Grant).
Muravchik, J. and Gedmin, J. (1997: July), 'Why Iran Is (Still) a Menace', *Commentary*.
Mutahhari, M., 'Islam and Iran: A historical study of mutual services', *Al-Tawhtd a Quarterly Journal of Islamic Thought and Culture*, VI (No.3).
Nelan, B. (1998: June 7), 'New Day Coming? – Responding to a Clinton suggestion for more normal relations, Iran's President opens the door a crack but still blames US policy for tensions', *Time Magazine*.
Neumann, S. (1948-49), 'The International Civil War', *World Politics*, 1.
Nielsen, J.S. (1994), *Islam and Europe* (Birmingham: Centre for the Study of Islam and Christian-Muslim Relations).
Nouri, A. (1378/1999), *A Hemlock for the 'Advocate of Reform'* (Tehran: n.p.).
Nu'mani, M. (1988), *Khomeini, Iranian revolution and the Shiite faith* (London: Furqan).
Omid, H. (1994), *Islam and the Post Revolutionary State in Iran* (London: Macmillian Press Ltd.).
Parsons, A. (1984), *The Pride and Fall: Iran 1974-79* (London: Jonathan Cape).
Parsons, T. (1966), *Societies: Evolutionary and Comparative Perspectives*, (Englewood Cliffs: N.J: Prentice-Hall).
Peters, F.E. (1994), *Muhammad and the origins of Islam* (Albany: State University of New York Press).
Pettee, G. (1971), *The Process of Revolution* (New York: Harper).
Plato (1966), *Plato's Republic* (Cambridge: Cambridge University Press).
'Power Struggle: Khatami liberalism under conservative attack', *Middle East Reporter Weekly*; (1998: August 6).
Qureshi, S. and Javed, K. (1989), *The Politics of the Satanic Verses – Unmasking Western Attitudes* (London: Muslim Community Studies Institute).
Qutb, M. (1964), *Islam the Misunderstood Religion* (State of Kuwait: Ministry of Awqaf and Islamic Affairs).
Rahnema, A. (1996), *An Islamic utopian: a political biography of Ali Shari'ati* (London: I.B. Tauris).
Rajaee, F. 'The social origins of political elite's in Iran: an historical review', *Iranian Journal for International Affairs*, VI (no. 1 & 2).
Ramazani, R. (1973), *The Persian Gulf – Iran's Role* (Virginia: Charlottesville University Press).
Ramazani, R. (1982), *The United States and Iran – Patterns of Influence* (New York: Praeger).
Ramazani, R. (1986), *Revolutionary Iran – Challenges and Responses in the Middle East* (Baltimore: Johns Hopkins University Press).
Ramazani, R. (1998: Spring), 'The shifting premise of Iran's foreign policy: towards a democratic peace?' *Middle East Journal*; 52.

Reeves, M. (2000), *Muhammad in Europe* (Reading: Garnet).
Rice, T. (1994), *May it fill your Soul* (Chicago: University of Chicago Press).
Rosen, B. (1985), *Iran since the Revolution, Internal Dynamics, Regional Conflicts and the Superpowers* (New York: Social Science Monographs).
Rouleau, E. (1980: Fall), 'Khomeini's Iran (Islamic tradition and political events)', *Foreign Affairs, 59*.
Rousseau, J. (1987), *Social Contract* (Harmonsworth: Penguin).
Roy, O. (1994), *The Failure of Political Islam* (London: I.B. Tauris).
Rubin, B. (1980), *Paved with Good Intentions – The American Experience in Iran* (New York: Oxford University Press).
Sabet, A. (1994: Spring/Summer), 'Islam, Iran and the Western Discourse: Behind the veil', *The Iranian Journal for International Affairs*, VI (no. 1 & 2).
Sadr, B. (1991), *My Turn to Speak; Iran, the Revolution and Secret Deals with the US* (Washington: Brassey's).
Said, E. (1997), *Covering Islam – How the Media and the Experts Determine How We See the Rest of the World* (London: Vintage).
Salamah, A. (1991), *Shia & Sunni Perspective on Islam* (Riyadh: Abul-Qasim).
Salvatore, A. (1997), *Islam and the political discourse of modernity* (Reading: Ithaca).
Savory, R.M. (1980), *Iran under the Safavids* (Cambridge: Cambridge University Press).
Sayeed Khalid bin (1995), *Western Dominance and Political Islam – Challenge and Response* (Albany: State University of New York Press).
Seyyed-Javadi, K. (1405/1984), *The Dawn of the Islamic Revolution* (Tehran: Ministry of Islamic Guidance).
Shaked, S. (1994), *Dualism in transformation: varieties of religion in Sasanian Iran* (London: University of London).
Shariati, A. (undated), *Tashiiyeh Alavi va tashiiyeh Safavi* (Tehran: Hoseinieyeh Ershad Publications).
Shariati, A. (1974), *Masuliateh Shia Budan (The responsibilities of being a Shia)*, (Tehran: Ketabkhaneh Melli).
Shariati, A. (1980), *Marxism and other Western fallacies: an Islamic critique* (Berkeley: Mizan Press).
Shariati, A. (1988), *School of thought and action* (Tehran: Kazi Publications).
Shepard, R. (1996: Summer), 'Muhammad Sa'id al Ashmawi and the application of Shar'ia in Egypt', *International Journal of Middle Eastern Studies* (28).
Sick, G., Rodenbeck, M. and Vivrst, M. (1998: Spring), 'The Middle East Confronts the Millenium', *The Washington Quarterly*, 21(2).
Siddiqi, M.M. (1953), *Islam and Theocracy* (Lahore Pakistan: Institute of Islamic Culture).
Simone, T. (1994), *In whose image?: Political Islam and urban practices in Sudan* (London: University of Chicago Press).
Simpson, J. (1988), *Behind Iranian Lines – Travels Through Revolutionary Iran and the Persian Past* (London: Robinson Books Ltd.).
Simpson, J. (1998), *Strange Places, Questionable People* (London: Macmillan).

Sivan, E. (1985), *Radical Islam – Medieval Theology and Modern Politics* (New Haven: Yale University Press).
Sliman, I.B. (1990), *The life of Mohammad: Prophet of Allah* (London: Studio Editions).
Smith, N.A. (1976), *The new enlightenment: an essay in political and social realism* (London: J. Calder).
Sorokin, P. (1969), *Society, Culture and Personality* (New York: Cooper Square).
Soroush, A. (2000: Summer), 'More Robust than Ideology', *Discourse Vol. 2, 1*.
Stempel, J. (1981), *Inside the Iranian Revolution* (Bloomington: Indiana University Press).
Sullivan, W. (1981), *Mission to Iran* (London: Norton).
Tabataba'i, M. (1975), *Shi'ite Islam* (London: Allen & Unwin).
Tarrow, S. (1989), *Struggle, Politics and Reform* (Ithaca: Cornell University).
The Book of light, a collection of Imam Khomeini's Guidelines (1990) (Tehran: The Organisation for Cultural Documents of the Islamic Revolution).
'The Iran Election', *Washington Report on Middle East Affairs* (1997: July 11).
Tilly, A. (1993), *European Revolutions 1492-1993* (Oxford: Blackwell).
Ullman, R. (1972), *Anglo-Soviet Relation 1917-1921* (Princeton: Princeton University Press).
'United Nations year of Dialogue amongst civilisations, 2001 launched with headquarters roundtable discussion', *UN Press Release GA/9747* (2000: September 5).
Vakili, V., *Debating religion and politics in Iran: the political thought of Abdolkarim Soroush* (New York: Council on Foreign Relations).
Waltz, K. (1979), *Theory of International Politics* (USA: McGraw Hill, Inc).
Watt, W.M. (1974), *Muhammad: prophet and statesman* (London: Galaxy Books).
Waxman, D. (1998), *The Islamic Republic of Iran: between revolution and realpolitik* (London: Research Institute for the Study of Conflict and Terrorism).
Wharton, B. (1998), *The Islamic resurgence in Egypt and its relationship with the EU* (Limerick: University of Limerick).
Wright, D. (1970), *The English Amongst the Persians* (London: Heinemann).
Wright, R. (2000), *The Last Great Revolution: turmoil and transformation in Iran* (New York: Random House).
www.seraj.com
www.ioanufind.com
Younessi, B. (1995: Summer), 'L'islamisme algerien: nebuleuse ou movement social?' *Politique-Etrangere*.
Ziring, L. (1984), *The Middle East Political Dictionary* (London: Clio Press Ltd.).
Zubaida, S. (1989), *Islam, the People and the State* (London: Routledge).

Index

Abadan incident 112
Abbasid Caliphate 12, 13, 15, 16
Abdul-Karim Ha'eri, Shaykh, influence on Khomeini 86, 87, 93, 179
Abu Bakr, Caliph 7
Abu Musa island dispute 162
Achemenian Dynasty (559-339 BC) 13
Afghanistan ix
  and the Taleban xvii, 30
Agents of Construction Party 133, 150, 153 n.5
Ali, Imam 6, 7, 10, 12, 88, 177
  death 9
American Revolution 47
Americans, in Iran, immunity proposals 91-2
Arabs, and Israel 25
Aristotle, on revolution 70
Áshúrá 9, 90, 97, 134, 180
Asrar-e Hazar Saleh 87
Atatürk, Kemal 107
'axis of evil' member, Iran as 161-2
Ayatollah, meaning 180

Bahonar, Hojatoleslam 117
Bakhtiar, Shahpour 115, 179
Bani Sadr, Abol Hassan 43, 117, 144-5, 175
  elected President 125
  impeached by *majlis* 128, 137
  and Iran/Iraq war 127-8
  undermined by *ulema* 125
basijj 137
  meaning 180
bazaar, economic role 130 n.7
bazaari merchants 16, 60, 90, 91, 96, 110
  Iranian Revolution, role 111-12, 116, 147, 164-5
Bazargan, Mehdi 117, 177
  forms government 118
  resignation 120, 122
  undermined by Khomeini 119-20
Beheshti, Ayatollah 117, 118-19, 122, 124, 175
Berlin Wall, fall, and spread of revolution 62-3
binary opposition
  and the Iranian Revolution 65, 68, 78-81, 143-4, 166
  measurement 71-3, 156 n.32
  model 73-8, 165
  revolution as xiii-xiv, 44, 71
Borujerdi, Mohammad Hosayn, Ayatollah
  death 88, 175
  influence on Khomeini 87, 93
Bureau for Solidarity 133
Byzantines, Sasanians, conflict 2

Caliph, Imam, difference 180
Carter, President 108
chador 180-1
Chinese Revolution 47, 144
Chosroes I 1
Chosroes II 4
Christianity, and Islam 5
clergy *see ulema*
Coalition of Islamic Societies 90-1, 110, 117, 176
Confederation of Iranian Students Abroad 176
Constitutional Revolution, Iran (1905-11) 16, 86, 95, 99
Corbin, Henri, on Shi'ism 16-17
Council for Constitutional Amendments, and Abdullah Nouri 140
Council for the Determination of Exigencies 148
coup d'état, and revolution 70, 71

democracy, oligarchy, comparison 70

Egypt
  conversion to Islam 5
  Islamic Brotherhood 11
élites, and revolution 51, 57
enhessar 150
equality, inequality, comparison 70
erfan 98
Esfahan 90
European Union, and Iran 159

faqih (plural *foqaha*) 99, 100, 101, 121, 122
  meaning 181
Farsi xii
fatwa, meaning 181
Feda'iyan-e Islam party 93, 110, 114, 123, 176
foqaha see fatih
Freedom Movement 176
Functionalism, and revolution 45, 49, 56-7, 66

Gadaffi, Colonel 25
Gandhi, Mahatma, and non-violent revolution 53-4
Glasnost 138
Guardian Council of Elections 133, 148, 149, 151
  membership 154 n.7
  power 168-9
  role 143

Haggani Seminary 176
Hamedan 169
Hanifnejad, Mohammad 177
Hasan, Caliph 9
hekmat 98
Heraclius, Byzantine Emperor 4
Hezbollah Party 176-7
  formed 122
  ideals 122-3
  violence 139
hijrah 3, 4, 20 n.12
  meaning 181
Hojatoleslam, meaning 181
Honorius I, Pope 4
Husayn, Imam 9, 12, 16, 90, 95, 134, 163, 177

ideology
  Khomeini's 55-6
  meaning 33
  and religion 33-4
  society's need for 34
ijtihid 36, 181
Imam, Caliph, difference 180
Imamis see Shi ism, Twelvers
inequality
  equality, comparison 70
  and revolution 70
intelligentsia
  and Khomeini 97
  ulema, alliance 35, 37
international order, and the Islamic movement 38-9
Iran
  Afghan invasion (1722) 36
  Constitutional Revolution (1905-11) 16, 86, 95, 99
  and the European Union 159
  factions 139-40
  foreign policy 157-61
  intelligentsia 35
  Iraq, war (1980-88) 29, 126, 145, 158
  Islam in 163
  Islamic Constitution 123
  Islamic movement 34-7
  as Islamic Republic 56, 72, 85, 120-1, 142-3
  Islamic Revival 11
  and the Islamic state 31-3
  meaning 21 n.48
  newspapers, closure 140
  and September 11 attacks 170, 173

Shi'ism, identification with 36
strategic position ix
and the Taleban 170, 172
as theocracy 24
ulema, power of 15-16, 29-30, 35, 36-7
United Arab Emirates, dispute 162
see also Iranian Revolution
Iranian Revolution
  bazaari classes, role 111-12, 116, 147, 164-5
  and binary opposition 65, 68, 78-81, 143-4, 166
  causes xii, 106-11
  consolidation 146-9
  as continuing process 67-8, 71, 144, 164, 165
  course of 111-15, 141-2
  disillusion with 141-3, 167
  economics
    centralisation 149
    control 147-8
    difficulties 124
  institutions, building 146-7
  and Khomeini 158-9
  nature of 50, 158-9
  and power change 69-70
  right wing control 149-53
  significance xi, 115-17
  student protest 109-10
  theocratic government 117-21
  and Theory of Rising Expectations 60-1, 66-7, 106-7
  Third Republic 132, 153 n.2
  ulema, role 111-12
  uniqueness 56
  women, role 112, 129 n.4
Iraq ix
  invasion of Iran 126
  Iran, war (1980-88) 29, 126, 145, 158
  Najaf 36
Islam
  and Christianity 5
  expansion 5-6
  extent 1
  in Iran 163
  and Jews 5
  and Marxism 23, 25, 98
  and the modern state 28
  nature of 2-3
  origins 1
  Shia-Sunni divide xiv, 6-11, 12, 17-18, 29, 95, 172
  turning point 3
  and usury 124
  Western Europe
    growth 1
    threat to 1
  see also Shi'ism; Sunnism
Islamic Brotherhood, Egypt 11
Islamic Constitution, Iran 123
Islamic Culture and Guidance, Ministry 167
  role 151
Islamic movement
  and the international order 38-9
  in Iran 34-7
  and Marxism 25
  and modernity 24-5, 27, 37-8
  and the oil crisis (1973) 25-6
  and political power 28
  and universities 26-7
  as urban phenomenon 25
  varieties 38
  and violence 25
Islamic Republic
  Iran as 56, 72, 85, 120-1, 142-3
  proposals for 120-1
Islamic Republican Party 125-6, 146, 177
  formed 122, 156 n.35
Islamic Revival, Iran 11
Islamic Revolution Guards Corps, and Abdullah Nouri 140
Islamic state
  and Iran 31-3
  and the Quran 29-30
  and Sunnism 30-1

Isma'ilis see Shi'ism, Seveners
Israel, and the Arabs 25
Ivory Coast, *coup d'état* 48

Ja'far as-Sadeq, Imam 12-13
Jalal ad-Din Farsi 85
Jalal Al Ahmed, influence on Khomeini 93-4
Jaleh Square massacre 113
Jamaat-i Islami, Pakistan 28
Jews, and Islam 5
jihad xi
 meaning 5, 20 n.22, 181
Jordan, Muslim Brotherhood 28

Karbála, Battle of 9, 12, 16
Karbaschi, Golam Hussein 138, 153 n.5
Karrubi, Mr 169, 170, 173 n.8
Kashani, Ayatollah 87, 103 n.21, 118, 175
Khalkhali, Sadeq, Hojatoleslam 122, 177
Khameini, Ayatollah 169, 174
 anti-Americanism 170
Khatami, Sayeed Mohammad, President 44, 174
 attempts to discredit 134-6, 138
 'Dialogue Amongst Civilisations' theory xiv, xv, 39, 135, 157, 160-1
 election xii, 132-4, 151
 foreign policy 160, 162
 liberalisation 140, 154 n.12
 Mikhael Gorbachev, comparison 138
 quietism 13
 reforms xv, 59, 136, 145-6, 151, 167-9
 strategy of government 137-40
 student demonstrations, handling 137-8
Khomeini, Ayatollah ix, x, xi, xiv, 12, 174
 Abdul-Karim Ha'eri, influence of 86, 87, 93, 179
 arrest 90, 91
 Bazargan government, undermines 119-20
 complexity xvi, 83
 exile
  in Najaf, Iraq 92
  in Paris 113-14
  in Turkey 92
 family background 86
 and 'Golden Age' of Islam 6
 government, philosophy of xv, 92, 99-102
 ideology 55-6
 influence 82-3
 and the intelligentsia 97
 and the Iranian Revolution 158-9
 isolationism xii
 Jalal Al Ahmed, influence of 93-4
 as moderniser 24-5
 Mohammad Hosayn Borujerdi, influence of 87, 93
 and the nation state 85
 National Front party, alliance 114
 nationalism 85
 and pan-Islamism 84, 85, 158-9
 as a populist 83-4
 quietism 87-8, 93
 Shah, opposition to 89-92
 Shi'ism, interpretation 14
 as a teacher 98
 ulema, hostility to 37, 56, 88, 92, 96-7
 as *Velayat-e Faqih* 32, 36, 37, 92, 98, 99, 101, 102, 105, 106, 120, 121, 147, 163
 works
  Islamic Government 182
  Khasf Al-Asrar 87
Khwarji sect 8-9
 formation 10
King, Martin Luther, and non-violent revolution 54
komitehs 119, 122, 123
 meaning 181

legality, and revolution 51-2
Loghmanian, Hossein 169, 170

Mahdavi-Kani, Ayatollah 117
Mahdi, Imam 10, 12, 13, 15, 177
majlis 125, 127
  Bani-Sadr impeached by 128
  meaning 181
Manichaeism 14
Mao Tse Tung 25
marja'taqlid 101
  meaning 181
Marxism
  and Islam 23, 25, 98
  and the Islamic movement 25
  and revolution 45, 49, 52, 54-5
Mashad 90
Mass Society, Theory
  and Nazism 58
  and revolution 45, 58
  and totalitarianism 58
Maududi 30
Mazdak 14
Mecca 2
Medina (Yathrib)
  Muhammad's move to 3
  siege 4
Milosevic, Slobodan, overthrow 48, 64 n.19
model, binary opposition 73-8, 165
modernity
  and the Islamic movement 24-5, 27, 37-8
  and religious revival 23
Montazeri, Ayatollah 30, 37, 141, 174-5
  memoirs 129
Mossadeq, Muhammad 87-8, 103 n.20, 106, 144, 156 n.34, 177
Mottahari, Ayatollah 98-9, 175
Mu'áwíyah, Caliph 9, 88
Muhammad
  Angel Gabriel, revelation from 2
  birth 1
  childhood 1-2
  death 4, 7
  diplomatic missions 4
  family 2
  marriages 4
  Medina, move to 3
  parents 1
  successor 7
  as a warrior 4
Muharram 89-90
  meaning 182
Mujahedin-e Khalq party 93, 110, 114, 127, 145, 177
mujtahid 32, 36, 181
  meaning 182
Músá, Imam 13
Musavi-Ardabili, Ayatollah 117
Musharraf, General 171-2
Muslim Brotherhood, Jordan 28
Muslim Peoples' Republican Party, formed 122, 131 n.20
Muzaffer Din Shah 115

Najaf, Iraq 36
Nasr Din Shah 115
nation state, and Khomeini 85
National Front party 178
  alliance with Khomeini 114
nationalism, of Khomeini 85
Nazism, and Theory of Mass Society 58
Negus of Ethiopia 4
Nixon, President 106, 108
Nouri, Abdullah x, 139, 175
  beliefs 141
  career 140
  and Council for Constitutional Amendments 140
  and Islamic Revolution Guards Corps 140
  trial 141, 142, 145, 155 n.30
Nouri, Nadegh 133, 154 n.8, 178

occultation, doctrine of 13
OIC *see* Organisation of the Islamic Conference

oil crisis (1973) 106
    and the Islamic movement 25-6
oligarchy, democracy, comparison 70
Organisation of the Islamic Conference
    x, 39, 178

Pahlavi Dynasty 14, 18-19, 178
Pakistan, *Jamaat-i Islami* 28
pan-Islamism, and Khomeini 84, 85, 158-9
Parsons, Anthony 115
Perestroika 138
Persia, conversion to Islam 5
Persian Gulf, extent xvi-xvii
personality, and revolution 46
politics, and power 69
power
    change, and the Iranian Revolution 69-70
    political, and the Islamic movement 28
    and politics 69
    and revolution 50, 166

Qajar Dynasty (1796-1925) 15-16, 18, 35, 178
qarbzadegi 93
Qom 86, 87, 89, 90, 91, 98, 111, 117-18, 178
Qotbzadeh, Saqeq 117, 125
Quran, and the Islamic state 29-30

Rafsanjani, Ali Akbar Hashimi, Hajatoleslam 117, 148, 174
    majlis Speaker 140
    President 132, 141, 149
Rastakhiz Party 72, 107, 109, 178
Refah 11
Reformation, The, as revolution 49
Relative Deprivation, Theory, and revolution 61
religion, and ideology 33-4
religious revival, and modernity 23

Repression of Instincts, Theory, and revolution 58-9
revolution
    Aristotle on 70
    as binary opposition xiii-xiv, 44, 71
    as continuing process xiii, 44, 67-8, 70-1, 144, 165
    and *coup d'état* 70, 71
    definitions xiii, 46-8, 50-1, 57, 62, 69, 116, 165
    and élites 51, 57
    examples 47-8
    Functionalist view 45, 49, 56-7, 66
    and inequality 70
    and legality 51-2
    Marxist view 45, 49, 52, 54-5
    nature of 43-4
    non-violent
        and Gandhi 53-4
        and Martin Luther King 54
    and personality 46
    and power 50, 166
    and social change 69
    and social structure 49
    spread 62-3
    The Reformation as 49
    theory xiv, 45-6, 62-3, 65-6, 158
        of Mass Society 45, 58
        of Relative Deprivation 61
        of Repression of Instincts 58-9
        of Rising Expectations 58, 59-60
    and values 47, 68
    and violence 47, 52-4, 66, 68-9
    see also Iranian Revolution
revolutionaries, characteristics 61
Revolutionary Council 118, 119, 125
    as caretaker government 124
revolutionary situation
    definition 62
    revolutionary outcome, comparison 62
Reza Khan, Shah (1925-41) 86-7, 95, 178
    abdication xvii, 87
    anti-Islam policies 107

westernisation 116
Reza Shah, Mohammad (1941-79) 89-92, 177
  exile 115
  health problems 108
  urbanisation 116
  US support 107-9
  White Revolution 106, 107
Rising Expectations
  theory
    and the Iranian Revolution 60-1, 66-7, 106-7
    and revolution 58, 59-60
Roohaniyun party 133, 153 n.4
Russian Revolution 43-4, 47, 71

Saddam Hussein 126
Safavi, Ismail, Shah 15
Safavid Dynasty (1501-1736) 14, 18, 178-9
  origins 35
  and Shi'ism 14-15, 35-6, 95-6
Sasanian Dynasty (224-651) 13
  Byzantines, conflict 2
Saudi Arabia 26
SAVAK 109, 112, 113, 179
SAVAMH 179
secularisation, growth of 23
September 11 attacks 38
  and Iran 170, 173
Seveners *see* Shi'ism, Seveners
Shar'ia, meaning 182
Shariati, Ali xiv, 34, 35, 36-7, 176
  on the *ulema* 94-6, 97
Shariatmadrai, Ayatollah 118, 122, 175
Shia, meaning 182
Shia-Sunni divide xiv, 6-11, 12, 17-18, 29, 95, 172
Shi'ism
  development 12
  Fivers 12
  groups 12-13
  Henri Corbin on 16-17

ideology 17, 18
Iran, identification with 36
Khomeini's interpretation 14
as minority sect 16
and the Safavid Dynasty 14-15, 35, 35-6, 95-6
Seveners 12, 13
Twelvers 10, 12, 13, 14
  doctrine 15
  varieties 24
Yemen 14
see also Shia-Sunni divide; Sunnism
Shiraz 90
social change
  measurement 69
  and revolution 69
Soroush, Dr xiv, 176
Special Clerical Court 148
Sunnism
  basis 17
  and the Islamic state 30-1
  meaning 182
  varieties 24
  and virtue 31
  see also Shia-Sunni divide; Shi'ism
Supreme Leader, power of 143
Syria, conversion to Islam 5

Taleban
  and Afghanistan xvii, 30
  and Iran 170, 172
Taleqani, Ayatollah 118, 175-6
Tehran 90
theocracy
  Iran as 24
  post-Revolution 117-21
Third Republic, Iranian Revolution 132, 153 n.2
Tobacco Protests (1892) 95, 115, 170
totalitarianism, and Theory of Mass Society 58
Tudeh party 93, 123, 179
Turkey, Virtue Party 11

Twelvers *see* Shi'ism, Twelvers

ulema 11, 13
  Bani-Sadr, undermined by 125
  intelligentsia, alliance, Iran 35, 37
  Iran 15-16, 29-30, 35, 36-7
  Iranian Revolution, role 111-12
  Khomeini's hostility to 37, 56, 88, 92, 96-7
  meaning 21 n.44, 182
  rulers, relationship with 15, 95-6, 163
  Shariati on 94-6, 97
Umar, Caliph 7, 14
Umayyads 8, 9, 11, 16
United Arab Emirates, Iran, dispute 162
universities, and the Islamic movement 26-7
US
  embassy in Iran seized 119-20, 122, 124, 158
  Iran as 'axis of evil' member 161-2
  Shah, support for 107-9
usury, and Islam 124
Uthman, Caliph 7
  death 8

values, and revolution 47, 68

Velayat-e Faqih 143, 152
  and Khomeini 32, 36, 37, 92, 98, 99, 101, 102, 105, 106, 120, 121, 147, 163
  meaning 182
violence
  Hezbollah Party 139
  and the Islamic movement 25
  and revolution 47, 52-4, 66, 68-9
  model 53
virtue, and Sunnism 31
Virtue Party, Turkey 11

West, the, threat from Islam 1
White Revolution 106, 107
women, in the Iranian Revolution 112, 129 n.4

Yathrib *see* Medina
Yazdi, Ebrahim 117, 176
Yazid, Caliph 9, 90
Yemen, Shi'ism 14
Yugoslavia 48

Zaidis see Shi'ism, Fivers
Zand Dynasty (1750 - 94) 35
Zoroastrianism 13-14